ENVIRONMENTS OF MAN

ENVIRONMENTS OF MAN

ENVIRONMENTS OF MAN

Edited by
JACK B. BRESLER
Tufts University

ADDISON-WESLEY PUBLISHING COMPANY

Reading, Massachusetts · Menlo Park, California · London · Don Mills, Ontario

This book is in the
ADDISON-WESLEY SERIES IN THE LIFE SCIENCES

This book is dedicated to Mark
Joel
Kenneth
Faye

Preface

Every so often in the biological sciences area, there is shown to exist a discipline-bridging theme which brings to the surface many unsuspected relationships. *Human Ecology* is such a theme and this book is concerned with human ecology. The beginning student is able to see how biology, geology, and anthropology may be linked, or perhaps in a more specific sense, how nuclear weapons, smoking, and mutations are linked.

It is, therefore, not surprising that this book may be recommended for many courses as an ancillary text.

It appears to me that this reader could be used in introductory or general biology courses, ecology courses, general or introductory anthropology courses, and physical anthropology courses. Many schools have general education courses, and this volume might be useful for these courses as well. In addition, it may be deemed useful for courses in other sciences.

In summary, man lives in many environments—physical, biological, and social—and this is what this book is all about.

J. B. B.

Newton, Massachusetts
June 1967

Acknowledgements

We wish to thank the following for permission to reprint the papers in this volume.

American Anthropologist	(Nos. 2, 10)
American Journal of Physical Anthropology	(No. 13)
American Journal of Public Health	(No. 15)
American Medical Association Archives of Dermatology	(No. 5)
American Review of Respiratory Diseases	(No. 22)
American Scientist	(Nos. 18, 20)
Annals of the New York Academy of Science	(No. 6)
Australian Dental Journal	(No. 3)
BioScience	(No. 1)
Bulletin of the Atomic Scientists	(Nos. 8, 19)
California Medicine	(No. 12)
Evolution	(No. 4)
Fertility and Sterility	(No. 11)
National Academy of Sciences	(No. 14)
Nature	(Nos. 7, 24)
Science	(Nos. 9, 16, 17, 21, 23)

Contents

This table of contents is also a bibliography of the collected papers.

INTRODUCTION

An ecologist is basically interested in three relationships. These may be phrased in terms of questions: How does the environment affect the organism? How does the organism affect its environment? How does one organism affect another organism in context of the environment in which they both live? In a very real sense, all of ecology is merely commentary on these three questions.

In recent years some ecologists have been concerned with man and his ecological problems; that is, "human ecology." This anthology contains readings in human ecology which are addressed to the above three basic questions. By editorial choice, the major emphasis in this anthology is given over to the problems of the environment affecting man—his development, his health, his numbers, and his evolution. A few of the readings are concerned with man's role in affecting his environment. Only two papers in this collection are devoted to interactions between humans.

The 23 papers and 6 letters of this volume were culled from 17 different journals of general science, biology, medicine, dentistry, anthropology, and social problems. This large number of journals is indicative of the broad range of areas incorporated into human ecology.

Three Appendices are provided at the end of this reader. Appendix A contains a glossary of those terms in the selected papers which are not typically found in elementary biology texts or in a common collegiate dictionary. Appendix B contains a brief summary of those statistical principles needed to understand portions of some of the papers. Appendix C contains a list of supplementary readings.

1

The first sections of the reader tend to emphasize the natural environments and the earlier ecological relationships involving man. There is a general historical progression throughout the volume so that the later sections are concerned with "man-made" environments and the latest developments in ecological relationships.

The first paper by Cole serves two purposes. It is an overall introduction or even a summary of the other readings in this anthology, and it also provides an excellent summary of the early history of the earth. A geological time table is provided (Table 1) which contains an easy reference for this paper as well as for other papers in the collection. There is a modest amount of elementary chemistry in this paper. However, the reader should have very little trouble in gaining adequate background from a high school or first-year college chemistry textbook.

The Cole paper presents a global view of human interactions with his environment and some may wish to re-read it at the end because of this point of view.

Man's Ecosystem

LAMONT C. COLE*

Introduction

My survey here will be superficial by scientific standards, will almost entirely neglect the very important sociological environments in which modern man lives, and will touch on areas in which I am dependent, at best, on second-hand sources of information. I make the effort less for ecologists than in the hope that the message will eventually reach an audience that has forgotten, or has never learned, that man is a part of nature.

The earth's atmosphere, hydrosphere, biosphere, and the superficial layers of its lithosphere all together constitute a vast ecosphere within which a change in any one component evokes changes in all the others. Man's survival will ultimately depend upon an understanding of the functioning of the ecosphere, and I here present my conception of how all these things reached their present state and of where they may go in the future.

Early history of the earth

We must start by referring to some astronomical accidents. First, the earth originated in, or settled into, an orbit at a distance from the sun such that, after it evolved its definitive atmosphere, temperatures permitted water to be present in the liquid state over most of the surface, most of the time. This must be a cosmic rarity but was vitally important to the origin of life as we know it. Second, the earth's axis of rotation turned out to be tipped away from normal to the plane of its revolution about the sun. This accident, of course, is responsible for the existence of seasons and thus greatly accentuated the diversity between regions in different latitudes. Another astronomical accident of some sort provided the

---

* Department of Biology, Cornell University.

earth with a moon which, after the oceans developed, was responsible for the existence of an intertidal zone where, eventually, organisms adapted to life in the sea could become tolerant of life out of water and so be prepared to colonize the land.

However the earth may have originated, some 4.5 billion (4.5×10^9) years ago by present estimates, all theories with which I am familiar agree that at one time it was at too high a temperature to retain an atmosphere composed of the gases that are now present. Oxygen was probably bound in hydrated silicates and metallic oxides, and nitrogen, carbon, and phosphorus may have been bound as nitrides, carbides, and phosphides which occur today in meteorites but which are unstable in an atmosphere containing oxygen and water vapor.

The oldest known rocks show evidence of volcanic activity, and I accept the conclusion of Rubey (1951) that the atmosphere and hydrosphere originated from the degrassing of rocks in the earth's interior after the surface had cooled sufficiently for its gravitational field to retain water vapor and other light gasses. I also see no reason to doubt that the primeval atmosphere was a reducing atmosphere lacking free oxygen, because we know that today there are enough reduced compounds of iron and magnesium alone in superficial layers of the lithosphere to extract all of the oxygen from the atmosphere in a geologically very short time, were it not for photosynthesis.

Whether the primeval atmosphere was a strongly reducing one consisting of ammonia, hydrogen, methane, and water, as postulated by Oparin (1936), and supported by observations on the atmospheres of the outer planets (Kuiper, 1951), and by the experiments of Miller (1953), or whether it was only weakly reducing as postulated by Rubey (1955) need not concern us here. Abelson (1957) has shown experimentally that electrical discharges can induce the synthesis of amino acids in weakly reducing gaseous mixtures containing oxidized carbon compounds so long as free hydrogen is present. In the more strongly reducing atmosphere, Miller obtained a complex mixture of amino acids, aldehydes, organic acids, and urea.

Electrical discharges doubtless occurred in the primeval atmosphere and, more important, ultraviolet radiation of high energy content per quantum would reach the earth's surface in the absence of atmospheric oxygen and drive unfamiliar chemical reactions. Whether or not carbides, nitrides, and phosphides existed in the primitive solid material of the earth, they must have arrived in meteorites and reacted with water to produce hydrocarbons and other compounds of biological interest.

So the primeval sea gradually became a dilute soup of organic compounds which Urey (1952) postulates may have reached a concentration of 1%. Amino acids polymerize readily and, given as much time as we care to postulate, it is not difficult to conceive of polypeptides or even primitive proteins arising under these conditions. A number of authors (Oparin, 1936) have discussed the possible origin of larger organic complexes through such mechanisms as adsorption on clay particles and there is no need to repeat these speculations here. In this complex primeval soup there may have arisen transient forms exhibiting some of the properties we associate with life; for example, scavenging molecules building large aggregates by ingesting other molecules and perhaps metabolizing them in some simple manner. It is even possible that some primitive photosynthetic process may have arisen because, at wavelengths shorter than 200 nanometers, photons have enough energy to reduce CO_2 and H_2O to carbohydrate as a one-step photochemical reaction. Such a process, however, would be self-defeating because some of the evolved oxygen would be ionized by sunlight to ozone which is responsible in our present atmosphere for limiting the short wavelength end of the solar spectrum to 300 nm where photons lack sufficient energy to drive photosynthesis in a single step. In any case, a single-step photosynthetic process would have had to be a transient phenomenon because the photochemical lysis of water vapor in the thin upper atmosphere would result in the loss of hydrogen to space and the addition of some oxygen to the atmosphere.

Whatever protoliving processes may have occurred in the primitive seas, nothing that we would today be willing to call "life" could exist until some organic system acquired the means of producing replicates of itself—the process of reproduction. It is clear that the formation of a nucleic acid was the key step. Once this step was taken, life in the primitive soup could expand rapidly. This, however, was an exploitive form of life, using up the nonrenewable resources of organic matter that had been accumulating for millions of years. Natural selection and speciation doubtless began to operate with different living forms competing for the energy in the organic compounds and with some forms adopting new modes of life as predators and parasites of other forms. Physico-chemical conditions, then as now, varied with differences of latitude and depth and some of these early living forms doubtless became specialists adapted to particular environmental conditions where they were competitively superior in acquiring the stored energy.

This primitive biosphere would have been destined to eat its way to extinction by virtue of its exploitive economy had there not been another large energy source in the form of solar radiation that could be tapped. As Lotka (1925) describes the situation: ". . . so long as there is an abundant surplus of available energy running 'to waste' over the sides of the mill wheel, so to speak, so long will a marked advantage be gained by any species that may develop talents to utilize this 'lost portion of the stream.' Such a species will therefore, other things equal, tend to grow in extent (numbers). . . ."

Pyrrole rings may have appeared as metabolic by-products and complete porphyrins may have been present. It was therefore not too tremendous a step to develop the talent of photosynthesis (Granick, 1957) and, with this process established, the atmosphere necessarily became oxidizing, if it was not so already, as a result of the photolysis of water. At this point life acquired the potential for a balanced nonexploitive economy—one not based on the destruction of nonrenewable resources.

All this took place in early pre-Cambrian time, for which, to speak gener-
ously, the geological and paleontological record is miserably poor. Possible
fossils of photosynthetic organisms from rocks 2.7 billion years old have
recently been reported (Cloud et al., 1965) and there is considerable evidence
for crude oils and other hydrocarbons of biological origin in rocks 1–2 billion
years old (Barghoorn et al., 1965). The deposition of such "fossil fuels," which
are potential sources of energy for organisms living in an oxidizing environment,
indicates that the biosphere did not at this time achieve the potentially permanent
state represented by the legendary "balanced aquarium," but the advent of
photosynthesis, employing visible light, certainly made life much less exploita-
tive and gave it a much greater expected duration than had previously been the
case.

Despite the poor fossil record we know that a major part of all organic evolution must have occurred in the pre-Cambrian because, immediately after a
geological revolution of vulcanism and diastrophism ushered in the Cambrian
some 600 million years ago, many modern phyla and even some modern classes
of animals were already distinct.

Thus the earth entered the Paleozoic era with a great variety of genetically
diverse organisms ready to compete for occupancy of its diverse habitats. At
first, no doubt, great quantities of mineral nutrients were washed into the seas
by runoff of water from land areas of rough topography that had been elevated in
the geological revolution. As erosion of the bare surface proceeded to level
mountains and hills, the transport of minerals to the seas decreased and the
earth gradually settled down into what Brooks (1949) calls "the normal state
of affairs on this our earth." This is a state of low relief of the land with great
arms of the sea extending far into the interiors of the continents, with warm
ocean currents able to reach high latitudes, and with greatly reduced climatic
contrasts between different latitudes. It is a state of arid conditions on land and
with freezing temperatures unusual or nonexistent.

By Silurian times plants colonized the land and they evolved greatly during
the Devonian, at which time animals began to follow them out of the water.
It is tempting to suggest that the great deposits of fossil fuels laid down in
Carboniferous times were a result of the fact that biotic communities on land
were incomplete—that animals and other heterotrophs had not perfected the
talent of land life to the point where they could radiate into all available ecological niches (roles in the economy of nature) and use up the organic matter
from plants as rapidly as it was produced. In any case, production of these great
unoxidized organic deposits probably brought the oxygen in the atmosphere
close to its present concentration of 23.2% by weight. It is a sobering thought
that if all of the fossil fuels on earth could be extracted and burned, the process
would virtually exhaust the oxygen of the atmosphere.

The Paleozoic ended with another great geological revolution of mountain-
building, vulcanism, and glaciation some 200 million years ago and with the
wholesale extermination of plants and animals which, under the pressure of

competition and natural selection, had become highly efficient by becoming highly specialized for exploiting environments that were wiped out in the geological revolution. Every plant species that became extinct probably took with it specialized herbivores and the specialized predators, parasites, and other dependents of these herbivores.

The same pattern repeated in the Mesozoic with gradual leveling of the land and assumption of the normal geological state of affairs, but this time the predominant organisms were different. Of particular interest to us is the fact that the amniote vertebrates and the flowering plants now came into their own. After some 130 million years of base-leveling of the land and specialization of the biota to outcontend competitors for the various ecological niches, the Mesozoic also ended with a geological revolution and the massive extinction of prominent plants and animals. At this point the geological record is clearer (Newell, 1962), and we know that the wave of extinction involved not just such conspicuous forms as the "ruling reptiles" and the ammonites but also even the marine plankton—a phenomenon which Bramlette (1965) has recently suggested may have been associated with the reduced supply of nutrients reaching the seas from land.

The Cenozoic era again repeated the geological story and, with the start of the Pleistocene, the earth may have entered a new geological revolution. Certainly, mountain-building, vulcanism, and glaciation today are far in excess of the geological norm. But in this particular highly abnormal instant of geological time, a new species, *Homo sapiens*, has risen to prominence.

Ecosystems

It is the nature of ecosystems that they tend toward a steady state in which the organic matter produced by autotrophs is all broken down by heterotrophs and other oxidative processes. We have indicated that there are exceptions and that the 1.2×10^{21} gm of oxygen in the atmosphere plus 1% of this amount dissolved in the oceans all represents organic matter that has not been used up and which is what we refer to as "fossil fuels." This is really a small quantity. Green plant photosynthesis releases one gram of oxygen in storing 3.5 kcal of energy, so the oxygen in the atmosphere represents 4.2×10^{21} kcal stored. I have estimated elsewhere (Cole, 1958) the net annual production of organic matter by plants at 5×10^{17} kcal, so the unused potential energy from all of geological time corresponds to about 8400 years of plant production which has gone unutilized in at least two billion years of photosynthesis. This figure is too small if, as Dr. John Cantlon has tried to persuade me, a major part of the earth's oxygen was originally bound as water. In that case, much of the oxygen now bound in oxides of iron and aluminum and in limestones also represents fossil fuel. Putnam (1953), employing such assumptions, has given a maximum estimate 18 times my figure, but even this corresponds to well under 1/100 of 1% of the total organic carbon fixation which has gone unutilized. The approximation to a steady state is evidently very close.

Implicit in the tendency of ecosystems to attain a steady state is the fact that an environmental situation to which it is difficult to adapt will have relatively few species present but that those that do adapt successfully will maintain the largest possible numbers and tend to maximize the energy flux through the system. We recognize this situation, for example, in the large populations of relatively few species living in arctic regions or in difficult habitats, such as salt lakes. On the other hand, an equitable environment where many forms can tolerate the physical and chemical features acquires a great variety of species, most of which become specialists at utilizing some very limited ecological niche within which they are superior to potential competitors. We meet the extreme of this situation in the tropical rain forest or on coral reefs where the energy flux is divided among many species and the mean number of individuals per species is accordingly relatively small. We have learned empirically that complex ecosystems tend toward stability in time while simpler systems are subject to numerical fluctuations often of violent proportions.

Whether simple or complex, just about all of the conceivable niches in any ecosystem tend to be filled because, so long as there remains a way to seize a share of the available energy, natural selection will favor any form that may develop the talent for doing so. Thus, selection pressure tends to produce similar ecosystems in separated regions of similar environment. The tropical rain forests of Africa, South America, and the Pacific area have similar organizations but different origins, and therefore different species (Richards, 1952), and many of the marsupial mammals of Australia are startlingly close ecological counterparts of placental mammals on other continents.

A mature ecosystem has autotrophic organisms producing organic matter, usually a variety of primary consumers, including grazers and decomposers, parasites and predators of these, and a complement of "opportunistic" species with a special talent for finding and colonizing the temporary habitats that appear following events such as fires, landslides, or geological revolutions, and then moving on when exposed to the pressure of competition from more efficient but more specialized forms. There is a balance between energy income and energy output, and a new species can only invade or rise to prominence by displacing forms that are already present.

Primitive man subsisted by hunting, fishing, and gathering wild foods. Of course, we shall never know for certain what forms may have had to suffer reduction of numbers or been brought to extinction to make room for man; or perhaps he appeared at a time when biotic communities were incomplete as a result of wholesale extinctions brought on by glacial periods and merely had to establish himself in a niche from which no competitor could displace him.

Human history

Primitive food gatherers had to learn something about ecology; they had to learn what forms were edible and when and where and how to find these. Early hunters probably used fire to drive game, and perhaps they noticed that this had a subsequent effect on the vegetation as, for example, by increasing berry crops and later by concentrating grazing ungulates. Something like this may have been man's first accomplishment in controlling the other species in his ecosystem for his own advantage.

By more than 10,000 years ago man had domesticated both plants and animals, and some of his accomplishments still merit admiration; for example, he did such a job with the corn (maize) plant that authorities are still not in complete agreement as to what wild species he started with. On the other hand, some species probably practically domesticated themselves. I would expect this of wild canids, and Helback (1959) interprets barley as originally a weed of wheat fields which, when man tried growing wheat with an admixture of barley seed in new environments, may have proved hardier than the wheat and have replaced it in some regions. Rye and oats may have had a similar history.

Food-gathering man probably had to make annual migrations to obtain food at all seasons, but early agricultural man could settle by the river flood plains that were easiest to farm and build permanent settlements that would grow into villages and cities. A this stage, if not before, man must have differentiated his activities into distinct professions comparable to ecological niches. Farming, production of meat and milk products, mining, and trading all seem to be about equally ancient ways of life. By selection of seed and breeding stock man "improved" his domestic forms and continued to bring other species under domestication. With the advent of trade, and probably growing populations, he expanded his agricultural activities and discovered that water shortage often limits plant growth and that he could circumvent this by irrigation.

In places, this type of agriculture was a spectacular success. The annual flood of the Nile was dependable both in time of occurrence and depth attained, and it brought to the flood plain not only water but also an alluvium rich in plant nutrients. Irrigation in Egypt goes back to at least 2000 B.C. and, after continuous use of the land, that country was still the principal granary of the Roman Empire.

Results were less happy in some other regions. At this stage man could hardly have been expected to anticipate that irrigation without adequate drainage would cause the water table to rise and produce waterlogged soils inimical to agriculture, or that evaporation of water moving upward would deposit a crust of salts on the surface, or that insidious erosion by wind and water, so slow as to be barely perceptible, could eliminate the fertile topsoil, ruin the plant cover, and end in violent erosion and gullying. These things had to be learned empirically and at great cost, for they were probably the principal factors causing the collapse of the great Babylonian Empire and other civilizations of the Middle East and Mediterranean regions.

By Plato's time (347 B.C.) a reflective scholar could write of deforestation and grazing as causing the drying up of springs and the destruction of the most fertile soils by causing water to "run from naked earth into the sea" so that lands "resemble the bones of a diseased body; such of the earth as was soft and fat being washed away, and a thin body of the country alone remaining." Virgil

(30 B.C.) recommended crop rotation with wheat following a legume (or vetch or lupine), leaving land fallow on alternate years, dressing exhausted soils with manure or ashes, weeding, repelling birds, and selecting by hand the best quality seed for planting. A century later Pliny (77 A.D.) told of man altering climates by changing river courses and draining a lake with the result that olives and grapes in the region were killed by frost. So, by the beginning of the Christian era, man had acquired a good deal of practical ecological knowledge. But, despite the eminence of these authors, this knowledge failed to enter the mainstream of Western thought.

Meanwhile, agriculture along somewhat different lines had developed under other types of climates. In forested regions the "slash and burn" technique, then as now, was the method of choice. After killing the trees, the land was burned over and crops grown for as long as profitable—then the process was repeated in a new location, giving the exhausted area a chance to recover. Land can often be cultivated less than 10% of the time in tropical regions where humus decomposes rapidly and accumulates little, so a large ratio of land to population is necessary.

Thus man achieved his dominance over the face of the earth, and there is no accurate way of estimating the number of extinctions and displacements that he may have caused by altering and eliminating distinctive habitats and increasing his numbers in an already saturated ecosphere. At the same time he created some new problems for himself. As he crowded into villages and later cities he created ideal conditions for the spread of pathogens and other parasites, and he thus became subject to devastation by frightful epidemics. As populations exhausted or outgrew the resources of their own territories, they came to covet the resources of their neighbors and developed the almost uniquely human institution of war. Man's agricultural technique of simplifying ecosystems to favor a crop plant of his choice also favored the opportunistic species that are present in all ecosystems but usually as a minor element capable of inhabiting temporary habitats by virtue of their hardiness, adaptability, great reproductive potential, and powers of dispersal. The tendency toward monoculture agriculture, often employing annual plants, was as if designed to favor these forms which do not compete successfully in a mature, diverse ecosystem, and they remain today as our important "pest" species.

Just as the crowding of man predisposed him to epidemics, so fields crowded with a single variety of plant provided ideal conditions for the spread of pathogenic fungi and the multiplication of larger consumers, such as insects and rodents. So man at this stage was also subject to mass destruction by famine caused sometimes by pests and sometimes by unfortunate long runs of unfavorable weather.

Despite these occasional setbacks, human numbers gradually increased, and this growth was eventually assisted by the exploitation of new lands, especially in the new world. Then, 300 years ago, the industrial revolution started and initiated a new cycle of population growth that has not yet ended.

Mankind today

The most significant feature of the industrial world is its dependence on the fossil fuels. In the early stages wood, charcoal, water, wind, and animal power could supply much of the necessary energy, but we are far past that point now; and it is doubtless true that half of all the fuel ever burned by man has been burned in the past 50 years. But the fossil fuels are nonrenewable resources so, for the second time in the history of life, it is running on an exploitive economy that will destroy itself if continued long enough.

As soon as the rate at which fuel is burned comes to exceed the rate of photosynthesis, the oxygen content of the atmosphere must start to decrease. I wish I could estimate how near we are to that frightening compensation point but I have found no reasonably satisfying way of doing so. For the United States, Putnam estimated in 1953 that: "If all the carbon fixed in one year . . . was burnt and the energy recovered, it would amount to about one and one-half times the present requirements of the national energy system."

If he was approximately correct, this country and some other industrial nations may by now have passed the compensation point. Fortunately, there remain vast areas, such as the Amazonian rain forest, that have not even started on this hazardous path, but we hear every year of exploitive interests bent on promoting "progress" that are casting covetous eyes on these "undeveloped" areas.

Even modern agriculture is industrialized. We boast of our efficiency in raising more food on less land with the labor of fewer people, but we are deceiving ourselves. If we were to deduct from the food calories that a farmer produces the calories consumed by his machinery, the calories used to build and transport that machinery, to mine raw materials, to process, transport, and apply fertilizers and pesticides and to process and distribute the food, we would see that modern agriculture is largely a device for exchanging the calories in fossil fuels for calories in food.

The modern world is divided up into a series of nations, each operating under the curious unecological assumption that it is beneficial to export each year more of its resources (including food which represents a portion of its soil fertility) than it receives in return. It is also considered desirable to maximize the rate at which resources such as minerals leave the ground, enter into products, and pass to the scrap heap. The creation of accelerated obsolescence, which some of us took to be a joke when we first heard of it, appears now to be a serious economic policy without concern for the renewability of resources.

I cannot remember at what age or in what young people's magazine I first encountered an arithmetic problem concerning a bowl containing an amoeba which every hour divided into two amoebae the size of the original, and where each descendant continued the process. The computations, of course, led to the ludicrous conclusion that the mass or volume of amoebae would soon exceed that of the earth. The actual human population today, like the hypothetical amoeba, is reproducing in a manner that, if continued, would cause it to double in every generation. The hypothetical consequences in this case are ludicrous also, but this is no hypothetical problem. Man has some other very serious problems to face but, unless he achieves a rational solution of the problem of his own population growth instead of leaving its control to wars, epidemics, and famine, I see little hope that he will be able to solve the technologically more difficult problems.

Man is damaging the earth in various ways, not the least of which is through environmental pollution. Products of erosion, sewage, and industrial wastes have been polluting environments for a long time, but the problem has become more acute as the population pressure increases. Agriculture has recently embraced the theory that the way to avoid damage from pest organisms is to make the environment poisonous. Naturally poisonous environments often teem with tremendous populations of the few opportunistic species that can adapt to them, and I think it is an ecologically sound prediction that long continued use of toxins with residual action will produce similar effects on agricultural land. After all, bacteria have recently evolved strains that require antibiotics for growth, and we can expect fungi and insects to be only a little slower in evolving. Some pesticides, notably DDT, have become virtually a normal constituent of the world environment and have turned up even in the fat of penguins from Antarctica, where, of course, agricultural chemicals are ridiculous. The frightening thing is that man brought this about in just a few years with an irresponsible disregard for possible effects on ecosystems. He did damage wildlife, but apparently he was lucky this time and did not upset any vital process, such as the activities of the various bacteria involved in the nitrogen cycle, without which man could not survive.

Contamination with radioisotopes is another modern problem that is not being approached with the intelligence or candor it merits. A committee of prominent scientists (Commoner, 1965) has recently called attention to the fact that millions of curies of radioactive fallout have dropped on the earth over the last 20 years, while, as late as 1962, the scientists responsible were "apparently unaware that iodine-131 constitutes the most severe immediate hazard." The finding (Weiss and Shipman, 1957) of high concentrations of the radioisotope cobalt-60 in clams 2 years after contamination of the water by fallout is instructive for two reasons. First, cobalt-60 is not a product of nuclear fission, so this shows the necessity for considering all of the possible interactions of radioactive materials with other components of the environment. Second, this illustrates the ability of an organism to take an unnatural chemical from an almost indefinitely dilute medium and concentrate it to hazardous levels. This biological concentration of novel materials has also often been a factor in the killing of wildlife by pesticides (Cottam, 1965) and it shows the necessity for a full understanding of the food chains in ecosystems before subjecting them to contamination.

Mankind must outgrow its ancient illusion that the atmosphere and hydrosphere represent waste receptacles of infinite capacity. In this country we are beginning to be disillusioned about this for rivers and lakes, and a few local areas are even beginning to try to do something about the pollution of the atmosphere and of harbors. However, the predominating attitude was illustrated less than 2 years ago by a leading news magazine (*Time*) which, in reporting a proposal to dig a new Panama canal with nuclear explosives, explained that the amount of radioactivity that would get into the water cannot be estimated, "but the strong current that will run through the canal should carry most of it away." And so it should, at the risk of making seafood from the Atlantic Ocean unsafe to eat!

I have been given to understand that solid-fuel rocket engines release beryllium into the atmosphere but, despite some inquiries, I know absolutely nothing about the quantities involved. I do know that there have been a number of reports of beryllium toxicity to vertebrate animals and that the 1938 *USDA Yearbook of Agriculture* reports that very low concentrations of beryllium are toxic to citrus cuttings in solution culture (McMurtrey and Robinson, 1938). I should like to feel confident that due consideration was given to this, and appropriate experiments performed, prior to the decision to test such rocket engines at ground level in southern California, but I do not expect such reassurance to be forthcoming. I offer this as a fairly typical example of the things that make ecologists distrustful of many of the decisions being made by society.*

I could go on listing things that, from an ecological viewpoint, man is clearly doing wrong, such as depleting the supply of fresh water and developing increased reliance on monoculture agriculture and animal husbandry, and I could draw up a long list of man-made changes I deplore. I regret that I can never expect to see a wild wolverine in the eastern United States, but I recognize that the wolverine's requirements and habits are incompatible with man's. I regret that the same processes that have made it possible for me to live in a house built of cypress have brought America's largest woodpecker, the ivory-bill, to the verge of extinction, but I recognize that some such displacements are inevitable when any species greatly expands its sphere of activity. However, I can see no excuse for the extinction, through reckless overexploitation, of species man values. One would think that the most primitive savage could understand that a species once gone cannot be restored, and that his greatest harvest in the long run depends upon always preserving a breeding stock. Yet today, whaling ships from scientifically and technologically advanced nations are threatening the existence of the largest animal that has ever lived on earth.

Conclusion

If the picture I have painted of man and his ecosystem appears to be a gloomy one, let me state that the situation is not hopeless. Man has the necessary technology to regulate his population size; what is needed is a consensus as to how

---

* Since this was written the toxicity of beryllium has been explicitly acknowledged (Glassman, 1965) and it is noted that ". . . currently, Be is under active investigation."

many people should be allowed to inhabit the earth at one time. Because our present economy is exploitive, we are in need of a breakthrough comparable in significance to the discovery of photosynthesis. Atomic energy does not quite represent such a breakthrough because it depends on a nonrenewable resource, but I think it can take us quite a way into the future if man will use it responsibly. Also, a large amount of deuterium is found in the oceans, and future technology may include a way to use that source of potential energy. And, finally, there is solar radiation, which must ultimately become man's energy source if the species persists long enough.

With an adequate energy supply assured, man can solve many of his other problems by methods that are shunned today as too expensive. He can distill sea water and transport the distillate to regions of shortage; the scrap heaps and junk yards of today can become mines tomorrow, and it will almost certainly become necessary to mine the ocean bottoms, at least for phosphorus fertilizer.

The problems I have dealt with here are all essentially ecological. I have not ventured to suggest what the world we are developing may do to man's mental

TABLE 1. Geological Time Table*

Era	Period	Epoch	Beginning of Interval (Million Years)
Cenozoic	Quaternary	Recent	
		Pleistocene	1
	Tertiary	Pliocene	13
		Miocene	25
		Oligocene	36
		Eocene	58
		Paleocene	63
Mesozoic	Cretaceous		135
	Jurassic		181
	Triassic		230
Paleozoic	Permian		280
	Carboniferous		345
	Devonian		405
	Silurian		425
	Ordovician		500
	Cambrian		600
— ? — ?	— ? — ? — ?	— ? — ? —	? —
Proterozoic			1400 (?)
Archeozoic			1850 (?)

* Based in large part on study by J. Laurence Kulp (1961, *Science* **133:** 1105–1116).

health, nor have I discussed the factors that have given man the capacity to render the earth uninhabitable almost instantaneously, nor the social factors that make it a real possibility that man will use that destructive capacity. The ecological problems are serious enough and, unfortunately, the most prestigious bodies of scientists, the ones that administrators listen to most intently, are woefully ignorant of ecology. I am encouraged that a prominent committee of scientists (Commoner, 1965), including no ecologists, has surveyed the current status of "the integrity of science" and has caught a glimpse of the fundamental role of ecology. I hope that this news will spread quickly.

REFERENCES

ABELSON, P. H. 1957. Some aspects of paleobiochemistry. *Ann. N.Y. Acad. Sci.,* **69:** 176–285.

BARGHOORN, E. S., W. G. MEINSCHEIN, and J. W. SCHOPF. 1965. Paleobiology of a Pre-Cambrian shale. *Science,* **148:** 461–472.

BARGHOORN, E. S. 1957. Origin of life. *Mem. Geol. Soc. Am.,* **67:** 75–86.

BRAMLETTE, M. N. 1965. Massive extinctions in biota at the end of Mesozoic time. *Science,* **148:** 1696–1699.

BROOKS, C. E. P. 1949. *Climate through the Ages.* Rev. ed. McGraw-Hill Book Co., New York.

CLOUD, P. E., J. W. GRUNER, and H. HAGEN. 1965. Carbonaceous rocks of the Soudan iron formation (early pre-Cambrian). *Science,* **148:** 1713–1716.

COLE, L. C. 1958. The ecosphere. *Sci. Am.,* **198:** 83–92.

COMMONER, B. (Chairman). 1965. The integrity of science. A report by the AAAS Committee on Science in the Promotion of Human Welfare. *Am. Scientist,* **53:** 174–198.

Cf. COTTAM, C. 1965. The ecologists' role in problems of pesticide pollution. *Bio-Science,* **15:** 457–463.

GLASSMAN, I. 1965. The Chemistry of Propellants. *Am. Scientist,* **53:** 508–524.

Cf. GRANICK, S. 1957. Speculations on the origins and evolutions of photosynthesis. *Ann. N.Y. Acad. Sci.,* **69:** 292–308.

HELBAEK, H. 1959. Domestication of food plants in the old world. *Science,* **130:** 365–372.

KUIPER, G. P. (ed.) 1951. *The Atmospheres of the Earth and Planets.* University of Chicago Press, Chicago.

LOTKA, A. J. 1925. *Elements of Physical Biology.* Williams & Wilkins Co., Baltimore, p. 190.

McMURTREY, J. E., JR., and W. O. ROBINSON. 1938. Neglected soil constituents that affect plant and animal development, in: Soils and man. *USDA Yearbook of Agriculture.* Govt. Printing Office, Washington, D.C., pp. 807–829.

MILLER, S. L. 1953. A production of amino acids under possible primitive earth conditions. *Science,* **117:** 528–529.

MILLER, S. L. 1955. Production of some organic compounds under possible primitive earth conditions. *J. Am. Chem. Soc.,* **77:** 2351–2361.

NEWELL, N. D. 1962. Paleontological gaps and geochronology, *J. Paleontol.,* **36:** 592–610.

OPARIN, A. I. 1936. *The Origin of Life.* (English translation, 1938.) Macmillan Co., New York.

ORO, J., D. W. NOONER, A. ZLATKIS, S. A. WIKSTRÖM, and E. S. BARGHOORN. 1965. Hydrocarbons of biological origin in sediments about two billion years old. *Science,* **148:** 77–79.

PLATO. ca. 347 B.C. Critias. in: *The Timaeus and The Critias or Atlanticus.* The Thomas Taylor translation. Pantheon Books, New York, 1944.

PLINY THE ELDER. ca. 77 A.D. *Natural History.*

PUTNAM, P. C. 1953. *Energy in the Future.* D. Van Nostrand Co., Inc., New York, p. 117.

RICHARDS, P. W. 1952. *The Tropical Rain Forest.* Cambridge University Press, New York.

RUBEY, W. W. 1951. Geological history of sea water. *Bull. Geol. Soc. Am.,* **62:** 1111–1148.

RUBEY, W. W. 1955. Development of the hydrosphere and atmosphere with special reference to the probable composition of the early atmosphere. *Spec. Papers, Geol. Soc. Am.,* **62:** 631–650.

Time Magazine, January 21, 1964, p. 36.

UREY, H. C. 1952. On the early chemical history of the earth and the origin of life. *Proc. Natl. Acad. Sci. U.S.,* **38:** 351–363.

VIRGIL. ca. 30 B.C. *First Georgics.*

WALD, G. 1954. The origin of life. *Sci. Am.,* **191:** 44–53.

WEISS, H. V., and W. H. SHIPMAN. 1957. Biological concentration by killer clams of cobalt-60 from radioactive fallout. *Science,* **125:** 695.

ADAPTATION
TO SOILS

*Where man settled is an ecological problem. What happened to man as a
sedentary animal after he settled down is another ecological problem. In this
section we shall look at two papers which examine the problems of settling down
and its consequences for man.*

*In her paper, Meggers discusses four types of agricultural potential.
According to her thesis, as the agricultural potential increases, the possibilities
of higher civilization also increase. Thus the potential, as indicated by soils
and other environmental factors, would determine or, more specifically, limit
cultural developments. This thesis is limited to those civilizations with no
technological advantages. In a later section, we shall read about the levels of
civilization which may be developed even in the absence of any agricultural
potential when sophisticated technological advances are employed.*

*The reader may wish to defer the section on page 37, application to the
Maya problem, to the later section on population and society.*

*The article by Meggers evoked some reactions from Ferdon and Bronson
(see Appendix C).*

*Ferdon said that agricultural techniques, cultural desires, and economic needs
were a great impetus to improve the natural environment in which man found
himself. Given sufficient technological development, even the most impossible
environment might be overcome. Bronson, in commenting about the ancient
Maya civilization, felt that the Mayan had a larger potential for cultural*

17

achievement than had been supposed by Meggers. His study included the high productivity of root crops as well as the grain produced in the area.

A reading of the papers by Ferdon and Bronson might lead one to believe that vast differences in points of view exist between them and Meggers. However, the exchange suggests that it is still possible to accept gross or global guide lines for the relationship of agricultural potential to cultural development if one is also prepared to accept a number of deviations from a set of norms as suggested by the Meggers' Types 1 through 4. It would seem, however, that peaks of civilization have indeed been reached where the nutrition potential has been high for whatever the cause and whatever the effect. Nutrition and higher civilization have always been intertwined.

Ludwig has shown that soils affect human life even today. Where soils have been shown to have a recent marine history, the teeth of the children living on these soils have been shown to have a lower caries incidence.

Environmental Limitation
on the Development of Culture*

BETTY J. MEGGERS

The relationship of culture to environment is one of the oldest problems in the science of anthropology and has provided a leading source of controversy. Early students, impressed with the ways in which cultures were adjusted to the unique features of their local environments, developed the concept of environmental determinism. As more field work was done by trained observers, the variability in culture patterns became more evident and the idea of determinism was rejected. Then, as individual cultures were grouped into culture areas and recognized as specific manifestations of a general pattern, the role of environment once again compelled attention. Wissler (1926:214) expressed the correspondence that exists between culture areas and "natural" areas in the form of a law: ". . . when two sections of a continent differ in climate, florae and faunae, or in their ecological complexes, the culture of the tribal groups in one section will differ from that in the other."

In the last two decades this situation has been examined in broad-scale analyses (Forde 1934; Kroeber 1939) and detailed field studies (Steward 1938) and the relationship between environment and culture has been clarified to such an extent that Coon (1948:614) could phrase it recently in more causal terms than Wissler could use two decades before: "Differences in environment . . . are the chief if not the only reason why historical changes have proceeded at different rates in different places, and why more complicated systems have not diffused more rapidly from centers of development."

* Various versions of this paper have been read by Marshall T. Newman, Philip Drucker, Waldo Wedel, Clifford Evans, James A. Ford and Gordon Ekholm. I should like to express my gratitude to them for their constructive comments.

There are few anthropologists today who would disagree with the general statement that environment is an important conditioner of culture. However, efforts to establish the relationship more specifically seem to give negative results. The potentialities of a particular habitat can be seen reflected in the subsistence pattern, the material culture, and by extension, in the social and religious aspects of the culture that is exploiting it, but when cultures of similar subsistence patterns or general features are compared they are not found to occupy similar environments. Hunting tribes, for example, may live in semi-deserts, swamps, forests, grasslands, or mountains, and in the arctic, the tropics or the temperate zone. Conversely, areas that seem similar geographically may differ greatly culturally. This has led to the conclusion expressed by Forde (1934:464):

> Physical conditions enter intimately into every cultural development and pattern, not excluding the most abstract and non-material; they enter not as determinants, however, but as one category of the raw material of cultural elaboration. The study of the relations between cultural patterns and physical conditions is of the greatest importance for an understanding of human society, but it cannot be undertaken in terms of simple geographical controls alleged to be identifiable on sight. It must proceed inductively from the minute analysis of each actual society.

Given the traditional conception of environment, no other conclusion is possible. However, in view of the very definite evidence that cultures have an ecological aspect, which can be shown to have a determinative character particularly on the lower levels (e.g., Wedel 1953), it does not seem likely that no more general relationship exists. It is more probable that, in attempting to discover it, we have not been distinguishing the fundamental factors involved. All the efforts to correlate culture with environment have utilized the landscape classifications set up by geographers. James (1935), for example, has summarized world environments under eight principal types: dry lands or deserts, tropical forests, Mediterranean scrub forests, mid-latitude mixed forests, grasslands, boreal forests, polar lands and mountain lands. It has frequently been noted that these categories do not represent cultural uniformities or even similarities. Desert cultures range from food gatherers to high civilizations; both polar lands and boreal forests, on the other hand, are exploited by food gatherers. Since environment does have an important effect on culture, and since the usual geographical classifications fail to discriminate culturally significant units, it is logical to search for some other basis for distinction.

Definition of environment

The primary point of interaction between a culture and its environment is in terms of subsistence, and the most vital aspect of environment from the point of view of culture is its suitability for food production. Until the discovery of agriculture, this was relatively equal over the major portion of the earth's surface.

In some areas game, wild plants or fish were more abundant than in others, but the range of variation was slight in comparison with what it became following the adoption of agriculture. The cultivation of cereals was designated by Tylor (1881:215) as "the great moving power of civilization," and the cultural revolution that followed in its wake has since been commented upon frequently (Peake 1940:127; Childe 1941:66; Steward 1949a:23; White 1949:371). Most anthropologists, however, do not carry the analysis beyond the effect that agriculture has had on culture to the effect that environment has on the productivity of agriculture. Differences in soil fertility, climate and other elements determine the productivity of agriculture, which, in turn, regulates population size and concentration and through this influences the sociopolitical and even the technological development of the culture. Once this point is raised, it is evident that differential suitability of the environment for agricultural exploitation provides a potential explanation for differences in cultural development attained around the world.

To be culturally significant, a classification of environment must recognize differences in agricultural potential. Areas that permit only limited, shifting cultivation because of the poverty of the soil must be distinguished from those of enduring fertility where intensive agriculture can be practiced over long periods of time. An examination of the methods of food production suggests that four types of environment can be recognized, each with a distinct agricultural implication:

Type 1.—Areas of no agricultural potential. This includes the greatest variety of natural landscapes because only one of the many components necessary for agriculture need be absent for the area to be unsuitable. The defective element may be soil composition, temperature, rainfall, short growing season, elevation, terrain, etc. Type 1 regions include tundra, some deserts, tropical savannas, swamps, some mountain ranges, and similarly uncultivable types of land.

A few areas with no agricultural potential are suitable for a pastoral economy. These constitute a special category of Type 1 because food gathering is replaced by food production and a higher level of cultural development can be attained than is typical of Type 1 areas. Some Type 3 areas have also supported pastoral cultures on the aboriginal level. However, since pastoralism is a minor source of food production compared to agriculture among the cultures of the world, and lacks both the environmental adaptability and the variety of potentiality for cultural development characteristic of agriculture, it will receive only brief mention in this discussion.

Type 2.—Areas of limited agriculture potential. Here agriculture can be undertaken, but its productivity is minimized by limited soil fertility, which cannot economically be improved or conserved. When the natural vegetation cycle is broken by clearing, planting and harvesting, the delicate balance between what is taken from and what is returned to the soil is upset. The soil is poor to begin with, and exposed fully to the detrimental effects of the climate, it is quickly exhausted of plant nutrients. The addition of fertilizer is not feasible on a primitive level or economically practical on a modern one. Since the major cause of this condition is abundant rainfall and high humidity, Type 2 environments may be restricted to the tropics, and a good example is the South American tropical forest and selva. This does not mean, however, that all tropical environments are necessarily Type 2.

Up to the present time, no method of maintaining such areas in continuously profitable, intensive food production has been found, in spite of our extensive knowledge of plants and soils (cf. Higbee 1948). Permanent and intensive production has been achieved in some places by the introduction of tree crops (cacao, coffee, bananas, citrus, etc.) and jute, but with the possible exception of the banana, none of these could provide an adequate subsistence base. Should a solution appear in the future, the "limited" designation for Type 2 might have to be modified, but since the obstacles to the increased productivity of food crops are infinitely greater than in Type 3, a distinction between the two should still be made.

Type 3.—Areas of increasable (improvable) agricultural potential. Areas of this type contain all the essentials for agricultural production that exist in Type 2. However, being in more temperate climates where rainfall and humidity are less detrimental, soil exhaustion is caused mainly by the raising of food crops. Under a slash-and-burn type of utilization, the productivity of the land is not much greater than that of Type 2 areas. However, crop returns can be appreciably increased by techniques such as rotation, fallow and fertilization, and the same fields can be kept in almost constant production over long periods of time if not permanently. Temperate forest zones like Europe and the eastern United States belong in this category.

Other Type 3 environments are less readily improved because the deficient element is not soil fertility, but water. The Imperial Valley of California is such a case, where agriculture is made possible by water brought long distances over mountains.

Further methods of increasing agricultural potential are by the introduction of more suitable plants, such as the replacement of dry rice by wet rice in Madagascar (Linton 1936: 348–54), and the introduction of new or improved tools like the animal-drawn plow in the North American plains.

Type 4.—Areas of unlimited agricultural potential. Here the natural environment approximates as closely as possible the ideal conditions for agriculture. Climate, water and terrain are suitable and soil fertility is for the purposes of this discussion inexhaustible, so that the land can support intensive food production indefinitely. The "cradles of civilization" all belong to Type 4.

The classification of an area into one of these types is theoretically independent of the time factor. Since the introduction of agriculture in most of the world, there has been little alteration in climate or topography that has affected the agricultural potentiality of the environment. Where changes have occurred because of climatic shifts, such as the gradual northward extension of the limit of agriculture in North America, the area can be reclassified in accord with its new potential.

For purposes of practical ease in identifying an area as to type, the year 1950 can be taken as a base line. If an area is improvable by modern agricultural techniques, it is Type 3, regardless of what might have been its primitive or aboriginal usage. If it cannot be shown to have been so improved, or to be comparable to some area where similar natural deficiencies in agricultural potential have been compensated for with modern knowledge and techniques, then it is Type 2 or Type 1, depending on whether agriculture is feasible or impossible. Type 3 areas, as will be seen, are most dependent on such technical advances to develop their potential. Type 4 areas are highly productive even with relatively primitive means of exploitation.

Since this is not a common approach to the classification of environment, it may be well to risk over-repetition in order to avoid being misunderstood. The characteristics and differences between Types 1, 3 and 4 are relatively clear-cut, and probably do not need further discussion. Type 2, however, contains two pitfalls: (1) It takes a stand on a question in much dispute, namely, the agricultural potentiality of the tropics, and (2) it leads to the identification of "tropical" with "Type 2," which is not intended. Comments and information bearing on these two points will be found in the succeeding pages, but a more specific statement here may help to orient the reader.

If one wishes to make an abstract argument about the opportunities for agriculture in the South American tropics, it can be documented with quotations from visitors to the area beginning with Raleigh and La Barre in the 17th century and continuing right up to the present (Price 1952). However, a careful examination will reveal the liberal use of qualifiers such as "could," "might," "probably," "if . . . , then," etc., and considerable emphasis on the luxuriance of the wild vegetation. Such arguments are hard to refute because of their indefinite character. However, if one examines archeological, ethnographical and historical data, the efforts to initiate large-scale agricultural programs, the climatic factors influencing the vegetation cycle, and so delves beneath the promising surface, one is forced to conclude that the latter is largely an attractive camouflage. Even to grant the possibility that parts of the Amazon Basin can be brought under successful agricultural production by the use of specialized techniques and crops does not invalidate the establishment of a separate category for this and similar areas in the environmental classification. Our goal is to explain differences in cultural development, and we can do this only by observing the facts and distilling from them a general hypothesis. The assumption that underlies this process is that the situations we observe are not fortuitous or arbitrary, but are caused. The fact that cultural evolution has proceeded farther in Type 3 areas than in Type 2 areas cannot be considered accidental and dismissed as irrelevant. Although it may seem to us, possessed of the knowledge of the 20th century, that the obstacles to agricultural exploitation are no greater in one type of environment than in the other, we are not justified in projecting this view into the analysis. Unless it is a conclusion derived from an examination of the data, it cannot be brought forth to refute other generalizations founded on these facts.

Since the primary cause of this low agricultural potentiality appears to lie in the low natural fertility of the soil, worn out and broken down by long and constant exposure to leaching, it was suggested that Type 2 environments may be exclusively tropical. This is not equivalent, however, to a statement that all tropical environments are Type 2. On the contrary, one need not look far around the world to gather evidence that this is not the case. There is no reason why it should be. The primary definition of "tropical" is in terms of latitude, and latitude is perhaps the least important and most generalized factor influencing agriculture. Soil fertility, topography, rainfall pattern, temperature and similar agriculturally significant variables differ among tropical areas as they do among temperate ones, and form the basis for this environmental classification.

In correlating cultural development with environmental potentiality, the two components must be treated on the same level. The classification of the environment has been made in terms of general features that unite the landscapes placed in one category and distinguish them from those in another. The basic or primary factor, agricultural potentiality, has been deduced or abstracted from the unique or variable features, temperature, rainfall, flora, topography, that are present in any given area. In order to detect possible relationships, culture must be reduced to a similar level of generalization and specific features categorized under concepts such as "social classes," "occupational division of labor," "hierarchy of gods," etc. This has been done frequently before, especially in culture-area formulations, and its philosophical validity has been discussed by Steward (1949a: 6–7), so that it does not seem necessary to add further justification here.

If we accept as a working hypothesis the existence of a definite cause and effect relationship between these four kinds of environment and the maximum cultural development they can continuously support, the next step is to examine from this point of view some of the evidence that has been assembled about cultures. Since limitations of space do not permit coverage of the world, the greatest temporal, spatial and cultural variety may be included by using South America and Europe as test areas.

Culture and environment in South America

The aboriginal cultures of South America have been analyzed and classified in recent years into four major culture areas: Marginal, Tropical Forest, Circum-Caribbean and Andean (Steward 1946–50). Although this division was made primarily in order to present the tremendous array of data in an intelligible order, it performs the secondary function of being one of the most remarkable demonstrations available of the limiting effect of environment on culture.

The habitats of the Marginal tribes are varied geographically, including swamps, savannas, sub-Antarctic forests and arid uplands, but all belong to Type 1 because they are unfit for agriculture. A subsistence derived from hunting, fishing and gathering will normally support only small groups and these must be constantly on the move to take advantage of seasonal food plants and moving game. The combination of small population concentrations and nomadic life exerts a very definitely limiting effect on the culture, keeping it on a simple level that permits the satisfaction of basic needs and little more. Technology is limited to the manufacture of essential tools and utensils that can be made in a minimum of time and with easily accessible materials: bows and arrows, spears, coiled baskets, nets and perhaps bark canoes. Shelters are crude and temporary. Social organization is on kinship lines, since the social unit is a single family, or at best an extended family or lineage. There is no division of labor except on sex and age lines, no differentiation in rank or status among adults. The family head is the band leader, but he has no privileges or enforceable powers and few duties. Supernaturalism is poorly defined and serves individual rather than group ends; there are no offerings, sacrifices, temples or idols. Even shamans are not frequent.

That the failure to achieve a higher level of culture in Type 1 areas in South America is not the result of isolation from sources of diffusion is noted by Steward (1949b:691 92):

> More advanced technologies were absent to a surprising degree, even among the tribes who adjoined or formed enclaves within the Tropical Forest peoples and would seem to have had considerable opportunity for borrowing. . . . For example, simple woven and twilled baskets are easier and faster to make than coiled or twined ones, loom weaving is more efficient than netting or finger twining, and in many localities even dugout canoes would have repaid the labor of constructing them.

To explain this as the result of "a certain recklessness toward the hazards of existence," as Steward does (p. 692), is to attribute to these people an attitude that may be present at our own level of development but if held by primitive groups would soon have led them to extinction. It seems more reasonable to conclude that a powerful deterrent beyond the influence of human wishes prevents these advances from being made. Since the culture is in such intimate relationship with the environment, it is logical to look for an explanation from this source. The evidence suggests that the environment exerts an unsurmountable limiting effect on the cultures it supports as long as it permits only a hunting and gathering subsistence pattern, and that this limitation exends to all areas of the culture, even those that seem remotely or not at all related to the subsistence requirements. No amount of inventive genius or receptivity to borrowing that might be theoretically attributable to the people psychologically is sufficient to overcome this barrier.

The tribes belonging to the Tropical Forest pattern of culture occupy an environment belonging to Type 2, with limited agricultural potential. The introduction of slash-and-burn agriculture to the subsistence brings a more reliable food supply, which in turn permits a denser and more sedentary population and a release of labor from subsistence activities that is reflected in an expansion of all other aspects of the culture. More time is available for the gathering and preparation of raw materials and for the process of manufacture, and this permits the introduction of pottery and loom weaving of domesticated cotton. Other new traits are woven basketry and dugout canoes. The settlement pattern consists of semipermanent villages composed of communal or single-family houses of pole and thatch construction.

Although it represents an increase in security of food supply, slash-and-burn agriculture is not sufficiently productive or permanent of locale to support large concentrations of population or stable settlements. This is reflected in the sociopolitical organization which remains basically along kinship lines, the headman or chief having limited authority and few if any special privileges. Division of labor remains on sex and age lines, but the shaman begins to emerge as a part-time occupational specialist. Crisis rites are elaborated, especially at birth and puberty, and surrounded with magical observances and taboos. Deities are still mythical beings rather than objects of worship, and the most important supernatural beings are "bush spirits."

The role of the environment in the formation of this type of culture pattern is clear, but the fact that a Type 2 environment prevents any further increase in the complexity of the cultures it supports may not be so obvious. The process of evolution being typically slow, there is a possibility that the Tropical Forest pattern was too recent a development for there to have been further progress before the advent of the Europeans. This would be in line with Steward's reconstruction (1948:14–15) of the spread of culture in South America: an early expansion of the Andean pattern with some deculturation to the Circum-Caribbean level, followed by diffusion from Venezuela down the coast and up the Amazon accompanied by the loss of more advanced sociopolitical and religious patterns. If this reconstruction were true, it would place a relatively late date on the origin of the Tropical Forest pattern, since it would have to postdate the development of culture in the Andean area to a level higher than that represented in the Circum-Caribbean area and allow for the occurrence of a deculturation in the latter region and a further decline in the Tropical Forest.

Archeological evidence from the Circum-Caribbean and Tropical Forest areas has greatly increased since the publication of Steward's hypothesis, and it indicates that the actual sequence of events was in the direction of evolution rather than degeneration. Rouse's analysis (1953) of the Circum-Caribbean archeological picture shows that cultures of the Tropical Forest level precede those identifiable as Circum-Caribbean. Field work in two Tropical Forest areas (the mouth of the Amazon and British Guiana) produces a sequence from Marginal to Tropical Forest culture, rather than the Circum-Caribbean to Tropical Forest sequence needed to support Steward's analysis (Evans and Meggers n.d.; Meggers n.d.). It appears that as agriculture diffused over the continent, culture in each area was elaborated to the limit determined by the environmental potential, and having attained that level remained relatively stationary. In the Tropical Forest area it advanced from Marginal to Tropical Forest; in the Circum-Caribbean area, from Marginal to Tropical Forest to Circum-Caribbean. Thereafter local diversification in details continued but there was no noticeable further advance.

A number of examples of the degeneration of higher cultures under the influence of the tropical forest or Type 2 environment exist and constitute important evidence of the limiting force of this type of environment, although they can no longer be considered as typical of the process that created the Tropical Forest cultural pattern. One of the most striking is the failure of the highly-organized and technically-advanced Inca culture to include any of the tropical forest as an effective part of the Inca Empire. Although numerous efforts were made to extend the boundaries in this direction, they were uniformly unsuccessful. This suggests that the subsistence resources of the lowlands were so meager that they could not support such an advanced culture even when it brought with it well-developed techniques for the mass production and distribution of food.

Even less highly organized groups that attempted to colonize the lowlands were unable to maintain traits that were more advanced than the Tropical Forest pattern. One of these, the Marajoara culture at the mouth of the Amazon River, has had sufficient archeological examination to permit the reconstruction of its course to decline in detail (Meggers 1951, n.d.). The sites consist of artificial earth mounds up to 250 meters long and 7 meters high, which were used either for habitation or for burial. The variety of complex decorative styles in the pottery, the details of the burial pattern, and the size and quantity of the mounds imply a social and religious organization of the Circum-Caribbean or Sub-Andean level, with well-developed leadership, social stratification, occupational division of labor, and a religion involving idols and probably priests. The history of this culture on Marajó Island begins suddenly with the technological and sociopolitical development in its most complex form. Mounds were begun, the potters set about their work, craftsmen and specialists of other kinds devoted themselves to their special tasks, while another segment of the population undertook to secure food for all. Initially, it would not be impossible, or perhaps even difficult, for a few people to supply the needs of the group in the new environment as they had in the old one. The forested western half of the Island must have provided considerable game, and the streams and lakes were bountifully stocked with fish. Birds are abundant today and must have been so in aboriginal times.

This condition could not continue indefinitely, however. With intensive exploitation, the game would grow more wary, the fish less abundant, the birds would seek safer spots and an increasing number of man-hours would be required to feed the community. The difficulties would mount when the limited area suitable for slash-and-burn agriculture had been cut over and had to be re-used before fertility was restored. More and more individuals would have to leave their special occupations and join the quest for food. This change is reflected in the pottery, which shows a consistent decline in quality of decoration, variety of shapes and technical skill. The more elaborate decorative techniques die out approximately in the order of their complexity, those requiring the greatest expenditure of time for their execution going first. The same degeneration must have taken place in the other categories of material culture. With the breakdown of the division of labor on occupational lines, and the basis for social stratification, came a disintegration of the social system reflected archeologically in the disappearance of differential treatment of the dead. The decline continued until the culture viewed archeologically is similar in all respects to the Tropical Forest cultures, in which state it survived until Marajó Island was overrun by an invading tribe of the Tropical Forest pattern.

The evidence just reviewed brings out two major attributes of the Tropical Forest culture area: (1) advanced cultural traits did not diffuse into it from the adjacent regions of higher culture in spite of frequent "opportunity"; and (2) more advanced cultures that attempted to colonize the tropical forest were unable to preserve their more advanced culture in so doing. The conclusion seems unavoidable that there is a force at work to which man through his culture must bow. The determinant operates uniformly regardless of time, place (within the forest), psychology or race. Its leveling effect appears to be inescapable. Even modern efforts to implant civilization in the South American tropical forest have met with defeat, or survive only with constant assistance from the outside. In short, the environmental potential of the tropical forest is sufficient to allow the evolution of culture to proceed only to the level represented by the Tropical Forest culture pattern; further indigenous evolution is impossible, and any more highly evolved culture attempting to settle and maintain itself in the tropical forest environment will inevitably decline to the Tropical Forest level.

The culture of the Circum-Caribbean pattern represents a higher degree of development than was achieved in the tropical forest, manifested primarily on the social and religious level. Technological improvements are mainly in quality and variety of products, the only new category of manufactures being metallurgy. The settlement pattern is characterized by large, compact, planned villages containing several hundred to several thousand persons, with special structures for temple, chief's residence and storehouses. Social organization is in marked contrast to what exists on the Tropical Forest level: stratification into three or four classes with status partly hereditary and partly dependent on individual achievement in warfare; a chief who receives tribute and who is distinguished in life by special insignia and in death by special burial practices; divsion of labor on occupational lines; and, on the political side, union of villages or tribes into federations. Religion becomes institutionalized. Celestial beings and ancestors are among supernatural objects of worship, represented by idols housed in temples served by the shaman or chief who made offerings that sometimes included human sacrifice. Warfare was an important activity and villages were often fortified for defense.

The Circum-Caribbean and Tropical Forest cultures occupy adjacent territory along northern South America, and it has already been shown that the differences between them cannot be explained as the result of lack of opportunity for diffusion. In the light of the environmental influences operating on Tropical Forest culture, it is pertinent to examine the Circum-Caribbean area environmentally to see what the differences are that will account for the greater cultural complexity.

A diversity of geographical features is included in the Circum-Caribbean area, ranging from lowland tropical forests and alternately dry and flooded savannas up to more temperate highlands, and including both islands of varying size and the mainland. If environment and culture are related, it would be expected that this environmental diversity would be reflected in cultural diversity, which is indeed the case. Certain of these environments are Type 3, suitable for relatively intensive farming (supplemented with a good supply of seafood), and it is in those situations that the typical Circum-Caribbean cultures are found. Attempts by these to expand to the Type 2 tropical forest are traceable archeologically, especially in Central America, but none of them were successful in producing enduring settlements (Johnson 1948:196). The main distinction between Tropical Forest and Circum-Caribbean culture is in the realm of social organization. Where a stable food supply permits the establishment of good-sized, permanent communities, an elaboration of the social structure is mandatory. The village is no longer composed of relatives, and kinship is no longer a sufficient basis for regulating interpersonal relations. Chiefs exacting tribute and exercising special privileges, social classes, and occupational division of labor do not at first glance seem closely related to food supply, but the degree of dependence is readily indicated by the loss of these features when the effort is made to transplant them to the less productive Type 2 environment of the tropical forest.

In the Andean culture area with a Type 3 and Type 4 environment, the highest cultural development in South America was achieved. The Peruvian coastal valleys furnish the longest uninterrupted prehistoric sequence, partly because favorable conditions for preservation accompany favorable conditions for human occupancy. Arts and crafts, social organization, and religion were elaborated to an extent that rivaled what had been achieved in Europe in the same century. Cotton and woolen textiles were produced by a variety of techniques, some so complex that they cannot be duplicated on modern machine looms, and often ornamented with elaborate designs. Pottery was mass-produced and of high quality. Metallurgy included casting, alloying, plating of gold, silver and copper. Massive fortifications, agricultural terraces, palaces, temples and lesser buildings were constructed of carefully fitted stone masonry or adobe. Minor arts and crafts existed in profusion. Settlements ranged from small villages to cities, some of which were administrative centers attaining an estimated population of 100,000. A network of roads facilitated communication and transportation of goods between towns.

The functions of government were handled by a hierarchy of officials of increasing rank and responsibility, culminating in the divine and absolute monarch. Class distinctions were clearly defined and hereditary, with distinctive garments, insignia and other privileges for individuals of the upper class. Governmental supervision touched all aspects of life; the duties and obligations of each individual were fixed, all activities were regulated. It is almost superfluous to add that occupational division of labor was advanced to modern proportions. The religious organization paralleled the governmental one, with a hierarchy of priests headed by a close relative of the ruler. These presided over temples dedicated to gods of varying importance and housing images and ceremonial paraphernalia. The gods were approached with blood sacrifice, fasting, prayer and offerings, and ceremonies were held in accord with the ritual calendar.

The existence of so elaborate a civilization depends upon the intensive production of food and its effective distribution. Large irrigation works increased cultivatable land in the valleys on the coast, and terracing with fertilization was employed in the highlands. Specialization in crops permitted each region to grow what was best suited to its climate, altitude and soil. The surpluses of one year or area were stored for distribution in time of need. These methods were so productive that many thousands of commoners could be levied for military service, labor on public works or similar specialized tasks that contributed nothing to the basic subsistence. The closeness of the correlation between these advanced technological and sociological features and the highly productive subsistence base is demonstrated by the failure of the Inca Empire to extend its boundaries into regions with lesser agricultural potential. The failure to expand farther north or south might be laid to the slow communication and consequent difficulties in maintaining control, which were compounded as distance from the center increased. This could not excuse lack of expansion to the east, however, nor would it have prevented the diffusion of advanced pottery and weaving techniques, which were not adopted to any extent by neighboring tribes.

The evidence summarized above leads to the following conclusion: In determining the degree of evolution that a culture or culture area can attain, geographical location (in terms of proximity to centers of diffusion), intelligence (or genius) and psychological receptivity to new ideas are not as important as environment as it is reflected in the subsistence resources. If the temperature, soil, altitude, rainfall, growing season, terrain or some other factor will not permit agricultural production, then only unusual circumstances in the form of a bountiful and permanent supply of wild food (as on the Northwest Coast), or the adoption of a pastoral food production (as in parts of Asia) will permit the cultural adaptation to go beyond nomadic family bands with a minimum of material equipment and social organization. Where other factors are favorable, but the soils are of limited natural fertility that cannot be artificially increased, agriculture can be carried on although it requires constant clearing of new fields to be maintained. Even with such limitations, the effect on culture is remarkable, bringing a radically altered settlement pattern and an increase in the inventory of material traits. However, unless a method of continuing fields under permanent production is found, the culture can never proceed beyond a simple level. Where soils are of increasable or unlimited fertility and capable of permanent productivity, cultural evolution has no environmental limitation.

The close correlation between environment and culture just sketched for South America could be accidental or unique, in which case the above conclusions would have no general validity. Whether or not this is the case can easily be discovered by reviewing the relationship between cultural evolution and agricultural productivity in another part of the world. One of the best documented is Europe, a predominantly Type 3 area.

Culture and environment in Europe

The term "Neolithic Revolution" originated to describe the revolutionary alteration that took place in European culture after the introduction of cereal cultivation from the Near East. For almost a million years man had been a roving hunter and gatherer of wild foods. During this time his tool inventory increased and more effective weapons were invented, but his sociopolitical organization remained basically the same. It was only after the introduction of agriculture that a marked alteration in culture took place. The effect was similar to what occurred in South America, and Childe's description (1951:86–87) of the Danubian I period in Central Europe sounds very much like that of the Tropical Forest pattern except that slash-and-burn cultivation was supplemented with domestic cattle and pigs rather than hunting. Villages were small, composed of communal as well as individual family houses. Arts and crafts include pottery and weaving. There are no indications of differences in rank or of occupational specialization. Nor are there any temples or other evidence of well-defined religion.

In the four succeeding Danubian periods, there is little alteration in the economy that can be considered an advance. The main differences are an increasing emphasis on the pastoral aspect of the subsistence and expansion of warfare and trade, especially after the introduction of bronze. A major transformation occurred in Danubian Period VI, however, as a result of two improvements in agricultural technique: the substitution of plow for hoe cultivation, and the substitution of crop and fallow for slash-and-burn exploitation (pp. 92–94). Sheep grazed on the fallow and stubble fields, which not only provided them with a more stable food supply but also were thereby fertilized. Bronze tools facilitated the clearing of farm land and the harvesting of the grain. These innovations increased the productivity of man-hours expended in subsistence activities and this is reflected in the emergence of distinctions in rank and of occupational division of labor. Chiefs exercised local authority, and enjoyed status and wealth above the common man. War was prominent and most villages were strongly fortified. Increased village size is reflected in enlargement of the associated cemeteries.

With the introduction of iron into Europe, corresponding to Danubian VII and continuing in Period VIII, further advances in agricultural technique were initiated (pp. 96–99). Iron tools were cheaper than bronze ones and consequently more generally available. The result was more extensive clearing of land on the one hand, and more efficient cultivation with iron plows on the other. Together with other tool improvements, these permitted increased food production that resulted in further cultural advance. The population density increased substantially, and fortified towns covering twelve or more acres made their appearance. Social classes developed, with slaves at the bottom and nobility at the top. The existence of political units greater than the local community is implied by the discovery of royal tombs. Occupational division of labor was advanced and utilitarian objects like pottery were mass produced. Local manufactures were supplemented by imports from the Classical civilizations of Greece and Rome. There is little evidence of religious development except the existence of small shrines.

As Childe (p. 116) points out, the sequence just reviewed represents "not stages in the evolution of a rural economy, but rather stages in the adaptation of a rural economy, based on exotic cereals and exotic sheep, to the environment of the deciduous forest zone." It is conceivable that some of these advances could have been made without the benefit of diffusion, but the cultural evolution would have been slower in that case. As it was, the growth of culture in Europe, stimulated by diffusion, followed the same basic pattern as it did in the Near East where the discoveries originated. This is not true of all Type 3 areas. Where the techniques needed for improvement of the agricultural potentiality are more complex, the culture may skip directly from food gathering to food production in modern proportions. These changes are not accomplished by diffusion, but by transplantation of personnel and equipment into the "underdeveloped" area. The point to be emphasized is that without the application of improved agricultural techniques, Type 3 environments limit the cultures they support to the simple level represented by the Tropical Forest pattern, or in some cases even to a food-gathering economy. With these improvements, they can produce and support as high a cultural development as can environments of Type 4. Were this not the case, the history of culture would have been quite different, since Type 4 areas occupy a very small portion of the surface of the earth.

The law of environmental limitation on culture

When the four levels or stages of cultural development that have just been traced in South America and in Europe are compared, the coincidence of basic features is remarkable (Fig. 1). The same kinds of advances in settlement pattern, social organization and technology follow the same kinds of improvements in agricultural production. The major difference lies in the fact that in South America these advances were achieved spatially as well as temporally and the culture was stabilized as the agricultural limit of each area was reached, while in Europe the productivity of the soil could be increased by the application of better agricultural methods and as each improvement was put into use the culture underwent a spurt.

Since this close correlation does exist between the increased productivity of agriculture and progressive cultural development, and agricultural productivity depends upon the potentiality of the natural environment, we can rephrase the statement that culture is dependent on agriculture to read that *the level to which a culture can develop is dependent upon the agricultural potentiality of the environment it occupies.* As this potentiality is improved, culture will advance. If it cannot be improved, the culture will become stabilized at a level compatible with the food resources.

A quick mental application of this rule to a random selection of cultures will reveal many "exceptions." These are not true exceptions in the sense that they invalidate the rule, but rather are instances in which local conditions have introduced elements that disturb the "natural" course of events. This is the usual situation with scientific laws, and we are more fortunate than those in other fields in that we do have examples that illustrate the functioning of this law. Many of the laws of the physical sciences refer to ideal situations and are always distorted when viewed in the real world. Variables such as temperature, pressure, friction and gravitation explain the discrepancies between actual events and the prescriptions of physical laws. A similar variable, technology, accounts for most of the "exceptions" to the law of environmental limitation on culture. Ideally, we should expect every culture occupying a Type 3 area to have reached the level of development achieved in Europe. In reality, the level to which a culture actually does develop, or did develop aboriginally in many parts of the world, depends on the success with which the full potential of the environment is utilized. The range of variation in this respect is greatest in Type 3 areas, where technology plays the greatest role in the exploitation. Where independent discovery of improved techniques did not occur, and distance from or absence of centers of diffusion eliminated the possibility of borrowing, a culture was often stabilized at a much lower level than that set by the environmental potentiality. One only need compare the aboriginal situation in areas such as the northeastern United States, the Great Plains, and the Imperial Valley of California with modern usage to recognize the difference that technology makes in agricultural productivity in Type 3 areas.

One of the most glaring of the "exceptions" is modern civilization, which has extended itself into swamps and similarly inauspicious regions all around the world. An examination of this situation in terms of the law, however, will reveal that the basic requirement is not violated. The proposition reads: "The level to which a culture *can develop* is dependent upon the agricultural potenti-

SOUTH AMERICA

Culture	Subsistence	Settlement Pattern	Technology	Sociopolitical System	Religion
Andean	Intensive agriculture Irrigation Fertilization	Cities to 100,000 pop.	Full occupational specialization	King Hierarchy of officials Social classes	Hierarchy of gods Hierarchy of priests Temples and idols Public ceremonies
Circum-Caribbean	Improved agriculture Seafood	Towns up to 3,000 pop.	Division of labor by occupation	Chiefs Social stratification	Shaman or chief acts as priest Temples and idols Offerings
Tropical Forest	Slash-and-burn agriculture Hunting, fishing, gathering	Villages of 50–1,000 pop.	Division of labor by sex and age	Headman No difference in rank	Bush spirits Shaman, mainly for curing
Marginal	Hunting, fishing, gathering	Nomadic single or multifamily bands	Division of labor by sex and age	Headman No difference in rank	Bush spirits

EUROPE

Culture	Subsistence	Settlement Pattern	Technology	Sociopolitical System	Religion
Danubian VII and VIII	Improved agriculture Iron plow Fertilization Fallow	Fortified cities covering 12 acres or more	Full occupational specialization	Kings and lesser chiefs Social classes	Shrines
Danubian VI	Improved agriculture Crop and fallow Wooden (?) plow Bronze ax and harvesting tools	Villages of about 38 houses	Division of labor by occupation	Chiefs with local authority Differences in rank	Ritual objects and charms
Danubian I	Slash-and-burn agriculture Domestic pigs and cattle	Hamlets of 13–26 houses	Division of labor by sex and age	No evidence of difference in rank	Female figurines
Paleolithic	Hunting, fishing, gathering	Nomadic bands	Division of labor by sex and age	No evidence of difference in rank	

FIG. 1. Correlation between agricultural productivity and culture.

ality of the environment it *occupies."* There is no evidence to indicate that the technology represented in a modern base in Alaska, a mining town in the West Virginia hills or a sponge fishing community in Florida could have been achieved indigenously or can maintain itself on local resources. On the contrary, it is obvious that the existence of modern civilization in these environments is based on the special products or services which are provided to the culture as a whole, and which warrant the "underwriting" of their subsistence support. The satisfaction of thousands of secondary needs that have assumed primary significance to the consumers has spread modern technology far and wide to take advantage of everything from local natural resources to lower tax rates, and the fact that these extensions owe their existence solely to the vast food-producing capacity achieved in Type 3 environments and the extensive facilities for distribution is often obscured. The ability to maintain this kind of regional specialization is a good measure of cultural advance and a simple means of indicating how far we have progressed beyond the level represented by the Inca Empire.

This law of environmental limitation on culture has bearing on numerous current problems in anthropology. It provides a basic explanation for what seems often to be an erratic operation of diffusion. Instead of concluding that diffusion usually moves from higher cultures to lower ones, but not always, one can examine the hypothesis that diffusion proceeds most rapidly from cultures in Type 4 areas to those in Type 3 areas, and only to a limited extent from Type 4 and Type 3 areas to those of Types 1 and 2. In other words, if this is a valid law, then the barrier to acceptance of a trait or complex may often be basically environmental. A further implication is that geographical proximity to centers of diffusion is not necessarily an important determinant of degree of cultural development. Environmental limitations in adjacent Type 1 or Type 2 areas may inhibit the adoption of traits that diffuse to distant areas of Type 3.

This concept of differential cultural potential inherent in different types of environment offers an interesting explanation of both the areal distribution of cultures and the lack of stability of certain culture areas through time. The four types of environment set different limits on the level of development which a culture can attain, and the amount of latitude permitted is closely related to the stability of the cultural adjustment. Cultures occupying Type 1 areas show little basic change over thousands of years and, in fact, comprise the hunting and gathering groups surviving into the 20th century. Cultures occupying areas of Type 2 reached their optimum level of elaboration shortly after their subsistence source shifted from food gathering to slash-and-burn agriculture, and have since shown great stability. It is in areas of Type 3 and Type 4 that the greatest variation in culture through time exists, and this situation has been one of the primary obstacles to the satisfactory definition of culture areas in Asia.

The assumption of this active relationship between environment and cultural development helps to clarify some of the puzzling distributional aspects of culture, in which enclaves of lower culture are found between those of higher levels, and even along routes of diffusion. Prominent examples are the "gap" between aboriginal Mexico and the American Southeast, and tribes of Marginal level between the Andean and Tropical Forest areas in South America. These tribes are like "whistle stops," occupying areas too low in agricultural (and therefore cultural) potential to share in or profit by the diffusion moving along their "line" except in the most limited way.

If this is a true cultural law, it must have no exceptions. Either it operates as specified or one or more variables in the local situation explain the failure of the expected result. In all of the illustrations cited thus far, the total picture is well understood and the application of the law simply places the specific instance in a larger general framework. One of the most useful aspects of scientific laws, however, is that they furnish a basis for prediction and thus direct investigation of problems away from variable factors into lines that are more likely to be fruitful. An analysis of the puzzling elements surrounding the origin and development of Maya culture will serve to illustrate how the law of environmental limitation on culture can open new possibilities for investigation.

Application to the Maya problem

No one will question the statement that the Maya rank with the Aztecs and the Inca at the peak of New World cultural development. Certain of their achievements, among them calendrical, mathematical, and writing systems, are unique in this hemisphere and compare favorably with contemporary attainments in the Old World. Now, however, the marvelous sculptured stone buildings that remain as monuments to the intellectual and religious achievements of the past lie broken and concealed by luxuriant vegetation. The incongruity of this magnificent civilization in a lowland, tropical forest environment has been noted by geographers (Platt 1942:501; James 1942:675) as well as anthropologists (Steward 1949a:17; Ruppert and Denison 1943:1). The circumstance is so unusual that it has required explanation, and the one most frequently given is that geographical location at the junction between two continents in the "crossroads of culture contact" provided sufficient stimulus to compensate for the deficiencies of the environment (Hoebel 1949:483; Kroeber 1948:786; White 1949:223). The preceding discussion, however, brings us to the conclusion that diffusion of this sort can operate only after the productivity of the subsistence pattern has been increased, which was not done in the Maya case. This means that a culture of the level attained by the Classic Maya could not have developed in the Type 2 environment where the archeological remains are found, but must have been introduced from elsewhere. Furthermore, since Type 2 environments lack the resources to maintain so high a level of culture, the history of the Maya occupation of the tropical forest should represent a decline or deculturation.

These conclusions can be tested against the archeological evidence. If Classic Maya culture is an indigenous development based on increasingly or indefinitely productive agriculture, we should expect to trace a gradual transformation from something approaching the Tropical Forest pattern through a stage comparable to the Circum-Caribbean, and beyond to the developed Maya, at which level it should remain. On the other hand, if Maya culture is an example of the effort of a high civilization to colonize the tropical forest, we should expect to find that: (1) it appears suddenly in a well-developed state; (2) it does not diffuse to adjacent areas; and (3) its history is one of gradual decline. An examination of the present evidence on these points gives a promising result.

Regarding the antecedents of Classic Maya culture, it is widely acknowledged that no very definite evidence has come to light. Pre-Classic horizons have been uncovered in the Guatemala highlands and coast, in southern Veracruz and Oaxaca, and in parts of the Guatemala lowlands, but none of these seems to be directly ancestral to the lowland Classic Maya development. It is important to note that many of these areas producing pre-Classic sites are Type 3 as, for example, highland Guatemala where rotation and fertilization permit a relatively intensive utilization of the agricultural land and give an average yield of maize comparable to that in the Peruvian coastal valleys (McBryde 1947:17–21). Pre-Classic manifestations in the tropical lowland forest can easily be explained as intrusions from areas more environmentally conducive to high cultural development. If they had not been stimulated by the influence bringing the Classic Maya culture, the operation of the law of environmental limitation on culture would have resulted in their petering out as did other similar expansions into Type 2 areas.

There is a lack of transition between pre-Classic and Classic Maya culture with its specialized art and architecture, its writing and calendrical systems, that should not exist if the latter is an indigenous development. This has been pointed out often. Kidder, for example, notes (Kidder, Jennings and Shook 1946:1): "Of the first steps toward higher culture we . . . know nothing; and why this should be is one of the great puzzles of New World prehistory." In speaking of the complex chronology, Morley says (1946:45–46):

> There are no simple beginnings, no elementary first steps which must have preceded the development of the perfected system. On the contrary, when we first meet it on these two earliest-known dated objects, it is already complete with all its intricacies—a flower in full blossom, with no preliminary bud stage having survived to show how it had developed.

Strong (1948:119) speaks of "a complete break in continuity" in Honduras; Longyear (1952:82) states that Maya Early Classic culture "still seems to spring into fully developed existence from nothing, in spite of our extensive researches of the past few years." To avoid this conclusion it has been suggested that many of the characteristic Maya traits originated in a perishable medium and were only executed in stone after they had already been developed to a high degree (Morley 1946:46).

On the second point, regarding diffusion of Maya traits to adjacent tribes or regions, evidence is once again negative. The situation has been summarized by Kroeber (1939: 114–15):

> A quality of narrowness of range applies to Mayan culture as a whole. . . . This culture never penetrated to any serious extent beyond the territory held by the historic Mayan tribes. There seems to be no true Maya stratum or archaeological horizon in Oaxaca and Vera Cruz, nor eastward beyond Salvador. Mayan relations or influences may be discernible as far as the Totonac and Chorotega. But influences are another thing from the presence of the culture; and at that, the distances in each direction are not great—less than from the mouth of the Mississippi to that of the Ohio. The generic Mayan as well as the specific Maya culture were nonexpansive, nonpropagandizing, self-sufficient, conservative. . . .

The third point is the question of whether the history of Maya culture reveals an advance or a decline. Evaluations of superiority in many aesthetic aspects of a culture are to some extent subjective, and in presenting data of this sort it is safer to rely on an evaluation made by another person who had no idea of using the result to demonstrate the point under discussion and therefore can be assumed not to have been prejudiced in its favor. The results published by Morley (1946: Figs. 1 and 2, Table XI and text) suit this qualification.

Maya history begins with the earliest preserved date, A.D. 320,* and ends with the European conquest in A.D. 1546. The intervening period is not characterized by a progressive advance as occurred in the Valley of Mexico, the Central Andes, or in the Old World centers. Instead, the culture reaches its climax about A.D. 790. All of the greatest achievements in stone sculpture, stucco modeling, wood carving, featherwork, textiles, clay modeling, pottery decoration, architecture and astronomy occurred before or about this date. The largest city (Tikal) and the largest and tallest buildings are also of this period. Not only are the arts and crafts most highly developed but the products are present in the greatest quantity. Dated monuments increase in abundance until 790 and thereafter rapidly decrease (Morley 1946: Fig. 1). In other words, there appear to have been 470 years of progress followed by more than 700 years of decline.

These figures are significant. The developmental period is too short to have produced so advanced a culture without outside influence. However, if Maya culture were brought into the area by a relatively small population equipped with skills and knowledge developed elsewhere, some time would be required to re-establish the culture in its former condition. An interesting and graphic reconstruction of how this process appears to be reflected in the archeological situation at Copan has been set forth by Longyear. He gives no explanation for the sudden termination of this apparently flourishing center, noting only that there is no evidence of violence or disaster (1951:92). This would not be inconsistent with the conclusion that the breakdown came because the sub-

---

* Since the present problem involves elapsed time rather than absolute dates, the choice between the correlations with the Christian calendar is immaterial.

sistence base, originally unsuited to the support of the occupational division of labor and other social features associated with advanced technology, was overtaxed to the point of collapse. The foundation weakened, the whole structure was doomed.

One question that is frequently raised at this conclusion is, "If this environment is so unsuitable, how could Maya culture have existed there for so long?" Unfortunately, no detailed study of the effect of intensive agriculture on the tropical forest environment has yet been made and theoretical analyses like that of Higbee (1948) or experiments of the type conducted by Morley (1946: 148) and Steggerda (Anon. 1938:222) are either not conclusive or not sufficiently broad to be relied upon for an accurate appraisal of the total region over a long time-span. Ecological studies examining the effect of intensive agriculture on the environment have been made, however, by Cook (1949a, 1949b) for Central Mexico, and the conclusions seem to fit the Maya archeological evidence very well. The essence of the result is expressed succinctly by Cook (1949a:54):

> So far as the Teotlalpan is concerned, it is quite clear that had Aztec (or Nahua) domination continued unchecked by external forces for another century or two, soil erosion, deforestation, and land deterioration would have reached the point where agriculture could not have supported the existing population, not to mention any further increase. At that crucial point the only solutions would have been famine and death, or wholesale emigration, which would have spelled the end of Aztec power and domination.

Here there was in the making a situation that would have ultimately caused the same sudden abandonment of flourishing centers that so puzzles us in Maya history. For a better appreciation of the way in which this interpretation fits the evidence we have on the Maya, and also because of the demonstration it makes of the importance of technology in exploiting the agricultural potential of a Type 3 environment, it might be well to quote Cook's reconstruction in greater detail (pp. 58–59):

> In the tenth century the Toltecs of Tula overran a relatively unspoiled but arid area then inhabited by Otomi who utilized the biotic environment through the use of the wild game, the nopal, the maguey, and probably some crops. The Toltecs then improved and expanded agriculture, thus permitting an increase in food supply. As a result, the population increased materially. The Toltecs were eliminated, agriculture diminished, and with it the population. During the thirteenth, fourteenth, and fifteenth centuries new races (Nahua and Otomi) entered the territory and gradually rebuilt a culture founded on agriculture, a culture which reached its peak at the end of the fifteenth and the beginning of the sixteenth centuries. As a consequence of the huge reservoir of food furnished by intensive cultivation of corn, beans, chia, huautli, and other crops and aided by extensive exploitation of the indigenous arid land plants, nopal and maguey, the population increased to the very high level of 477,000 people on 900 square miles or a density of 530 persons per square mile. This increase was possible because of a successful adaptation to the then existing physical environment, and for no other reason.

But this adaptation caused a reciprocal modification or adaptation on the part of the environment itself, and in the reverse direction. The latter consisted of a loss in agricultural potency mediated directly by erosion and indirectly by a diminution in soil water because of erosion and partial deforestation. Had events proceeded uninfluenced by external, extraneous factors [the Spanish Conquest] there would have followed a period of population decline running parallel to the diminishing food supply until at some subsequent date a new equilibrium would have been established at a lower population and agricultural level.

This area appears to have a Type 3 environment, which the application of soil conservation techniques, perhaps supplemented by other means of maintaining soil fertility, could have maintained indefinitely at the maximum level of production. In the absence of these, the environment was exploited in a manner comparable to areas of Type 2. The result was overtaxation followed by exhaustion, with marked effects on the incumbent culture. This was not an immediate thing, but required several centuries of gradual aggravation to reach the crucial point where a radical adjustment was forced on the part of the culture. This whole reaction closely fits the known archeological circumstances of Classic Maya development and decline and suggests that a similar process of increasing imbalance between the demands of the culture and the ability of the environment to meet them was in operation there. While this interpretation appears to have justification on the basis of present knowledge, only a detailed study of Maya environment in terms of subsistence capacity and the effects of intensive agriculture similar to that undertaken by Cook for central Mexico can establish finally and conclusively whether a similar reaction actually did take place.

Having suggested how this law may be of use in cultural interpretation, it may be pertinent to be equally specific about what it cannot do. It is not to be confused with a universal explanation for cultural decline. Cultures decline for a great many reasons other than the deficiencies of the environment, and have frequently done so in areas of Type 3 and Type 4. The environmental explanation is only primary when a highly developed culture invades a Type 2 area, and thereby taxes the environment beyond its capacity. Nor can this law explain the differential level of development attained aboriginally by cultures in areas of equal agricultural potentiality in different parts of the world. Western Europe and the eastern United States are both Type 3 areas, yet in A.D. 1492 the cultural level attained by the former was far above that of the latter. In terms of environment, both had equal opportunity, so that environment is obviously not the cause of cultural evolution. Nor has it been so stated or implied. The environmental limitation on culture simply establishes a ceiling on indigenous cultural evolution. Whether or not this limit is reached depends upon many other factors, some of which may turn out to be constant, others of which are undoubtedly local and "accidental." This law gives us a clue to why certain areas produced high cultures while in others cultural development was stabilized at a much lower level. Its application in many instances, however, consists in establishing the potential ceiling to cultural evolution, so that the local conditions that prevented the culture from realizing the environmenal possibilities are brought into sharper focus.

In concluding, it may be well to state specifically that it is not my intention to convey the impression that the analysis and conclusions presented here are in any way the final and complete answer to the problem of the relationship between environment and culture. They are only tentative and will require much more exploration than has been given here before we can confidently accept or reject them. In either event, the conclusion should be based on the evidence itself. To dismiss this hypothesis because of conflicts that might exist between it and other generalizations on this subject is unfair not only to this attempt and to the other theories, but harmful to our science as a whole. Only by continually re-examining our conclusions in the light of new data and confirming or rejecting them as the new situation warrants can we discover new avenues of investigation and continue to advance our understanding of culture and its behavior.

Summary

The relationship between environment and culture has been of increasing interest to anthropologists in recent years. There has also been a certain amount of attention directed to defining the relationship of the subsistence pattern to the sociopolitical and religious aspects of a culture. Since subsistence is dependent on environmental characteristics and appears also to be largely responsible for the level of development attained by the culture it supports, some cause and effect relationship between environment and culture is implied.

Since geographical classifications of environment do not isolate culturally significant types, an attempt was made to subdivide environments on the basis of their subsistence potential in terms of agriculture. Four types of environment were distinguished: Type 1, with no agricultural potential; Type 2, with limited agricultural potential; Type 3, with increasable agricultural potential; and Type 4, with unlimited agricultural potential. An analysis of the cultures of South America in areal terms and those of Europe in historical terms suggests that definite limitations and possibilities for cultural development are associated with each of the four types of environment. These were expressed in the form of a law: the level to which a culture can develop is dependent upon the agricultural potentiality of the environment it occupies.

If this analysis is valid, it suggests that previous attempts at explaining differences in level of cultural development in terms of geographical position, proximity to continental junctions, accessibility to centers of diffusion, genius or other psychological factors attributable to the population may not penetrate to the level of primary cause. Absence of a suitable source of diffusion can explain the failure of a culture to realize the potentiality of the environment it occupies, but where the environment is Type 1 or Type 2, no amount of opportunity for diffusion can effect a cultural advance beyond the limitations set by the environment.

REFERENCES

ANONYMOUS 1938 Maize and the Maya. Carnegie Institution of Washington News Service Bulletin, School Edition, Vol. IV, No. 26.

CHILDE, V. GORDON 1941 Man makes himself. Thinker's Library, No. 87. London. 1951 Social evolution. London.

COOK, SHERBURNE F. 1949*a* The historical demography and ecology of the Teotlalpan. Ibero-Americana 33. Berkeley. 1949*b* Soil erosion and population in central Mexico. Ibero-Americana 34. Berkeley.

COON, C. S. 1948 A reader in general anthropology. New York.

EVANS, CLIFFORD and BETTY J. MEGGERS n.d. Field notes on British Guiana archeology.

FORDE, C. DARYLL 1934 Habitat, economy and society. London.

HIGBEE, EDWARD 1948 Agriculture in the Maya homeland. Geographical Review 38:457–64.

HOEBEL, E. ADAMSON 1949 Man in the primitive world. New York.

JAMES, PRESTON 1935 An outline of geography. Boston. 1942 Latin America. New York.

JOHNSON, FREDERICK 1948 The post-conquest ethnology of Central America: an introduction. Handbook of South American Indians 4:195–98. (Bureau of American Ethnology Bulletin 143.)

KIDDER, A. V., J. D. JENNINGS and E. M. SHOOK 1946 Excavations at Kaminaljuyu. Carnegie Institution of Washington, Publication 561.

KROEBER, A. L. 1939 Cultural and natural areas of native North America. Berkeley. 1948 Anthropology: race, language, culture, psychology, prehistory. New York.

LINTON, RALPH 1936 The study of man. New York.

LONGYEAR, JOHN M., III 1951 A historical interpretation of Copan archeology. The Civilizations of Ancient America, Selected Papers of the XXIX International Congress of Americanists, pp. 86–92. 1952 Copan ceramics: a study of southeastern Maya pottery. Carnegie Institution of Washington, Publication 597.

MCBRYDE, F. WEBSTER 1947 Cultural and historical geography of southwest Guatemala. Smithsonian Institution, Institute of Social Anthropology, Publication No. 4. Washington.

MEGGERS, BETTY J. 1951 A pre-Columbian colonization of the Amazon. Archeology 4:110–14. n.d. The archeological sequence on Marajó Island, Brazil, with special reference to the Marajoara culture. Ph.D. dissertation on deposit at Columbia University, New York.

MORLEY, S. G. 1946 The ancient Maya. Stanford.

PEAKE, HAROLD E. 1940 The study of prehistoric times. Journal of the Royal Anthropological Institute 70:103–46.

PLATT, ROBERT S. 1942 Latin America: countrysides and united regions. New York.

PRICE, WILLARD 1952 The Amazing Amazon. New York.

ROUSE, IRVING 1953 The circum-Caribbean theory, an archeological test. American Anthropologist 55:188–200.

RUPPERT, KARL and J. H. DENISON, JR. 1943 Archaeological reconnaissance in Campeche, Quintana Roo, and Peten. Carnegie Institution of Washington, Publication 543.

STEWARD, JULIAN H. (ed.) 1946–50 Handbook of South American Indians. Bureau of American Ethnology Bulletin 143, Vols. 1–6. Washington, D.C.

STEWARD, JULIAN H. 1938 Basin-plateau aboriginal sociopolitical groups. Bureau of American Ethnology Bulletin 120. Washington. 1948 The Circum-Caribbean tribes: an introduction. Handbook of South American Indians 4:1–41. (Bureau of American Ethnology Bulletin 143.) 1949*a* Cultural causality and law: a trial formulation of the development of early civilization. American Anthropologist 51:1–27. 1949*b* South American cultures: an interpretative summary. Handbook of South American Indians 5:669–772. (Bureau of American Ethnology Bulletin 143.)

STRONG, W. D. 1948 The archeology of Honduras. Handbook of South American Indians 4:71–120. (Bureau of American Ethnology Bulletin 143.)

TYLOR, EDWARD B. 1881 Anthropology. New York.

WEDEL, WALDO R. 1953 Some aspects of human ecology in the central plains. American Anthropologist 55:499–514.

WISSLER, CLARK 1923 Man and culture. New York. 1926 The relation of nature to man in aboriginal America. New York.

WHITE, LESLIE A. 1949 The science of culture. New York.

Recent Marine Soils
and Resistance to Dental Caries*

T. G. LUDWIG†

Introduction

This report describes a relationship between resistance to caries and recent marine soils at Napier, New Zealand. This finding has been made during an intensive investigation which has been in progress in New Zealand for the past eight years to determine whether the prevalence of caries can be influenced by soil conditions. The general organization of the study at Napier has been previously described.[1] Briefly, dental examinations of Napier children have shown that they had a considerably lower caries-experience than children resident in the adjacent city of Hastings. It has been found that there are virtually no differences between Napier and Hastings in climatic conditions (hours of sunshine, mean annual temperature and rainfall), socio-economic conditions, the racial composition of the populations and the eating habits and types of foods consumed in the two places. The reticulated water supplies of the two cities are drawn from the same artesian strata, the normal fluoride content of this water as reflected at Napier being 0.15 p.p.m. They have a common milk supply.

The principal difference between the two cities is that they are situated on different types of soils. In 1956 Mr. T. L. Grant-Taylor, Geological Survey Division, D.S.I.R., initially drew attention to the fact that while both places are situated on soils derived from similar alluvial parent materials, those at Napier

* Sponsored by the New Zealand Medical Research Council, the Soil Bureau, Department of Scientific and Industrial Research; and during 1958–1961 by the United States Navy Dental Corps. The investigation has been supported in part by U.S. Public Health Grant D–965.
† Director of the Dental Research Unit, New Zealand Medical Research Council, at Wellington, New Zealand.

are saline soils and have a recent marine history. The salinity of the Napier soils is the result of the uplifting and draining of an extensive salt-water lagoon in the major Hawke's Bay earthquake in 1931. In comparatively recent years much of the residential section of Napier has extended onto the marine soil area and the salinity of the soils has been reduced to the level where they are now used to produce a substantial proportion of the market and home-garden vegetables used in the city.

The water supply of Hasting was fluoridated late in 1954 and in making subsequent evaluations of caries prevalence in Napier, comparisons have been made with the city of Palmerston North. Palmerston North is similar to Hastings in many respects and is, moreover, situated on recent alluvial soils which are closely comparable to those at Hastings.

In this report detailed dental findings of the investigation are described. The investigation has involved an extensive analytical programme of soils, vegetables, drinking waters and urine samples, results of which have been reported elsewhere.[2] Analyses of teeth from humans and teeth, bones and other tissues from animals raised on the soil areas involved are in progress.

Methods

Dental examinations of Napier and Hastings children were undertaken in 1954–55 and of Napier, Hastings and Palmerston North children in 1957 and 1961.

Subjects selected for examination represented all children of European extraction who had lived in the cities throughout life, who consumed only the city water, who were between the ages of five and sixteen years (inclusive) at the time of examination and who were attending school on the day of the dental examiner's visit. Information regarding the residential history of the children, the nature of the water supply available to them and their date of birth was obtained from questionnaires to parents and by questioning the children themselves.

All dental examinations were made by the author under good artificial light using sharp explorers, dental mirrors and hand chipblower. Pit and fissure defects were not considered as carious unless there was visual evidence of caries or unless the explorer sank into soft dentine. For all children eleven years of age and over, bitewing roentgenograms were taken. Interpretation of all roentgenograms was made by the author.

The findings for each tooth were called off by the examiner and recorded on Bodecker-type charts by an assistant. The statistical evaluation of data has involved a contingency analysis by means of the X^2 test. Since the X^2 test does not fully assess the degree of variability within samples, wherever this test indicated that a significant change occurred in the prevalence of caries the finding was confirmed by the use of Student's "t" test. Significance was set at the level of 1 percent. In this report results are presented for males and females combined. Results were, however, also evaluated separately for males and for females.

Results

Caries prevalence in the permanent teeth of Napier and Hastings children in the initial survey are shown in Table 1. This shows that in 1954–55 Napier children aged 6, 7 and 8 years had respectively 57, 46 and 21 percent fewer permanent teeth with caries experience than children of the same age in Hastings. Caries experience in the deciduous teeth of Napier children was also lower than in Hastings. It will be seen from Table 1 that the difference in caries tended to disappear at the age of 9 to 10 years.

At the time of the initial examinations in 1954–55 it was considered that either the caries resistance in Napier was of a transitory nature, confined chiefly to the first permanent molar and being rapidly lost; or it was of a more permanent nature, the apparent loss of caries resistance being due to the protective factor having come into operation only comparatively recently. It was considered important to determine whether the caries resistance in Napier would later extend to older children. For this reason further comparisons of caries prevalence in Napier and Palmerston North children were made in 1957 and 1961.

The results of these subsequent comparisons showed that indeed the effect was of a more permanent nature and its benefits had extended to older children. In 1957 Napier children up to the age of 10 years had a lower caries experience than Palmerston North, the caries experience of Palmerston North children in 1957 being closely comparable to that of Hastings children (Table 1) in 1954–55. It will be seen from Table 2 that by 1961 the higher resistance of Napier children had extended through to children aged 12 years and at this age the dif-

TABLE 1. Comparison of caries prevalence in permanent teeth of Napier and Hastings children in 1954–55.

	Napier 1954–55			Hastings 1954–55			
Age in years*	No. of children	No. perm. teeth present	Mean no. perm. teeth D.M.F.† per child	No. of children	No. perm. teeth present	Mean no. perm. teeth D.M.F. per child	Percent difference
6	144	807	0.61	216	1254	1.41	57
7	218	1880	1.49	246	2170	2.75	46
8	224	2496	2.93	202	2247	3.73	21
9	171	2249	4.06	145	1921	4.45	9
10	134	2148	5.25	157	2665	5.48	4
11	101	2023	7.36	122	2385	7.12	3
12	144	3466	9.52	139	3407	9.47	<1
13	120	3187	12.18	147	3819	11.82	3
14	122	3266	13.80	128	3455	14.35	4
15	67	1809	14.94	88	2404	16.80	11
16	27	740	16.74	41	1100	16.61	<1

* Age taken as at last birthday.
† D.M.F. = decayed, extracted due to caries; or filled.

TABLE 2. Comparison of caries prevalence in permanent teeth of Napier and Palmerston North children in 1961.

	Napier 1961			Palmerston North 1961			
Age in years*	No. of children	No. perm. teeth present	Mean no. perm. teeth D.M.F.† per child	No. of children	No. perm. teeth present	Mean no. perm. teeth D.M.F. per child	Percent difference
6	202	1158	0.59	134	813	1.24	52
7	193	1719	1.49	198	1778	2.54	41
8	179	2040	2.93	210	2436	3.61	19
9	201	2732	3.81	189	2505	4.58	17
10	177	2900	4.18	214	3546	5.55	25
11	131	2760	5.80	131	2959	7.84	24
12	112	2687	6.88	202	4908	10.07	32

* Age taken as at last birthday.
† D.M.F. = decayed, extracted due to caries; or filled.

ference in caries between Napier and Palmerston North was of a substantial order.

Table 2 shows that 6- to 7-year-old Napier children had from 40 to 50 percent fewer permanent teeth with caries experience than Palmerston North children. The differences at 8 and 9 years of age were not as marked. From Table 3, which shows a comparison of caries rates in different types of permanent teeth, it will be seen that this effect was due to there being initially a large difference between the proportion of caries-affected first permanent molars. The degree of protection given these teeth in Napier, however, to a large extent was lost by the age of 8 years. On the other hand it will be seen from Table 3 that for the permanent incisors, Napier children aged 8 to 12 years have more than 50 percent fewer of these teeth affected by caries than Palmerston North. While the proportion of D.M.F. permanent incisors in Napier children was considerably lower, it is of interest that the difference between the proportion of D.M.F. bicuspids in Napier and Palmerston North was relatively small. The results for the permanent cuspids are not shown since even at the age of 12 years less than 1 percent of these teeth were affected by caries in either locality.

Evaluation of the findings on the basis of D.M.F. surfaces gave results which were closely comparable to those described above where scoring was based on D.M.F. teeth. As may be expected in children aged 6 to 8 years the lower caries experience of Napier children was primarily reflected in the number of D.M.F. occlusal surfaces since in this age group pit and fissure surfaces in the permanent teeth are the predominant surfaces at risk. In older children the lower caries prevalence in Napier children was reflected about equally in the number of D.M.F. occlusal surfaces and in the number of D.M.F. proximal surfaces but to a much greater extent in the number of D.M.F. buccolingual (gingival) surfaces.

TABLE 3. Comparison of caries prevalence in different types of permanent teeth in Napier and Palmerston North children in 1961.

Age in years	First permanent molars				Permanent incisors				Bicuspids			
	Napier		Palmerston North		Napier		Palmerston North		Napier		Palmerston North	
	No. 1st molars present	Percent. 1st molars D.M.F.	No. 1st molars present	Percent. 1st molars D.M.F.	No. incis. present	Percent. incis. D.M.F.	No. incis. present	Percent. incis. D.M.F.	No. bicusps. present	Percent. bicusps. D.M.F.	No. bicusps. present	Percent. bicusps. D.M.F.
6	624	19.2	421	38.5	533	0	395	1.0	1	0	0	0
7	738	38.6	768	63.6	973	0	1007	1.3	2	0	6	0
8	718	70.9	835	78.3	1270	1.3	1522	6.9	29	0	33	0
9	820	83.8	759	88.9	1558	4.8	1466	12.1	219	1.8	157	7.6
10	789	78.8	927	90.2	1404	8.0	1692	18.5	456	1.3	777	4.9
11	729	76.3	752	83.9	1045	11.2	1041	28.2	645	13.2	759	12.1
12	721	72.3	1316	90.3	902	14.9	1611	32.7	694	21.8	1279	26.1

Discussion

The results presented show that Napier children have a higher resistance to caries than have children in the adjacent city of Hastings or in the city of Palmerston North. This difference in susceptibility cannot be related to a higher intake of fluoride by Napier children since their urinary-fluoride levels showed a mean of 0.15 p.p.m. (Malthus, R. S., unpublished data). The chief factor which distinguishes Napier from the other two places is that it is situated on an area of soils which have a recent marine history and we believe that the lower caries experience of Napier children is related to their consumption, particularly during the early years of life, of vegetables which are grown in market and home gardens on these marine soils. We have shown[2] that vegetables grown on the saline soils at Napier contain higher amounts of molybdenum, aluminium and titanium and lower amounts of manganese, copper, barium and strontium than those grown on the soils at Hastings. Adler and Straub[3] and Nagy and Polyik[4] have suggested that molybdenum, either in soils or drinking waters, may be associated with low caries prevalence in humans and a number of investigators[5,6,7,8,9] have shown that caries prevalence in the rat can be influenced by the intake of elements such as B, Cu, Mn, Mo, Sr and V as well as by fluoride.

Other aspects of this investigation which have yet to be reported will show that the author and co-workers have obtained additional evidence to support the belief that low caries prevalence in Napier is related to soil conditions and in particular that the mineral ash of a vegetable grown on the saline Napier soils has a caries-reducing effect in rats.[10] At present we think that the factor involved is more likely to be molybdenum acting either alone or in association with other elements.

It may be considered that the degree of protection afforded Napier children is not important when considered in relation to the effect produced by an optimal intake of fluoride. It must be realized, however, that it is not yet known whether the caries-reducing factor in Napier is operating at an optimal level. Especially in urban communities, water fluoridation will effectively reduce caries prevalence by as much as 60 percent. The present need is for other, perhaps less spectacular, anti-caries agents to be searched for which will reduce the remaining 40 percent.

The possibility of soils influencing the composition of foods produced on them and ultimately affecting the prevalence of dental disease is an intriguing one. For epidemiological studies in this field it would seem necessary that certain conditions should be met, namely, that one should be dealing with a uniform racial population whose food habits are fairly constant; the population under study should be reasonably dependent on local soils for their food production and there should be a minimum of "population drift." In this regard it is an advantage to be working in an area where a mild climate is associated with an extended growing season, and where detailed and extensive information is available on local soils. In studies of soil-caries relationships a low fluoride intake and internal differences in caries prevalence amongst the population are pre-requisites.

All these conditions are met in New Zealand.

Summary

An enhanced resistance to caries in children resident on saline, recent marine soils at Napier, New Zealand has been described. Caries prevalence in Napier was initially assessed in 1954–55 by comparison with that in children in the adjacent city of Hastings, which is situated on recent alluvial soils. The resistance to caries of Napier children has been confirmed by further comparisons in 1957 and 1961 with children in the city of Palmerston North. Evidence has been obtained to show that caries resistance in Napier has now extended through to older children. It is suggested that the caries-reducing factor in Napier is related to an increased intake of certain microelements from vegetables grown in market and home gardens on the recent marine soils.

REFERENCES

1. LUDWIG, T. G., W. B. HEALY, and F. L. LOSEE, An association between dental caries and certain soil conditions in New Zealand. Nature, 186: 695–696 (May 28), 1960.
2. HEALY, W. B., T. G. LUDWIG, and F. L. LOSEE, Soils and dental caries in Hawke's Bay, New Zealand. Soil Science, 92: 359–366 (Dec.) 1961.
3. ADLER, P., and J. STRAUB, Water-borne caries-protective agent other than fluorine. Acta med. Acad. Sc. hung., 4: 221–227, 1953.
4. NAGY, Z., and E. POLYIK, A devavanyai ivoviz specialis vizsgalata femnyomokra, Fogow, Syle, 48: 154, 1955.
5. KRUGER, B. J., The effect of "trace elements" on experimental dental caries in the albino rat: I. Austral. D. J., 3: 236–247 (Aug.) 1958.
6. KRUGER, B. J., The effect of "trace elements" on experimental dental caries in the albino rat: II. Austral. D. J., 3: 298–302 (Oct.) 1958.
7. MUNCH, J., and M. WINIKEN, Effect of manganese on caries susceptibility. Zahnärztl. Praxis, 10: 173–174, 1959.
8. RYGH, O., Recherches sur les oligo-elements: I. Bull. Soc. chim. biol., 31: 952–1061, 1949.
9. GEYER, C. F., Vanadium, a caries-inhibiting trace element in the Syrian hamster. J. D. Res., 32: 590–595 (Oct.) 1953.
10. LUDWIG, T. G., R. S. MALTHUS, and W. B. HEALY, A demonstration in rats of an association between soil conditions and dental caries prevalence. Nature, 194: 456–458, 1962.

ADAPTATION TO
PHYSICAL FACTORS

Like all other animals, man must learn to live with a complex of physical factors involving temperature, light, humidity, barometric pressure, altitude, wind, and many other influences. This section contains two readings which deal with physical factors and their influence on human life.

If one examines the general range of scientific articles on physical factors, one can identify three groups of papers. By far the largest number of papers is related to external temperature. A lesser number of articles is concerned with all other physical factors as they affect human beings. Lastly, only a handful of articles deal with dual or multiple interactions involving two or more factors and their concurrent effect on humans. It is important to make this observation of the stated literature because the beginner in human ecology is apt to be misled into thinking that the volume of papers on one particular phase of human ecology accurately reflects the true importance in the life of man. In the case of temperature, the large volume of papers may represent the ease with which temperatures are studied.

To pursue these thoughts even further, it is fruitful to compare the two papers in this section. The one by Schreider is a sophisticated synthesis of 52 previously published studies on only one phase of temperature effects. The other paper is by Allison and Wong on a study dealing with sunlight and its effects on man. It is possible, but not very likely, that as many as 52 papers exist in the total literature on the effects of natural light on man.

Now as to the contents of each of these papers, Schreider's survey of the literature presupposes some knowledge of Bergmann's and Allen's rules. Berg-

mann said that, within a single species of warm-blooded animal, the races in colder climates generally obtained greater body size than those in warmer climates. Allen's rule holds that warm-blooded animals living in cold climates have decreased in the size of their extremities and appendages.

There is a simple principle that is found in both these rules. In the north, a human would have a heavier weight or a larger volume/body surface ratio, whereas near the equator, he would tend to have a lighter weight or smaller volume/body surface ratio. In effect, a thicker or chunkier organism would have less cooling propensities, whereas a thinner organism would have greater cooling propensities. The rules would indicate a mechanism whereby the heat radiating from the body surfaces is regulated. A group of physiologists (Scholander, for example—see references cited) have questioned this position held by many anthropologists and evolutionists claiming that warm-blooded animals have significant heat-dissipating devices which are adequate for adaptation to both cold and hot environments. This controversy has raged for many years, and Schreider's paper is an attempt to synthesize the findings of these opposing views.

In the Du Bois formula on page 58, cm^2 represents centimeter squared and kg represents kilogram. A multiplication sign is implied before the factor 71.84.

Pages 61–63 may be regarded as an optional reading.

The article by Allison and Wong presents a number of interesting comments about skin cancer. The first observation shows that the Caucasian group does appear to have significantly higher incidence of skin cancer than the non-Caucasian groups. The authors are also aware of the relationships of the incidence of skin cancer with latitude. They show that the higher the latitude, the higher the incidence of cancer within the Caucasian group. However, Blum, as cited in their report, feels that the incidence change is related to carcinogenic radiation or shorter ultraviolet wave lengths rather than to the latitude as indicated. Nevertheless, the original report by Blum does mention the fact that carcinogenic radiation is correlated with latitude. Thus it is still useful to use latitude as a convenient index in the measure of skin cancer.

Ecological Rules, Body-Heat Regulation, and Human Evolution

EUGÈNE SCHREIDER

During the last ten years ecological rules related to body-heat regulation have been discussed by many authors.* It seems to me that their points of view can be summarized as follows:

Supporters of classical rules, named after Bergmann (1847) and Allen (1877), believe that variations in size and body-build of a homeotherm species, observed in different parts of its geographical range, must be considered as evolutionary adaptations to thermal environment. Zoologists are mostly concerned with size, while anthropologists usually put the stress on body-build.

An opposite view is held by some physiologists in whose opinion the actual existence of geographical gradients of this kind is doubtful, as there are many exceptions to the rule. Be that as it may, such gradients could not be explained by adaptive changes because the adaptation to thermal environment is achieved by physiological, rather than by anatomical means.

A third point of view has been expressed by some authors who do not seem to be generally concerned with ecological rules, but who emphatically deny their applicability to human species. In their opinion, man modifies his natural surroundings so efficiently that he escapes the pressure of climatic factors.

In my own opinion, these points of view should be revised critically, but sympathetically, as, in spite of conflicting conclusions, the evidence quoted in support of them is generally good.

---

* Among the recent authors, entirely or partly favorable to ecological rules, the following should be quoted: Baker (1960), Bodenheimer (1957), Coon et al. (1950), Coon (1955), Garn (1958), Mayr (1956), Newman (1953), Rensch (1959), Salt (1952), and Snow (1954, 1958); the "rules" have been criticized mostly by Hensel (1959), Scholander, (1955, 1956), Irving (1957), and Wilber (1957). A "synthetic" view, which is not inconsistent with the present writer's opinion, has been expressed by Hamilton (1961).

The efficiency of artificial microclimates

Although the idea that man can modify his environment at will is largely correct, it leads to faulty interpretations if it is forgotten that far-reaching changes continue to take place even in our time, without the demands of the human organism being taken into account.

Regarding protection against extremes of temperature, the situation varies considerably according to the technique standards used, the materials available, and local customs. Wherever social distinctions are marked, it also differs according to economic resources. Even in modern houses, heating, for economic reasons, may be highly inadequate.

Tradition and routine may also impede changes desirable from the physiological point of view. The average temperature in most houses in the British Isles is markedly lower than in American dwellings. From the physiological viewpoint it is insufficient, so insufficient, in fact, that some doctors are of the opinion that in certain conditions it is responsible for perinatal mortality: "prevention which is of paramount importance because of high mortality, can be achieved only by safeguarding against a fall of room temperature" (Mann and Elliot, 1957).

The American microclimate is more satisfactory probably because the harder winter demands stricter precautions being taken. Negligence is more liable to occur in countries whose winter is reputedly mild. This explains why chilblains are more common in France and Italy than in Russia, Sweden, or Canada.

Improvements are possible only if knowledge and technical means permit. Numbers of Arctic populations have been unable to solve the problem of heating. The portable tent used by certain Siberian autochtons provided no effective protection against low temperatures (Bogoraz, 1901, 1904–1909). A similar observation has been made about certain Canadian aboriginal tribes (Stefansson, 1943). The Eskimo igloo, with its "tropical" heat, should not be too exclusively singled out for quotation. The igloo is of relatively recent invention, and is not the only dwelling known to the Eskimos. In certain Eskimo huts, it may be cold (Birket-Smith, 1937).

Man, however, even with inferior material resources, but with a knowledge of fire going back to time immemorial, is capable of protecting himself with varying success against the cold. On the other hand, even with advanced techniques, he is generally defenseless against excesses of heat. Air conditioning is an extremely rare privilege, and the thermal environment in which, for instance, farm work is done, cannot be modified at will.

In damp tropical countries, as well as in deserts, the heat puts the organism to a severe test. Shade does not necessarily offer protection. In dry regions in Soviet Asia, the temperature in summer may reach 40°C. inside the homes. In some regions of the Sahara, the heat is so hard to bear, even at night, that, for part of the year, the inhabitants of certain towns sleep on terraces, unless they leave their permanent dwellings for reed huts (Rochefort, 1957).

It is true that in certain hot and arid regions the nights, at least in winter, are very cold. It has sometimes even been thought that it is the cold, rather than the heat, to which the inhabitants must have adapted themselves. Now, whatever the level of civilization, man has to work in order to live, and his work is generally done before nightfall: *the daytime environment counts above all,* for this is the environment in which his active life is lived, with the main expenditure of energy and the highest calories production (Schreider, 1962).

In the lower latitudes, the daytime environment, unless moderated by altitude or other local peculiarities, is characterized by the intense heat which man, impelled by economic needs, cannot escape. However ingenious he may be, he cannot entirely withdraw from the climatic environment, particularly the heat. It is therefore impossible to dismiss the problem of selective pressure exercised by the thermal environment.

Human ecological gradients

Let us now study the question whether gradients exist in man. A certain regularity in the geographical distribution of human characters was observed by the early naturalists. They noted, for example, that the inhabitants of cold mountainous regions are short but compact, whereas those of the neighboring lowlands with a damp, warm climate are more slender in form (Orbigny, 1839). Some authors judged it possible to group Eskimos and Fuegians in a single "hyperborean race," by basing their argument on the fact that all of them are of short and massive build.

Other similar generalizations have been made more recently, and they are on the whole correct. However, like the earlier conclusions, they are still based on impressions, rather than upon direct evidence, and, for want of quantitative data, propose one simple gradient for a given morphological "character," such as "body-build," without taking into account that the same biological result can be obtained, as we shall see, in different anatomical ways.

I have chosen a strictly biometrical approach to the problem. The first stage was the study of ten metric characters in eleven human populations, which permitted an approximate estimation of trunk volume and surface. It then appeared that the volume/surface ratio is very similar in groups as distinct as Parisian workmen and Somali nomads. It fluctuates around 0.5 liter per square decimeter, which leads one to believe that in spite of their obvious imperfection, estimated volume and surface reflect an anatomical fact. And, despite the small variation, the ratio appeared higher in European populations than in tropical populations.

If the body weight/estimated trunk surface ratio is found, closely related figures are still obtained, the European samples, however, forming one group (1.26–1.30 kg/dm^2), and the tropical samples another (1.09–1.24 kg/dm^2) (Schreider, 1950a, 1951a). These initial observations allow the assumption that a geographical gradient exists for the body weight/body surface ratio (W/S).

In fact, it proved impossible to pursue the work along these lines, because human samples, for whom measurements are available allowing the estimation of the trunk volume and surface, are extremely rare. I therefore had to use the much greater number of samples for which each individual body height and weight was known; this allowed the calculation of the body surface, by means of a well-known formula: Surface area (cm^2) = Weight in kg$^{0.425}$ Height in cm$^{0.725}$ 71.84 (Du Bois).

Published information so far relates to a hundred or so male samples, which represent all the main subdivisions of the human species, and about twenty female samples. For all these samples, the body height, the body weight, the body surface, and the body weight/body surface ratio are known, but in a fairly large number of cases, additional measurements are available, allowing the body structure to be estimated, which is highly important.

Figures now available confirm on the whole the geographical gradient of the W/S ratio, which tends to decrease in hot countries. They reveal, however, a more complex situation than had at first been thought, for they suggest that there is either an exception to the rule, or else that there is a plurality of distinct gradients for the various races.

As regards the European leucoderm group, no complication occurs. In Europe itself the ratio which can attain 39 kg/m^2 in Germany, more than 38 in northern Ireland and Finland and 37.9 in France, falls to 37.0 in Calabria and 37.4 in Sicily. It drops still further in North Africa (37.1–36.5), to 36 among the Arabs of the Yemen, and to 35.4 in a Berber population in the Sahara. The existence of the W/S ratio gradients in the white races has been moreover confirmed in the United States (Newman and Munro, 1955).

The only important exception to the W/S ratio gradient concerns the melanoderm (black) racial group. This exception is less important than one might believe at first sight, for although it is represented by almost twenty populations, it is limited geographically to neighboring tribes all grouped in the west of Africa (partly Mali and especially Haute Volta).

Beginning with this group of tribes whose W/S ratio fluctuates between 37.2 and 37.9 kg/m^2, the figures decrease towards the north, in the direction of the Sahara (36.5–36.8), towards the Atlantic coast (35.9–36.6), as well as towards the interior of the African continent, where the average figures are in the region of 33.5–36.2. If this territorial unit of relatively high values did not exist, the conclusion might have been reached that there is one single gradient of the body weight/body surface ratio, with progressive decrease in figures from northern Europe to East Africa (32.8–36.3) and South Africa (33.9).

Several populations of Somalia, a country close to the hot desert, give averages ranging between 34 and 35. We do not know whether it is permissible to include these human groups in the Black gradient, as their anthropological status is uncertain. And we naturally have to put in a class apart the Bushmen (30.2), as well as the Congo Pygmies (31.4–31.5) who give low figures but cannot mingle with the racial groups of Black Africa.

It has not been possible to find documentary material concerning the Siberian or Central Asiatic populations. We know, however, that the inhabitants of hot Asiatic countries, whether Tonkinese or Southern Indians, give low averages, especially the latter (32.4–34.6). Low figures are also found for a small group of Autochtons in the Australian desert (35.6) and for the pygmy inhabitants of the Andaman Islands (32.4), the Philippines (31.4–31.9), and Malaya (30.91).

There is a distinct shortage of information about the aborigines of the New World. Nevertheless, the few figures available clearly suggest the existence of a gradient. The highest are found in cold climates, among the Mapuches in the Andes (39.2), the Eskimos of Greenland (38.0) and of Canada (39.1), and some distinctly lower values in Guatemala (36.9), Venezuela (35.6), and Mexico (34.9–36.4).

This undoubtedly tallies with the classical ecological rules, and provides a satisfactory biometric confirmation of them. But I have further attempted, by testing it on human populations, to verify the rule that in closely related homeotherm forms, protruding and exposed organs tend to become shorter as the average temperature of the habitat decreases (Allen, 1877). In order to carry out this verification, I found the ratio, to the body weight, of the total length of the limbs,* which, as was shown long ago in physiology, are "thermolytic" organs (Bernard, 1858, 1878). It then appeared that the limbs/weight ratio shows a definite increase in populations dwelling in hot climates (Table 1).

The collected results confirm, therefore, the generalization made over ten years ago, namely, that "in races or closely related homeotherm species, the relative value of the body surface, expressed as a ratio of the volume or the mass, increases in climates which, at least during part of the year, subject the thermolytic mechanisms to stress. The inverse tendency appears in climates which over-facilitate the elimination of heat" (Schreider, 1951a). This last sentence should, I think, be emphasized, since the idea that the heat stress alone plays a role has been erroneously ascribed to me. This, however, concerns the interpretation of the results, to which we shall have occasion to return later. For the moment, the essential fact is the existence of gradients, namely anatomical changes whose parallelism with certain aspects of the enviroment it is hard to deny.

What, one may ask, are these anatomical changes? A number of anthropologists apparently consider that there is a correlative modification of stature and body-build, somewhat short stature and thickset, stocky figures typifying Arctic peoples, whereas inhabitants of the tropical belt tend to be characterized by tall stature combined with slenderness (Coon et al., 1950; Coon, 1955). The example, popularized by a number of publications (e.g., Barnett, 1961), is given, on the one hand, by the Eskimo, with its bulky shape, and on the other, by the tall, thin Nilotic. This conception is an oversimplification of the facts, and is utterly incompatible with the anthropometric data and the two gradients brought to light by my results.

---

* Total length of limbs = [(acromion − dactylion) + symphysion height] × 2.

TABLE 1. Limb length/body weight ratios (cm/kg) for adult males (Schreider, 1957a and b and unpublished data).

	Limbs/weight ratio		Body height average
	Average	SD	
73 Parisian workers	4.88	0.47	168.8
47 Finns	4.89	0.41	169.5
80 French soldiers	4.91	0.47	166.2
50 French students	4.94	0.43	174.6
300 British soldiers*	5.00	—	170.9
113 French soldiers	5.02	0.41	168.9
504 Ukrainians*	5.08	—	167.3
120 Sicilian soldiers	5.09	0.43	169.1
100 Tonkinese	5.37	0.36	159.9
82 Otomis (Mexico)	5.51	0.49	157.6
31 Arabs (Yemen)	5.63	0.47	162.2
18 Asheraf (Somalia)	5.64	0.56	170.9
119 Nhungues (Mozamb.)	5.66	0.52	167.9
123 Darod (Somalia)	5.74	0.54	172.2
119 Rahanoween (Somalia)	5.83	0.59	169.4
51 Gobaween (Somalia)	5.90	0.51	168.4
47 Dir (Somalia)	6.01	0.49	172.9
26 Antumba (Mozambique)	6.06	0.64	164.9
87 Hawyah (Somalia)	6.21	0.51	170.0
18 Korana (S. Africa)	6.21	0.58	159.8
35 Indians (Madras)	6.61	0.71	168.4
95 Aka Pygmies (Congo)	6.98	0.67	144.1
115 Basua Pygm. (Congo)	7.03	0.77	144.3

* Calculated from published averages. All other figures calculated from individual measurements. Data concerning Finns and Madras Indians communicated by M. Pelosse (Paris) and Dr. Henrotte (Liége), respectively.

In fact, if brachymorphic Eskimos give a high W/S ratio (38–39), the Otomi of Mexico, like other Indians of the tropical regions, are also brachymorphic, but show a much lower figure (W/S ratio = 34.9; stature = 157.6), which is close to that of the Darod of Somalia, leptomorphs of tall stature (W/S ratio = 35.1; stature = 172.2), whose anatomy is rather similar to that of Nilotics. There is no *exact* parallelism between the two gradients shown by my results, and the geographical distribution of weight, stature, or body-build. This is explained by the fact that the same result, like the reduction of the W/S ratio, is obtainable by different anatomical variations, namely, the diminution of all body dimensions, as in the case of the Otomi, and, to a more marked extent, the Pygmies; or by the considerable shortening of the trunk, accompanied by lengthening of limbs, as in the case of Somalis.

The opposition of the Eskimo and the Nilotic is, therefore, in some way fallacious and even from the didactic angle, it may lead to error. There exist in tropical regions brachymorphs of small size, with a low W/S ratio and a high limbs/weight ratio. The facts are such that there appears to be a convergence for the biologically important ratios in human groups which originally did not enjoy the same evolutionary opportunities. But, before we can accept this conclusion, we must be backed by a number of guarantees of certainty.

The value of basic data

The first task is to find how much reliance can be placed in the figures which allowed the existence of the weight/surface and limbs/weight ratios to be shown. Some understandable initial reserve can be expressed on the account of the body surface having been estimated by using a formula in which weight is a factor. In connection with this, it is worth recalling that the first rough draft of a gradient was obtained in a totally different way, the trunk surface having been estimated from a set of anthropometrical measurements. The facts show that the weight/total surface ratio gives the same results as the weight/trunk surface ratio.

By way of a check, we have also worked out, separately for the two sexes, correlations between the weight/*surface calculated by the formula* ratio, and the weight/*surface measured by integrator* ratio: these correlations amount to 0.83 for adult males, and 0.84 for females (Schreider, 1951a). There is a sufficient degree of agreement, if it is borne in mind that we have only to compare the averages.

It is true that the formula used for obtaining the total surface was established on individuals of white race, so that some correction might be necessary before applying it to other human groups. No correction appears, however, to be needed for the Eskimos (Rodahl, 1952); and for the yellow races, if one is necessary, it is not an extensive one (Necheles and Loo, 1932). The formula seems to imply a relatively important error only in the case of African and Australia black races, because it does not take into account the considerable length of limbs which characterizes the two racial groups. But if this is the case, a corrected formula could only still further accentuate the geographical gradient of the W/S ratio (Newman, 1956).

Doubt can, however, be expressed about the value or the significance of a character such as weight. The question is important, but is directly related to the biological interpretation of the gradients, and they will be studied together.

The biological meaning of gradients

In an interesting study confirming the geographical gradient of the W/S ratio in the United States, two American authors reach the conclusion that the cause of it is to be sought in the influence of the climate over food consumption, the latter being greater in regions where cold winters are experienced (Newman and Munro, 1955).

No one will question the influence of nutrition on body weight, and since this is the case, one is tempted to think that the low W/S ratio of populations living for the most part in underdeveloped countries is simply a reflection of their insufficient nutritional state. This explanation is too simple to be correct. Body weight's normal fluctuations are *loosely* correlated with calorie intake (Thomson et al., 1961). And as far as I know, I did not take into account data concerning populations stricken by famine or abnormally overnourished.

Certain samples, indeed, benefited from unusually plentiful nourishment, but they are found in tropical countries, and are military series from former colonial armies, whose average weight is greater than that of civilians of the same origin. However, their W/S ratio generally does not reach temperate climate figures. Such is the case, notably, of certain Somali samples. This is also the case of our Tonkinese, who were studied while stationed in France. Inversely, French soldiers who had, on the average, lost some kilograms during the last war, gave a W/S ratio comparable to that of the French samples studied in less exceptional circumstances. Other similar cases could be quoted.

This may well appear strange should it be forgotten that, if nutrition influences body weight, it is not the sole determining factor. The situation becomes clearer if, instead of confining oneself exclusively to weight, one takes into account a set of anthropometric data. Fortunately this is possible in a number of cases. It is then observed that, in the populations under study, the *average man* is neither skeleton-like nor obese, whatever his weight. In fact, the average weight of a population is dependent primarily on its average dimensions and its morphology, which limit ponderal fluctuations.

The short trunk and very long limbs of the Nilotics, Somalis, and Australians (Abbie, 1957, 1958), can no more be explained by a particular nutritional status than can the structure of the trunk of European populations which, out of geometrical necessity, shows excessive volume in relation to its surface (Schreider, 1950a). Moreover, direct observation of some human groups showing a low W/S ratio or a "deficient" body weight leads one to state that their nutrition is sufficient (Schreider, 1953–1955; Roberts, 1960).

One of the main arguments against the purely nutritional interpretation of the weight/surface ratio differences resides in the fact that the W/S ratio gradient, which is so clearly defined in men, is *non-existent in women,* who are nevertheless represented by about twenty populations (Schreider, 1950a, 1951a, and unpublished material). It is difficult to conceive that the men's diet should be insufficient, whereas the women of the same tribe may sometimes appear overnourished, for their averages, for both body weight and the W/S ratio, may even be above the male averages: such is the case of Andaman Islands aborigines and two populations of Somalia.*

---

* The fact of women showing no gradient comparable with that of men may be explained by the fact that body-heat regulation in females has peculiarities not found in males (Hardy and Milhorat, 1939; Hardy, Milhorat, and Du Bois, 1941; Du Bois, Ebaugh, and Hardy, 1952). Account has also to be taken of the possible influence of sexual selection, which favors corpulent women (Baker, 1960).

It is, in short, impossible to suppose, when human groups whose dimensions and body structure are fairly well known, that the differences in their average body weight are due solely, or even essentially, to the nutritional regimen. Food may be a disturbing factor likely to invert the ranking of similar averages, without, however, perturbing the whole gradient.

The problem is somewhat different for irregularities appearing as true departures from the rule. Exceptions, in the case of certain animals, had been known for some time. They are partly explained by ecological adaptation, i.e., by the behavior characterizing the species. Moreover, various physiological mechanisms may reduce the role of the body mass in relation to its thermolytic surfaces. It is, nevertheless, equally certain that the importance of the W/S ratio is not to be dismissed in homeotherms as a whole, as seems to be the opinion of physiologists who deny all relationship between anatomical dimensions and structures, on the one hand, and climatic characteristics on the other. In polar bear, whose coat, when completely soaked with water, offers no protection, the heat is probably retained by peripheral vasoconstriction. However, "the polar bear is also a very large animal with large heat capacity and has a proportionately small surface" (Scholander et al., 1950). If it is granted that the polar bear benefits from its very considerable mass compared to its relatively small surface, it is difficult to see why it should not be the case with other mammals, particularly with man.

As regards the human species, the problem is simplified for man's hairy coating does not show physiologically important variations. Moreover, we have multiple proofs of the influence exercised by the W/S ratio over his thermal balance. In heat, individuals with a high ratio perspire more freely than others, but this is useless waste, since the excessive sweat drips away and is largely lost from a physiological point of view (Schreider, 1951b). On the other hand, we observe, in 120 French soldiers, that those who stand up to heat well include a high proportion of individuals having a W/S ratio lower than 36 kg/m^2, whereas this proportion is low in those who find it difficult to stand high temperatures. The difference between the two percentages is equal to 23.2% $\pm$ 6.4 and the probabilities are fewer than one in a thousand that this is due to mere chance. Furthermore, by keeping men walking at a speed of 7 km/hr for fifteen minutes on the treadmill, we find, despite the short test time, a positive correlation of 0.31 between the W/S ratio and the final temperature of the subjects.

Does the limbs/weight ratio, in its turn, play a part in thermoregulation? In heat, with an environmental temperature of 35°–36.9°C., the negative correlation between the body temperature and the ratio amounts to -0.38 ($P = 0.03$). Like the previous one, this correlation is not very marked, but there is no reason to suppose that it ought to have been more so; the anatomical conditions of thermoregulation are not the only determining cause of this. The plurality of cross-factors partly explains why, in physiology, correlations are generally low. If we neglected the low coefficients, we should run the risk of rejecting, one by one, all the factors which, taken together, ensure the physiological success of the species (Schreider, 1958, 1960).

Summary

There are serious grounds for considering geographical gradients of biometrical characters such as the weight/surface ratio or limbs/weight ratio as true ecological gradients, linked in the course of evolution to climatic conditions and thermoregulation. We must not be deterred by the existence of exceptions. The sole important exception in man known at present is limited territorially to part of West Africa. It may be due to compensating physiological mechanisms, or be considered as the beginning of a gradient peculiar to African melanoderms: our present state of knowledge allows no clear choice to be made between these two hypotheses. Finally, it has to be borne in mind that certain exceptions might well be due to relatively recent migrations.

The most plausible hypothesis is that these ecological gradients are, in fact, the product of natural selection. Nutritional habits cannot explain the gradients even if they may influence them. The wide differences revealed by the figures do not admit of this interpretation: both gradients, like the average body mass of the populations, are linked in the first place to the very marked variations in average sizes and anatomical proportions which are largely, if not exclusively, hereditary. The outstanding fact is that, in similar climatic conditions, populations differing greatly in stature, weight, or other metric characters give closely related and sometimes identical figures for the weight/surface or limbs/weight ratio. This can only be explained by a phenomenon of convergence which, in partly differing anatomical ways, but under similar environmental conditions, has led to biologically equivalent results.

REFERENCES

ABBIE, A. A. 1957. Metrical characters of a central Australian tribe. Oceania, **27:** 220–243.
——. 1958. Timing in human evolution. Proc. Linn. Soc. N. S. Wales, **83** (2): 197–213.
ALLEN, J. A. 1877. The influence of physical conditions in the genesis of species. Radical Review, **1:** 108–140.
BAKER, P. T. 1960. Climate, culture and evolution. Human Biol., **32:** 3–16.
BARNETT, A. 1961. The human species. Revised ed., Penguin Books, Harmondsworth.
BERGMANN, C. 1847. Ueber die Verhaltnisse der Wärmeökonomie des Thiere zu ihrer Grösse. Göttinger Studien, **3:** 595–708.
BERNARD, CL. 1859. Leçons sur les propriétés physiologiques et les altérations pathologiques des liquides de l'organisme. **Vol. I,** Paris.

————. 1878. Leçons sur les phénomènes de la vie communs aux animaux et aux végétaux. Paris.

BIRKET-SMITH, K. 1937. Moeurs et coutumes des Esquimaux. Payot, Paris.

BODENHEIMER, F. S. 1957. The ecology of mammals in arid zones. Recherches sur al Zone Aride. Ecologie humaine et animale, p. 100–137, UNESCO, Paris.

BOGORAZ, W. C. 1901. Otcherk materialnovo byta olennikh Tchouktchei. Sbornik Muzeia po anthropologhii i etnografii. Vol. 2, St. Petersbourg.

————. 1904–1909. The Chukchee. Memoires of the Jesup North Pacific expedition. Vol. 7, Amer. Mus. Nat. Hist., New York.

COON, C. S. 1955. Some problems of human variability and natural selection in climate and culture. Amer. Nat., **89:** 257–280.

————, S. M. GARN, and J. B. BIRDSELL. 1950. Races. Thomas, Springfield.

DU BOIS, E. F., F. G. EBAUGH, and J. D. HARDY. 1952. Basal heat production and elimination of thirteen women at temperatures from 22°C. to 35°C. J. Nutr., **48:** 257–293.

GARN, S. M. 1958. A comment on Wilber's "Origin of human types." Human Biol., **30:** 338–340.

HAMILTON, T. H. 1961. The adaptive significance of intraspecific trends of variation in wing length and body size among bird species. Evolution, **15:** 180–195.

HARDY, J. D., and A. T. MILHORAT. 1939. Basal heat loss and production in women at temperatures from 23 to 36°C. Proc. Soc. Exp. Biol. Med., **41:** 9.

————, ————, and E. F. DU BOIS. 1941. Basal metabolism and heat loss of young women at temperatures from 22 to 35°C. J. Nutr., **21:** 383.

HENSEL, H. 1959. Heat and cold. Ann. Rev. Physiol., **21:** 91–116. Palo Alto.

IRVING, L. 1957. The usefulness Scholander's views on adaptive insulation of animals. Evolution, **11:** 257–259.

MANN, T. P., and R. I. K. ELLIOTT. 1957. Neonatal cold injury. Lancet, **272:** 229–233.

MAYR, E. 1956. Geographical character gradients and climatic adaptation. Evolution, **10:** 105–108.

NECHELES, H., and T. C. LOO. 1932. Uber den Stoffwechsel der Chinesen. I. Die Körperoberflache. Chinese J. Physiol., **6:** 129.

NEWMAN, M. T. 1953. The application of ecological rules to the racial anthropology of the aboriginal New World. Amer. Anthr. (n.s.), **55:** 311–327.

————. 1956. Adaptation of man to cold climates. Evolution, **10:** 101–114.

NEWMAN, R. W., and E. H. MUNRO. 1955. The relation of climate and body size in U.S. males. Amer. J. Phys. Anthr., **13:** 1–17.

ORBIGNY (D'), A. 1839. L'homme américain. Vol. I, Par

RENSCH, B. 1959. Evolution above the species level. Methuen, London.

ROBERTS, D. F. 1960. Effects of race and climate on human growth as exemplified by studies on African children. *In* Tanner, J. M., Human growth, p. 59–72, Pergamon, London.

ROCHEFORT, R. 1957. Les effets du milieu sur les communautés humaines des régions arides, adaptation de ces communautés aux conditions locales de milieu. *In* Recherches sur la zone aride, VIII, Ecologie humaine et animale, p. 11–42, UNESCO, Paris.

RODAHL, K. 1952. The body surface area of Eskimos as determined by the linear and the height-weight formulas. Amer. J. Phys. Anthr., **10:** 419–426.

SALT, G. W. 1952. The relation of metabolism to climate and distribution in three finches of the genus Carpodacus. Ecol. Monogr., **22:** 122–152.

SCHOLANDER, P. F. 1955. Evolution of climatic adaptation in homeotherms. Evolution, **9:** 15–26.

———. 1956. Climatic rules. Evolution, **10:** 339–340.

———, R. HOCK, V. WALTERS, and L. IRVING. 1950. Body insulation of some arctic and tropical mammals and birds. Biol. Bull., **99:** 225–236.

SCHREIDER, E. 1950a. Les variations raciales et sexuelles du tronc humain. L'Anthropologie, **54:** 67–81, 228–261.

———. 1950b. Geographical distribution of the body-weight/body-surface ratio. Nature, **165:** 286.

———. 1951a. Race, constitution, thermolyse. Rev. Sci., **89:** 110–119.

———. 1951b. Anatomical factors of body-heat regulation. Nature, **167:** 823–825.

———. 1953. Régulation thermique et évolution humaine. Bull. Mem. Soc. Anthr. Paris, (10) 4: 138–148.

———. 1953–1955. Recherches anthropologiques sur les Otomis de la région d'Ixmiquilpan (Mexique). L'Anthropologie, **57:** 453–489; **59:** 253–296.

———. 1957a. Ecological rules and body-heat regulation in man. Nature, **179:** 915–916.

———. 1957b. Gradients écologiques régulation thermique et différénciation humaine. Biotypologie, **18:** 168–183.

———. 1958. Les régulations physiologiques. Essai de révision biométrique du problème de l'homéostasie. Biotypologie, **19:** 127–215.

———. 1960. La biométrie. Presses Univ. de France, Paris.

———. 1962. Anthropologie physiologique et variations climatiques. Natural Sci. Dept., Arid Zone Report, UNESCO, Paris (in press).

SNOW, D. W. 1954. Trends in geographical variation in Palaearctic members of the genus Parus. Evolution, **8:** 19–28.

———. 1958. Climate and geographical variation in birds. New Biology, **25:** 64–84.

STEFANSSON, F. V. 1943. The friendly arctic. Macmillan, New York.

THOMSON, A. M., W. Z. BILLEWICZ, and R. PASSMORE. 1961. The relation between calorie intake and body weight in man. Lancet, **1:** 1027–1028.

WILBER, C. G. 1957. Physiological regulations and the origin of human types. Human Biol., **29:** 329–336.

Skin Cancer:
Some Ethnic Differences*

SAMUEL D. ALLISON
AND K. L. WONG

Skin cancer is 45 times as common among Caucasians as among non-Caucasians in Honolulu, Hawaii. This was revealed in an undertaking sponsored by private physicians and governmental and volunteer agencies in 1955 and 1956.

Cooperation can solve problems

The cooperative efforts of private physicians and governmental and volunteer agencies can elucidate problems not easily solved by independent action. Such cooperative effort was utilized in a skin cancer project designed to determine the incidence of skin cancer in the various ethnic groups in Hawaii.

The island of Oahu which makes up most of Honolulu County lies at about 21 degrees north latitude. The climate is mild; the percentage of available sunshine is high, and the average temperature is 75°F. The peoples of Hawaii represent several distinct ethnic groups, the major ones being noted in Table 1.

All Honolulu dermatologists cooperate

All of the seven dermatologists in private practice in the County of Honolulu participated in this study. It is believed that they see a representative selection of the various races. These dermatologists reported their cases of skin cancers

* A project of the Hawaii Dermatologic Society and the Department of Health, Territory of Hawaii, in cooperation with the Cancer Committee of the Hawaii Medical Association and the Hawaii Cancer Society. Dermatologists cooperating in this project were (in addition to the senior author): H. L. Arnold, Jr., C. V. Caver, E. K. Chung-Hoon, H. M. Johnson, W. H. Kurashige, and C. W. Loo.

TABLE 1. Estimated average population of Honolulu County by race 1955 and 1956.

Caucasian	99,977
Hawaiian and Part-Hawaiian	62,907
Chinese	31,453
Japanese	126,936
Filipino	35,947
Korean	5,607
Other	11,618
Total	374,445

to a central register at the Department of Health. In 1956 reports on cases of skin cancer diagnosed by non-dermatologists in the Territory were obtained through the cooperation of pathologists and general physicians sending biopsy specimens to them. As these reports did not differ much from those reported by dermatologists, this review is confined to 293 reports of cases seen by dermatologists on residents of Honolulu County during 1955 and 1956.

Multiple lesions of the same etiologic type were recorded as one case. Multiple lesions of different etiologic types were assigned as many times as there were types. A case diagnosed more than once, i.e., recurrence or new lesion of same type, was counted once.

Ethnic differences exist in cancer

Specific types of cancer are known to affect various ethnic groups at different rates. For example, studies in Hawaii[1,2] have revealed a high incidence of stomach cancer in Japanese males and a low incidence in non-Japanese males; a low incidence of breast cancer in Japanese females and a high incidence in Caucasian females.

It is common knowledge that skin cancer occurs less often in Negroes than in whites. It has long been recognized in Hawaii that Orientals have less skin

TABLE 2. Skin cancer cases by race and type of cancer, Honolulu County, 1955 and 1956.

Race	Squamous-Cell	Basal-Cell	Other	Total No. Cases
Caucasian	124	135	17	276
Non-Caucasian	10	7	—	17
Korean	2	—	—	2
Chinese	3	—	—	3
Japanese	4	5	—	9
Hawaiian and Part-Hawaiian	1	1	—	2
Filipino	—	1	—	1

cancer than Occidentals, and in 1946 Arnold[3] made some interesting observations concerning this. In 1955 and 1956 of 293 cases reported 94% were Caucasians; this group made up 27% of the population. Table 2 shows the racial breakdown of the skin cases.

Skin cancer rare in Orientals

From Table 3 it can be seen that the rate per 100,000 population for Caucasians is 138.0 and the rate for non-Caucasians is 3.1, or a ratio of approximately 45 to 1. This difference is highly significant. The differences in observed rates among the non-Caucasian groups are not statistically significant.

TABLE 3. Skin cancer incidence rates per 100,000 population by race, Honolulu County, 1955 and 1956.

Race	Rate
Caucasians	138.0
Non-Caucasians	3.1
Korean	17.8
Chinese	4.8
Japanese	3.5
Hawaiian and Part Hawaiian	1.6
Filipino	1.4

Lower latitude sunshine more carcinogenic

The white population of Hawaii apparently has more malignant neoplasms of the skin than do the white populations of selected mainland areas. While no true comparison between Hawaii and other areas is available, and recognizing the errors involved in comparing data from different types of surveys, some comparisons are made in Table 4.

It is to be repeated that Hawaii's figure is based on reporting by seven dermatologists only, comprising less than 2% of the total physicians practicing in the

TABLE 4. Skin cancer annual incidence rates per 100,000 white population, Honolulu County, 1955 and 1956; selected mainland areas,[4-6] 1947, 1948.

Area	Year	Rate
Honolulu	1955 and 1956	138
Dallas	1948	109
San Francisco	1947	90
Philadelphia	1948	39

County. On the other hand, the mainland rates are based on reports from "every hospital and clinic and from over 94% of the physicians."[4-6]

Blum[7] has presented convincing evidence that such differences noted in Table 4 are due not to total sunlight but to "carcinogenic radiation," relatively more abundant in the lower latitudes.

Most cases confirmed by biopsy

Microscopic confirmation was obtained in 93% of the 293 cases reported. Twenty cases (7%) did not have such confirmation, of whom all were Caucasians except for one Japanese. This latter case represents one of the five basal-cell epitheliomas diagnosed in Japanese.

Thirty-seven cases had more than one lesion of the same histologic type present at the time of diagnosis. Forty-four cases were reported to have had two or more types of lesions at one time or another. All were Caucasians, except for one Caucasian-Hawaiian.

The predominance of skin cancers on the head and face is borne out again in this series of cases. It is interesting to note, however, the occurrence by type of cancer by body site. In Hawaii, the physician cannot rely on the location of lesion as an aid in determining its type. Both of the common types of skin cancer occur on all parts of the body. Data illustrating this are presented in Table 5.

TABLE 5. Distribution of lesions by site and type of cancer, Honolulu County, 1955 and 1956.

Site	Total	Squamous-Cell	Basal-Cell	Malignant Melanoma	Other
Head and face	187	78	104	2	3
Lip and chin	23	11	12	—	—
Buccal cavity	1	1	—	—	—
Neck	13	5	6	1	1
Shoulder, chest, back, breast, abdomen	32	15	10	1	6
Upper extremity	29	22	6	—	1
Lower extremity	5	1	3	—	1
Not stated	3	1	1	—	1
Total	293	134	142	4	13

Summary

Independent dermatologists can aid in elucidating the epidemiologic pattern of certain diseases by a cooperative approach to a problem.

Caucasians in Hawaii suffer a much higher incidence of skin cancer than do Japanese and certain other ethnic groups.

REFERENCES

1. RHEA, T. R., A Comparative Study of the Mortality from Gastric Cancer in Hawaii, Hawaii M. J. 13:107–112 (Nov.–Dec.) 1953.
2. QUISENBERRY, W. B., I. L. TILDEN, and J. L. ROSENGARD, Racial Incidence of Cancer in Hawaii, Hawaii M. J. 13:449–451 (July–Aug.) 1954.
3. ARNOLD, H. L., JR., Incidence of Dermatoses in Office Practice in Hawaii, Arch. Dermat. & Syph. 53:6–9 (Jan.) 1946.
4. MARCUS, S. C., Cancer Illness Among Residents of Dallas, Texas, PHS Publication No. 178, Public Health Service, 1952.
5. GRODOWITZ, W., Cancer Illness Among Residents of San Francisco and Alameda Counties, California, PHS Publication No. 65, Public Health Service, 1951.
6. CUTLER, S. J., and S. C. MARCUS, Cancer Illness Among Residents of Philadelphia, Pennsylvania, PHS Publication No. 244, Public Health Service, 1952.
7. BLUM, H. F., Sunlight as a Causal Factor in Cancer of the Skin of Man, J. Nat. Cancer Inst. 9:247–258 (Dec.) 1948.

THE ENVIRONMENT, OTHER ORGANISMS, AND DISEASE PATTERNS

Man must adapt to other organisms which live together with him. Frequently, a relationship between man and another organism is shown to exist under certain environmental conditions or in a specific geographical location. In further study, it may be discovered that an environmental factor determines the distribution and activity of the other organism. The organism, in turn, is responsible for the disease pattern in man.

These relationships are shown in the two papers included in this section.

May cites the relationship of delta inhabitants with malaria and Anopholes minimus. *The disease would represent a maladjustment of the culture of the delta inhabitants to the activities of the mosquito which are determined by the environment.*

Burkitt indicates the relationships of central African children with cancer, virus, and a mosquito. Since the mosquito is confined within a geographical range which is determined by temperature, rainfall, and altitude, the cancer is also limited to this geographical range. This study has aroused much attention because it represents presumptive evidence that a virus is related to Burkitt's tumor and the very similar disease of leukemia. A viral-cancer link in certain diseases has been suspected in other recent research projects.

The applications of ecological principles to human diseases represents an exciting development.

73

The Ecology of Human Disease

JACQUES M. MAY*

A famous French playwright once quipped: "A healthy person is nothing but an unrevealed patient." I have a great fondness for this definition, and I think there is much more to it than meets the eye. I like it because it stresses the fact that what we call health is nothing but a struggle between mysterious forces that occur below the horizon. Nothing happens in the visible field that does not stem from deep, invisible, and unknown roots. It has been said that one of the traits that distinguishes man from animals is that man suspects there is another value to the appearance of what he observes. A second reason I like this definition is that it mentions the hidden traits that the challenges of the environment may cause to be revealed in a person when he becomes a patient. We shall see a little later that these hidden traits that really stem from the genetic make-up of the patient are of great importance in our understanding of the ecology of disease and have been far too often neglected in the past in favor of what is merely visible. Thus the French playwright's remark implies that some day the challenges of the environment will reveal the strength and the weakness of the person and give us a measure of his ability to adjust to this environment.

The adjustment of man to the world around him is the study that should interest physicians more than it has in the past. If only patients were to read this paper there would be no need for me to give a definition of disease. However, readers will include physicians also, and I know that physicians are in great need of such a definition.

Disease is that alteration of living cells or tissues that jeopardizes survival in their environment. I like this definition not only because I think I have coined it but also because it introduces the idea of the *environment* in any concept of

---

* American Geographical Society, New York.

disease. Indeed the environment is extremely important since one phenomenon that may appear to be disease in one place is not the case in another place. When we find eight or nine million red cells per cubic millimeter in the people living on the highest plateaus of the Andes, we do not consider this pathological because it helps them to survive in that particular environment. If we should make the same observation at sea level, however, we might worry whether this would not overburden the tissues with oxygen, and it might be considered pathological. In the same way an aggressive, mentally ill patient would be more readily acceptable in the environment of a large farm of the Midwest than in a two-and-one-half room apartment on the east side of Manhattan.

This definition stresses as its criterion *survival,* which is, of course, the basic dynamic force of any living thing. I believe it is better to define disease in terms of survival than to define it in terms of health, since health is also a very relative concept. Finally, I think this definition is an opportune reminder that there is no function without structure. It places the phenomenon of disease in the tissues, where it belongs. We have heard so much in the past 50 years of so-called purely functional diseases, and much time has been wasted in discussing this without referring to the indispensable basis for any function, which is structure. A structure may be nothing more than a cell built around a few molecules, but it is a structure nevertheless. If we remind ourselves that there is no function without structure, most of the discussions about dysfunctions become idle if they are not supported by careful scrutiny of the underlying structure.

Having now defined disease let us explore a bit further and try to find out how disease occurs. This should seem to be a rather simple undertaking. While everybody believes he has a good conception of disease and how it occurs, I do not think our thoughts are as clear on the subject as they ought to be.

Disease, any disease—and let me remind you that by disease I mean maladjustment to the environment—can never occur without the combination of three orders of factors converging in time and space, that is, there must be stimuli from the environment, there must be responses from a host, and there must be the conglomeration of thoughts and traits that we call culture. In order to understand disease and maladjustment, let us review these three orders of factors in succession.

The stimuli from the environment can be classified into physical stimuli, biological stimuli, and emotional stimuli. Of course these three classes of stimuli interpenetrate each other, and this is only a convenient way of presenting the subject. Strangely enough we know very little of the real effect of physical stimuli on man. It has always been extremely difficult in the past to dissociate what is really the action of climate from the action of the biotics that occur in these climates. Some time ago Douglas Lee built up an interesting curve showing the combinations of temperature and humidity that result in comfort and well-being in most human individuals. Below or beyond certain areas on the curve, physical stress occurs that may eventually lead to death. Except for these computations little else is known. We can assume only that unchartered forces occur that are specific to certain areas on the surface of the earth that must have an enormous importance in eliciting survival-worthy responses from, or on the contrary, cause the detrimental alteration of living tissues. For example the so-called solar flares that we know can disturb electronic communications on the surface of the earth are probably not ineffective in disturbing electronic communication inside the tissues. At least it seems to me that it would be improvident on our part not to give them some credit and to explore these new stimuli from the point of view of their action on man. We know very little about the forces that combine to create the climate at any given point of the earth and about their effect on living things, man, and the surrounding biotics upon which man is so very dependent in so many ways.

If we now consider the action of these biotics, their challenges are numerous and, of course, much better known. I go as far as to say that my generation has been quite guilty in giving them primordial importance in our concept of disease. I think that we have been very near to committing the major sin in disease etiology, that is, to consider that what we call disease may have a single cause. There is no such thing. A multiplicity of causes is always needed to produce that alteration of tissues creating maladjustment. These biotics, many of them more or less harmful parasites of our tissues, live in very definite environments of which we know little; their ecology is of great importance in our understanding of transmissible diseases. Last but not least we must always remember that these biotics live in societies like all living things, and that this social structure of very small or very large living objects dominates the picture. An example of this could be given by a study of what happens when we introduce *Penicillium notatum* or streptomycin into a society of bacteria.

In the same way that I gave to physicians my definition of disease, I think I should give to social scientists my concept of society. From the ecologist's point of view society is an organization of living things based on a pattern of mutual tolerance that occurs for a brief period of time after the dynamism of reciprocal exclusion has been temporarily exhausted. If we accept the idea that this is at least one aspect of what we call society, it is no wonder that every single unit living under such a climate will experience considerable stresses. By this I mean that stressful situations will occur and that, depending upon the host, these stressful situations may or may not translate themselves into actual physiological stress. Thus we have a brief sketch of the environmental stimuli that make up one third of the factors needed to produce that alteration of tissues that we call disease.

The second term of this equation is the host. I stress that I think this subject is the field of the future. Our forefathers had a good awareness of the importance of the individual, which they called "the terrain," in shaping the clinical forms of disease. Following the enlightening Pasteurian discoveries we have been mesmerized by the action of a single stimulus to produce disease, and have forgotten completely to explore the reasons that make the host respond in the way he does.

One of the fondest memories I have of my early days at medical school is that of my bewilderment when a professor of bacteriology told us that it was impossible to inoculate leprosy into animals and, vice versa, that certain bacteria that found themselves quite at home with animals could not, if inoculated into the human system, produce the symptoms that were observable in animals. Although I did not realize it at that time, this introduced the very potent idea of the genetic make-up of the host, and its importance in the kind of responses offered to environmental stimuli by the host. It is as though I had on a table three dolls, one of glass, another of celluloid, and a third of steel, and I chose to hit the three dolls with a hammer, using equal strength. The first doll would break, the second would scar, and the third would emit a pleasant musical sound.

This concept should never be forgotten (1) when we study the occurrence of transmissible diseases and the response of populations to the biological stimuli mentioned above; (2) when we study degenerative diseases and the response of individuals to the absorption of certain foods and poisons; and (3) when we study the so-called field of behavioral disorders in which we have had such a great tendency in the past to limit our investigations to stimuli, completely neglecting the more important host and the reasons for his responses.

In recent years we have learned to recognize the importance of certain blood groups, meaning certain genes, in increasing or diminishing our susceptibility to such diseases as duodenal peptic ulcer or carcinoma of the colon. We have learned the importance of the type of hemoglobin possessed by certain persons in relation to their susceptibility to malaria. We have begun to understand, as L. C. Dunn points out in his "Introductory Remarks," the role played in evolutionary processes by these genetic susceptibilities. We must now forge ahead in this field and try to map the various susceptibilities of the human host to the long list of known environmental challenges. This seems to me to be one of the most fascinating fields of the future.

The third order of factors that plays an important role in shaping disease patterns is, of course, culture. In the same way that I felt I should give a definition of disease to physicians and of society to social scientists, I owe to the anthropologists my definition of culture. Culture to me, as a disease ecologist, is the sum total of the concepts and techniques used by individuals or populations to control the environment in which they live. Of course, a culture trait may not always be survival-worthy, that is, may not promote survival. It may be erroneously conceived. It may have been received traditionally from ancient generations who had conceived it at a time when it had a purpose in a different environment, and may have been carried over faithfully throughout the centuries. Be that as it may it is useful for the disease ecologist and the public health worker to consider cultural traits observed in different populations as either promoting or preventing the survival of these populations. The sanitarian does not find it necessary to pass on the historical origin of these traits. He merely has to say whether the trait brings together the stimulus and the host or whether it keeps them apart. There are traits that do both, and they can be considered ambivalent. The revolting habit of smoking, now deeply ingrained in our society, may on the one hand precipitate death by cancer of a significant number of our population, while at the same time promoting survival if it soothes people's nerves to the point where it prevents them from rushing at each other's throats under the social emotional stresses alluded to previously. This role of culture as either a link between stimulus and host or a wall between them is, I think, a capital one.

A small Chinese village that I knew three decades ago may illustrate this linkage. To the epidemiologist, a puzzling problem was offered. One half of the inhabitants of this village were literally decimated by a very heavy hookworm infestation, while the other half enjoyed good health, at least from that point of view. An exploration of the local cultures revealed that almost all the patients were rice growers, while the healthy people bought their rice and had nothing to do with its cultivation. It was further found that the rice growers spent all their working days knee deep in mud thoroughly mixed with night soil which, of course, explained the introduction through skin penetration of the hookworm larvae. The healthy part of the population was engaged in silkworm farming, and spent their working days on ladders tending the mulberry trees.

In northern Vietnam many interesting situations, illustrating the role of culture in the disease patterns, occur. The country, from a geomorphological point of view, may be considered as composed of two parts: (1) a very fertile delta and (2) a much less fertile hill region. In the delta rice is grown. In the hill region some rice is grown, but there is considerable forest cover, and lumber is abundant. These are not the only two reasons for the differences in culture, but they are important nevertheless. As a result of these two situations the people of the delta build their houses on the ground. They have their stables on one side of the house and their kitchen on the other. Meals are brought into the house after they are cooked. The people in the hills, on the other hand, build their houses on stilts, and their living rooms usually are located about eight to ten feet above the ground. They keep their animals under the houses, and they do their cooking in the living rooms, which are usually full of smoke.

It happens that a very fierce malaria vector, *Anopheles minimus,* is found in the hill region, but the flight ceiling of this vector seldom exceeds nine to ten feet of elevation, so that during its flight it encounters only the animals under the houses. The fumes that emanate from the living rooms, where the people congregate, play a role in driving away any mosquitoes that might find themselves up there.

In the delta, on the contrary, there is no such malaria vector. When the people from the delta, under the economic pressure of overpopulation of the fertile land, seek relocation in the hills where space is more abundant, they take with them their delta culture. They build their houses on the ground floor, keep their animals outside, and see that their living rooms are free of smoke by cooking their food outdoors. As a result *Anopheles minimus,* which prefers human blood when it has a choice, becomes an active transmitter of malaria, and the people of the delta have become discouraged from participating in relocation schemes, feeling that there are evil spirits in the hills that do not like the delta people.

In the Vietnam delta itself we are confronted with three dominating factors: (1) the waters; (2) the aquatic life the waters cause to exist; and (3) the rice the waters help to grow. The water, represented chiefly by the Red River, is an important factor in the local culture. The mighty river not only has deposited its alluvial soil on the fields but continues pouring it deep into the China Sea. As a result the coastal population has developed no interest in sea fishing, the sea waters being too shallow and there being no fish along the coast. The Red River, fed by the snows and the rains of the eastern ranges of the Himalayas, has a shifty course, and it is very hard to predict its location for the next year. In addition to this it is subject to sudden rises, and the problem of flood control has been a major one in the area for centuries. Dams have been built for the triple purpose of protection, irrigation, and drainage. This has resulted in two important phenomena. The harvest does not occur at the same time in all parts of the delta, and repairs to the dams cause the necessity for a migrant labor force to rush where needed to keep the waters under control.

These dams have created conditions in which aquatic vegetation, snails, crayfish, and other biotics abound. Crayfish form an important item in the diet of the people.

From the waters the people also get their water-borne diseases, such as cholera, the dysenteries, and the typhoid fevers. From the migration of the labor force they get the pattern of these diseases that are transmitted from one point to the other by the migrant worker moving around wherever the need for his labor arises. From the snails they get their *Schistosoma japonicum;* from the aquatic vegetation, crayfish, and other biotics, they get their paragonimiasis and clonorchiasis.

However, from these soils and waters they also get their rice, which they prefer white and well polished. The polishing of the rice is done by machines in the more advanced villages. In the more backward villages it is done by mortar and pestle. As a result, the advanced villages get more beri-beri, while the backward villages get less, since hand polishing removes less of the thiamin-rich husk than does machine polishing.

All over the world numerous examples of the close interrelationship of culture and disease patterns could be given. As a result of the above I may say that the old art of reading symptoms and treating them by what appears to control them best is disappearing fast. The ancient formula of one ill, one pill, one bill, which seems to have been the credo of physicians for many generations, should be abandoned. Disease is a biological expression of maladjustment. This is what should be taught to our students in medical school, and this phenomenon against which they are going to fight all their lives cannot be understood without an ecological study in depth that should give equal importance to the three approaches: the environment, the host, and the culture.

A Children's Cancer
Dependent on Climatic Factors

DENIS BURKITT*

The incidence of many cancers varies enormously in different races. Notable examples are bowel carcinoma, so common in European races and so rare in the Bantu, and primary liver carcinoma with the reverse relationship. These and other tumours probably owe their differing racial incidence more to environmental than to genetic factors, as negroes in America show a tumour pattern approximating much closer to the white population there than to the pattern observed in Africa[1].

Until recently no cancer has, to my knowledge, been shown to occur only in certain clearly defined geographical locations, and within these boundaries to affect different tribes and races without discrimination.

Five years ago a number of hitherto unconnected tumours affecting children were recognized as being but different manifestations of a single tumour syndrome[2]. At about the same time it became evident that this tumor was very prevalent in certain parts of Africa while it was quite unknown in other parts[2].

The tumour has been histologically identified as a malignant lymphoma[3,4], but the condition is recognized rather as a clinical syndrome than as a specific tumour. Malignant lymphomata, presenting usually with generalized lymph-node enlargement, occur throughout the world. The unusual anatomical distribution of this tumour syndrome[2,4-7] is apparently unique, and with one exception, which will be referred to later, is confined to certain areas of tropical and sub-tropical Africa.

The age incidence differs from that observed in any other tumour. Nearly all cases recorded have occurred between the ages of 2 and 14 years, with a peak

* Department of surgery, Makerere University College Medical School and Mulago Hospital, Kampala, Uganda.

incidence at 5 years. The incidence appears to be approximately the same in both sexes[2,5].

This tumour syndrome accounts for more than 50 percent of all children's cancers seen in Uganda[2,7]. More than 200 cases have been recorded during the last eight years.

This tumour appears to traverse all barriers of race and tribe. Although unknown in India, it has been observed in Indian children domiciled in Africa in the proportion expected from the relative population figures[5].

The clinical characteristics have already been reported[2,5-7]. The distribution of tumour deposits throughout the body is totally unlike that observed in any other tumour. Moreover, the virtually simultaneous development of multiple tumours in sites where tumours were hitherto least expected to occur presents a strikingly characteristic clinical picture. Although there is a remarkably constant pattern of distribution, the presenting features vary, and are dependent on the particular lesion most in evidence at the time.

The most characteristic feature of this syndrome is the remarkable tendency for tumours to grow in the jaws. In more than 140 of the cases recorded in Uganda, tumours were present in the jaws, and in a high proportion of these more than one quadrant, and in 16 cases all four quadrants were involved. The tumours grow rapidly and cause gross disfigurement. The maxillary tumours commonly invade the orbit, presenting as an exophthalmos and eventually destroying the eye. These lesions have frequently been mistaken for retinoblastomata.

Other striking features are the bilateral ovarian tumours, present in more than 70 percent of female patients who have been submitted to laparotomy or come to autopsy, the bilateral thyroid tumours and the very high incidence of multiple renal tumours, which are also usually bilateral. The adrenals, heart and stomach are frequently involved, and lesions in the spinal canal make this tumour the commonest cause of paraplegia in children in the areas where the syndrome occurs.

Although tumours have been observed in many of the long bones, these lesions are relatively rare compared with the jaw tumours. Despite the fact that a more or less generalized enlargement of the lymphatic glands and spleen is the most prominent feature of malignant lymphoma as generally understood, clinical enlargement of these structures is exceptional in this syndrome. This unusual pattern and the rarity of pulmonary involvement constitute some of the most characteristic and unusual features. Untreated, the tumours grow exceedingly rapidly and terminate fatally, usually within six months.

Epidemiological aspects have also been discussed[2,5-8]. In view of the fact that the characteristic jaw tumours cannot easily be mistaken for any other condition these have been used to determine the geographical distribution of the tumour syndrome.

After wide distribution of illustrated leaflets accompanied by a questionnaire it became obvious that the tumour syndrome occurred right across tropical Africa from the coast of East Africa to Dakar in the extreme west (Fig. 1). In West

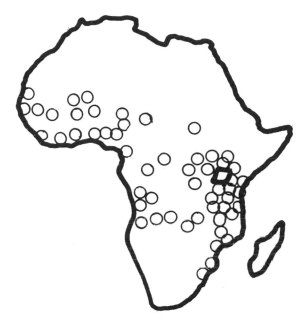

FIG. 1. Map of Africa showing the known distribution of the tumour syndrome. Each circle represents an area where this tumour has been recognized. (*Reproduced by kind permission of the Annals of the Royal College of Surgeons of England.*)

and Central Africa the northern limit of the tumour belt is about 15° latitude; but this line falls below 10° in the east. Populations fall off, in many instances to virtual desert, along this line so tumour incidence naturally tends to disappear. The condition is common in West Africa as far south as the sea coast and has been recognized as far south as the middle of Angola.

A much more detailed study, including a 10,000-mile roads safari, has been undertaken in East and Central Africa. Geographical plotting of all cases observed in Uganda showed that the only factor, other than population, affecting tumour distribution was altitude. Near the equator the tumour does not appear to exist above an altitude of about 5,000 ft.

East and Central Africa with its varying contours produced mountain ranges and the two limbs of the Great Rift Valley were examined in some detail to determine the areas of tumour distribution. The findings of this survey can be summarized as follows:

(1) Throughout Uganda, Kenya and Tanganyika the tumour can occur anywhere except at altitudes of more than about 5,000 ft. with the possible exception of the southern part of Tanganyika. (2) The off-shore islands of Zanzibar and Pemba are a notable and significant exception. No case of this syndrome has been observed in these islands with a population of more than a quarter of a million. (3) Throughout the Federation of Nyasaland and Southern and Northern Rhodesia, the syndrome is found only in or near the great river valleys, and on the shores of Lake Nyasa. (4) It is common throughout the

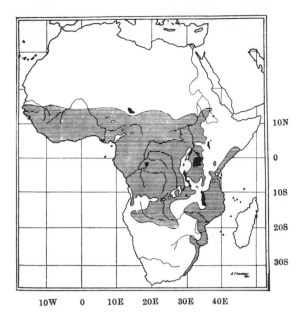

FIG. 2. Map of Africa from which have been eliminated (1) all areas where the temperature falls below 60° F, and (2) areas where the rainfall is below 20 in. a year. (*Reproduced by kind permission of the Annals of the Royal College of Surgeons of England.*)

coastal plain of Mozambique. (5) It is virtually unknown in South Africa. (6) This pattern of distribution does not coincide with population densities.

It is thus evident that the critical altitude above which the tumour is not observed falls progressively as the distance from the equator increases. Altitude is therefore only a limiting factor in so far as it reflects temperature. The actual limiting factor would appear to be a minimum temperature of about 60°F in the coldest season of the year (July) (Fig. 2).

There is no evidence that this tumour occurs in any country outside Africa with the exception of a few cases reported from New Guinea (Ten Saldam, personal communication, 1960).

The fact that the tumour distribution is dependent on climatic factors strongly suggests that some vector, perhaps a mosquito, is responsible for its transmission. This would naturally suggest that some virus may be the responsible agent.

No human tumour has yet been shown to be virus-induced but a number of virologists are now investigating the virological aspects of this tumour syndrome.

It was Prof. J. N. P. Davies who first suggested to me the possibility that this tumour might be virus induced. Dr. A. J. Haddow, director of the Virus Research Institute at Entebbe, has greatly assisted me in correlating tumour distribution to climatic factors.

I thank the Chief Medical Officer, Ministry of Health, Entebbe, for permission to publish this article.

REFERENCES

1. OETTLÉ, A. G., *J. Nat. Cancer Hosp.,* **24,** No. 3, 610 (1960).
2. BURKITT, D., *Brit. J. Surg.,* **46,** 218 (1958).
3. O'CONNOR, G., and DAVIES, J. N. P., *Paediat.,* **56,** 526 (1960).
4. O'CONNOR, G., *Cancer,* **14,** 258 (1961).
5. BURKITT, D., *Cancer,* **14,** 258 (1961).
6. BURKITT, D., *Ann. Roy. Coll. Surg.* (in press).
7. BURKITT, D., *Post-grad. Med. J.,* **38,** 71 (1962).
8. BURKITT, D., and DAVIES, J. N. P., *Med. Press,* **245,** 367 (1961).

FOOD, WATER,
AND ENERGETICS

Ecological energetics, sometimes termed production biology, identifies a phase of ecology which is concerned with energy received from the sun, the plant utilization of this energy and the transfer of this energy, now food, to animals and man. This is sometimes referred to as the "web of life." The role of water and the functions it fulfills in the production of his food is basic to this story of man.

The three papers in the section indicate some phases of man's relations to food availability and water in his environment.

It seems most appropriate to begin this section with the paper by Jones. The term "economy" in his title is useful from two standpoints. First, the economy of the sea indicates a well-run organization involving a food web of many trophic levels. In this sense, energy in food is continually cycled. The economy of the sea may also be used in the sense of commercial applications and financial gain. Jones gives a number of appropriate examples of this aspect as well. In Fig. 1, there is a diagram of the food web described in the paper.

Bradley's paper discusses water for human needs and water as a limiting factor to population growth. We are surprised to learn that the "generous American" diet could not be given to all the people living today on earth because there is simply not enough water to support it. However, on a vegetarian diet, the world would be able to support approximately 17 billion people, or approximately seven to eight times as many people as there are presently alive.

Newman has summarized many studies relating human nutritional stress to the world's climates, seasonal associations, and socioeconomic class structures. Since Newman's survey of the literature was undertaken, evidence has been presented that malnutrition can result in a significant depression of the intelligence in humans.

The Living Economy of the Sea

GALEN E. JONES*

An area of nature's realm that has received relatively little scientific attention is the sea, which covers over 70 percent of the surface of this planet. Yet the oceans have held a matchless fascination for the minds and hearts of some men. For less than 100 years the oceans have been studied in a systematic way by a few dedicated oceanographers whose ranks have been swelling, particularly since World War II. It is now believed that the sea may be the unique phenomenon characterizing this planet, that life originated in the sea, that understanding the evolution and interrelations of life in the sea may unlock a fabulous wealth of food and mineral resources. To promote a greater understanding of these problems, last year the U.S. government outlined a program that would commit $2.3 billion to the study of the sea over the next 10 years.

The oceans originated three to four billion years ago, one or two billion years after the formation of the planet Earth itself. The most widely held concept concerning the origin of our solar system presumes the coalescing of massive, moving clouds of gas drifting through space into a central nucleus of a hot ball of gas, the sun. In addition to this single nucleus, a group of satellite bodies attracted to the central nucleus and originating from the same gas cloud that gave birth to the sun rotated around the sun much as electrons move about the nucleus of an atom. These electrons became the planets of the sun and the earth was born as one of them.

The planet Earth contracted but never reached the high temperatures of the sun. The sea still did not exist but water vapor was trapped in the interior magma

* Department of Microbiology and Director of Jackson Estuarine Laboratory, University of New Hampshire.

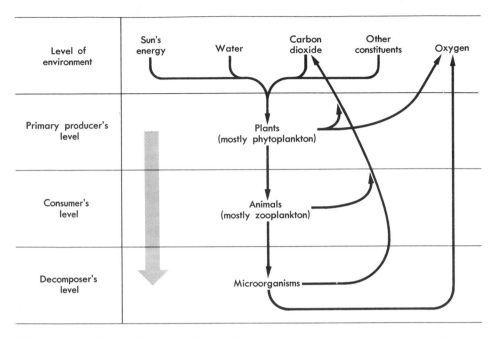

Fig. 1. Simple food web and trophic levels diagram based upon the economy of the sea.

and rock. As the temperature of the earth's surface dropped below the boiling point of water, water vapor spewed forth from the belly of the infant earth into great cloud masses. This steam condensed, fell, was converted to steam again until the earth became cool enough to permit the collection of rain water in its basins. Thus, the primeval ocean was created over many thousands of years as a great body of fresh water. In the millions and millions of years since this first water started to accumulate on the surface of the earth, water vapor has continued to pass through volcanoes and fumaroles to contribute to the moisture of the atmosphere and the seas. Today, the sea contains 330 million cubic miles of water (18 times the area of land above sea level).

The properties of water have probably provided the greatest advantages to this planet. The temperature of the earth is moderated by the stabilizing properties of water, especially its high specific heat, its high heat of vaporization, and its high heat of fusion. The surface temperatures of the earth are held near or between the very narrow range within which water remains a liquid, 0° to 100° centigrade. Most of the matter in the universe is either frozen or a blazing flame.

The sea acts as a massive reservoir of heat, tempering the cold of winter and cooling the high temperatures of summer. Ice formation is unique in that water expands by 9 percent when it freezes. Thus, ice floats on water and is exposed to the sun's rays, preventing the oceans from freezing solid, limiting the spread of ice, and permitting the formation of great ocean currents which aid in moderating the temperature.

Living cells must be supplied with foods and oxygen in aqueous solution. A cell anywhere, therefore, must always be in contact with water. Over 70 percent of living protoplasm is composed of water. When water is lost from protoplasm, life is suspended or lost. It is not surprising that life itself is believed to have originated in the sea.

Dissolved minerals

Water is the most effective solvent on earth, meaning it dissolves more substances than any other liquid. As a result, the seas have gradually become more and more salty. The salinity of seawater today is about 3.5 percent. One cubic mile of seawater contains 166 million tons of salt, 139 million tons of which is sodium chloride. Six other major ions, magnesium, calcium, potassium, sulfate, carbonate, and bromide, together with common salt, constitute over 99 percent of the chemical species dissolved in seawater.

Commercial possibilities for utilizing these dissolved minerals of the ocean seem obvious but they are not without problems. Common salt has been recovered by evaporation of seawater for thousands of years by many cultures, but the relative amount required from the ocean is slight. In fact, one of the great problems in mining seawater is to determine what to do with the overabundance of sodium chloride. Magnesium has been supplied to the nation since 1941 by the Dow Chemical Company from seawater, and the Ethyl Corporation has been successfully recovering bromine from the sea since 1924. Many other valuable minerals are present in seawater as totally less than 1 percent of the dissolved substances. One of the main reasons that elements like phosphorus, iron, copper, manganese, cobalt, and nickel are present in such small amounts in a soluble form is that they are concentrated from seawater by living creatures. Tunicates concentrate vanadium in their bodies by more than a factor of 100,000 over the concentration of vanadium in seawater. Oysters concentrate zinc and cobalt by a factor of more than 10,000. Thus, the remains of some of these marine creatures could be sources of valuable minerals. Oceanographers have long been aware that the sea bottom contains ore deposits comparable with those on land. Marine oozes and clays are rich in aluminum. A particularly promising accumulation of mineral resources is a cobblestone-like formation of iron-manganese nodules covering vast areas of the ocean floor. Even though these dark lumps of manganese oxide and iron hydroxide have been known since the eighteen-seventies, when the famous British *H.M.S. Challenger* expedition dredged them up from the bottom, no one really knows how they were formed.

In my laboratory, we are working on a solution to this problem. We know that the iron-manganese nodules usually contain less than 1 percent copper, cobalt, and nickel but significant amounts of these elements on a tonnage basis. We know that the nodules are formed, concentrically, at a rate of 0.01 mm.– 10 mm. per thousand years, often starting on an inert surface such as a shark's tooth or a whale's earbone. The growth rate is not necessarily even. They usually are formed in water deeper than 500 meters where the temperature of the water is $-1°$ to $2°$ C. Our hypothesis on their origin is that tiny marine bacteria are attracted to an inert surface and start scavenging very dilute organic matter which is swept by in the seawater. This organic matter often contains iron and manganese organometallic compounds. When the marine bacteria come in contact with the organometallic compounds, they consume the organic matter and deposit the metal. The bacterial activity is primarily regulated by the availability of organic matter and the temperature. We are growing iron-manganese nodules in the laboratory with the aid of marine bacteria and checking their composition with that of nodules formed in the sea.

If these nodules could be recovered in quantities of thousands of tons per day, they would be of great commercial value. The Newport News Shipbuilding and Dry Dock Co., in cooperation with John Mero, formerly at the University of California, is attempting to harvest these nodules now. Phosphorite nodules, rich in the valuable fertilizer phosphate, may also be mined from the oceans soon.

Plants

The great groups of living things in the oceans of the world today are performing functions which have their parallels on land. However, the life of the sea has been evolving for a longer period of time and the intricate, dynamic balances involved have been maintained for eons of time.

In the living economy of the sea, the most indispensable single group of organisms is the manufacturers—the plants. It is these organisms which have the ability to build up their own food supply by utilizing energy from the sun and two basic ingredients in the environment, water and carbon dioxide, in the amazing and still baffling process of photosynthesis that determines existence for almost all other life. Plant growth requires other constituents, such as minerals and, in the case of many plants, preformed accessory growth factors, i.e., vitamins, amino acids, nucleic acids, etc. These substances are necessary in very small amounts (parts per billion or parts per trillion).

Beside the production of organic food (carbohydrates, proteins, fats, etc.), plants give off large amounts of oxygen gas through the process of photosynthesis. Almost all higher plants and animals as well as many microorganisms require a continuous supply of oxygen in order to remain alive. Interestingly, the photosynthetic process itself is an anaerobic phenomenon (takes place in the absence of oxygen gas) and is believed to be the source of gaseous oxygen on this planet. The product, free oxygen, is derived from splitting oxygen from the water molecule and not from the carbon dioxide molecule. The atmosphere of the primitive earth was anaerobic. Life arose in the absence of oxygen gas. The evolution of green plants (about two billion years ago) produced an oxygenated atmosphere and oxygenated oceans. Green plants, like animals and many modern bacteria, depend on oxygen for their respiratory processes.

When one thinks of plants in the sea, the large seaweeds which surround the continental land masses may flash across the imagination first. These ancient algae are indeed important members of the marine community and include such important genera as *Macrocystis, Fucus, Polysiphonia, Gelidium,* which lie in great beds off the coasts and are attached in profusion to rocks in the intertidal zone. A commercial product of note which results from these seaweeds is alginic acid, derived from the giant California elk-kelp, *Macrocystis pyrifera.* Alginic acid goes into a wide variety of commercial products including wallboard, adhesive tape, insulation for housing, as a stabilizer for some ice creams, and in the manufacture of pharmaceuticals and cosmetics. Agar for solidifying bacteriological media is derived from seaweeds. Many oriental peoples prepare tasty soups from seaweed fronds.

Phytoplankton

In the overall economy of the sea, these seaweeds play a small part compared to the microscopic plants. The phytoplankton, floating freely in great abundance and diversity in the upper sunlit waters of the seas, carry out most of the photosynthesis and are responsible for over 95 percent of the primary production. It has been calculated by the Danish phytoplanktologist, Steemann Nielsen, that their production is of the same order of magnitude as all of the photosynthesis on land.

These drifting single-celled specks of life are often restricted to water of a particular temperature, salinity, and nutrient content. About 60 percent of the phytoplankton are single-celled algae called diatoms, whose minute architecture is one of the wonders of the natural world. Diatoms have a wide variety of shapes and sizes and are transparent.

Other members of the phytoplankton community are blue-green algae, coccolithophores, nannoplankton, and dinoflagellates. In the marine food-chain or food-web, the well-being of these tiny forms of life ultimately determines the well-being of larger and more advanced forms of life. Great diatom and other phytoplankton blooms are known to occur when nutrient-rich water from the deeps rises to the surface during upwelling or when excessive run-off from land occurs after torrential rains. These observations have led to the idea that much of the time phytoplankton populations are controlled by a limiting factor or factors lacking or in small supply in the sea. Indeed, pure culture investigation of the nutrition of marine phytoplankton tends to support this hypothesis, since necessary organic compounds such as vitamins and some elements available in very small amounts may be limiting. Available nitrogen and phosphate, two constituents of great importance to land plants, are also vitally important to phytoplankton. These substances are not present in abundant amounts in the sea, and it is a matter of some controversy whether they, too, are often limiting.

Primary production is commonly investigated today by the use of the radioactive isotope carbon 14, which is added to seawater or a pure culture of a phytoplankter as $NaHC^{14}O_3$, which is a readily available source of carbon dioxide. After a few hours' incubation at a specific temperature, some bottles are kept in the light and others in the dark under experimental nutrient conditions. Then the contents of the experimental bottles are filtered, dried, and the amount of radioactive carbon 14 assimilated by the phytoplankton cells in the light is determined and corrected by the amount of carbon 14 assimilated in the dark to provide a measure of photosynthesis. Another common technique is to extract a certain volume of seawater for chlorophyll *a*, which all phytoplankton contain, and measure this directly with a spectrophotometer as an estimate of plant standing crop.

John D. H. Strickland of the University of California's Institute of Marine Resources has recently stated, "Looked on as the primary source of energy and organic matter in the marine food web, the phytoplankton poses endless problems. The field is so challenging and the number of workers so few that those of us fortunate enough to be engaged in this research find an unlimited feast of problems. One can easily succumb to gluttony, and the difficulty is to restrict one's interest to match the available resources."

Consumers

In the living economy of the sea, there is a vast array of consumers—the animals. Many of these animals are as small as the phytoplankton and wander with the open ocean currents. These organisms are called zooplankton and they make their living by devouring phytoplankton. Among the most abundant and important members of the zooplankton are the multicellular copepods, which figure importantly in oceanic food chains.

Other members of the community of zooplankton include myriads of single-celled protozoans such as radiolarians and foraminifera, which have been slowly evolving for perhaps a billion years. Their siliceous and carbonaceous cases have been slowly but steadily deposited on the ocean floor to become part of the sedimentary accumulation which has provided evidence for the process of evolution by gradual changes in their structure. The age of the sediments has been estimated by observing these distinct structures. In ways such as this, living history has been recorded. Mysids, krill, euphausids, salps; larvae of snails, lobsters, and sea urchins; fish eggs and many kinds of newly born fish; sea worms and sea combs, as well as the larger floating forms such as jellyfish and Portuguese men-of-war are representative of the zooplankton.

Larger animals such as clams, abalone, lobsters, corals, many fish, and even some whales can live directly by filtering plankton from the seawater. However, many marine fish and other large predators prefer their meals in more appetizing packages so they eat the smaller fish. These in turn are eaten by slightly larger creatures until a few tycoons remain, such as the marlin, the swordfish, the dolphin, the shark. Vast billions of planktonic creatures are necessary directly or indirectly to nourish each of these protein-rich denizens of the open sea. In this environment, the strong live—until they meet something stronger. Disease is not common among marine creatures. Two explanations may be offered for this phenomenon: the weakened, diseased creatures are soon eliminated by the ruthless competition within the environment; and marine biologists have not become sufficiently aware of diseased plants or animals due to lack of enough detailed observations.

There are some beautiful examples of cooperation in the sea: little fish and shrimp that enter the mouths of large fish to pick the parasites from their gills while other large fish wait patiently for the service; the small fish, *Nomeus,* which lives among the tentacles of the Portuguese man-of-war, immune to its sting, and receives the crumbs from the table of the host. However, nature's ocean is not a gentle region but a highly competitive meeting place for the diverse forms of life which have gradually been evolving there.

Microorganisms

The living economy of the sea would not be complete without discussing the group of organisms which perform the street cleaner, junk-man services—the microorganisms. All plants and animals excrete wastes and eventually die, contributing their dead bodies back to the sea. If no agency were present to remove these wastes and dead materials, the accumulation of organic compounds useless to the living community would soon stifle life in the sea.

The first forms of life on earth are currently believed to have been tiny bacteria which lived on organic chemicals formed in the ancient seas through the action of electrical discharge, radiations, heat, etc., from such simple starting materials as water, ammonia, hydrogen gas, and methane through a strictly chemical process (chemical evolution). Therefore, it is not really proper to consider the removal of organic compounds by microorganisms from the present oceans as a service for plants and animals. Rather, the more recently formed plants and animals are able to provide organic matter for the microorganisms now that plants through the production of oxygen gas have changed the world's atmosphere from anaerobic to aerobic. This change in the content of oxygen in the atmosphere and seas has retarded or stopped chemical evolution. The production of organic matter by chemical evolution was a much slower process than photosynthesis.

Marine bacteria, fungi, actinomycetes, and even some marine algae derive their energy from these organic compounds, converting them back to simple substances again, such as water, carbon dioxide, phosphate, ammonia, and hydrogen sulfide. When the oxygen content of the water or marine sediments becomes very low, complex organic matter usually does not decompose as completely, allowing the release of organic phosphates, organic acids, such as lactic and acetic acids, glycerol, fatty acids, and many other organic compounds. Many marine microorganisms secrete organic compounds as part of their life processes, contributing vitamins, phospholipids, and a number of other substances to the seawater. Many of these organic compounds can be assimilated by the phytoplankton and other microorganisms, and, in fact, are vital, in very small amounts, to their well-being.

For the past several decades, marine algologists have been isolating marine phytoplankton from the sea and growing them in carefully defined media, bacteria free, to determine their nutrient requirements. Of the two hundred individual species studied in this manner, 55–60 percent require detectable (parts per million to parts per trillion) amounts of vitamin B_{12} (cyanocobalamin); 40–45 percent require vitamin B_1 (thiamine); 5 percent are dependent upon the vitamin biotin. Studies with soil and marine bacteria show that many of these bacteria secrete tiny amounts of these vitamins. So the implications are clear: a dynamic interchange of micronutrients between the secretion and decomposition of organic compounds by the bacteria and fungi on one hand, and the rapid assimilation and utilization by the phytoplankton during primary production on the other hand. Yet the levels of soluble organic matter which can be detected in the seas are small (from 0.1–2 parts per million of soluble organic carbon in the open ocean to almost 100 parts per million in shallow productive bays). This is many levels less than the concentrations of organic compounds believed to have been present in the "organic soup" in which life arose. It tends to emphasize the competition for these substances which exists in the ocean today. However, should one think of these levels of organic matter as insignificant, the sea generally contains 5 to 10 times more organic matter in a soluble state (less than 0.5 μ in size) than is present as particulate matter or as living cells. Certainly much of the soluble and particulate (detritus) organic matter is relatively inert. We need to understand more about the specific structure of this organic matter, where it came from, and how it was formed.

Besides the mineralization of organic compounds and the secretion of accessory growth factors, marine microorganisms can secrete inhibitory substances. Blooms of various marine dinoflagellates, diatoms, and green algae are often associated with biologically active substances. Very few of these substances have been carefully identified. The potential for recovering new drugs from marine creatures of all sizes is great. Potent substances may be recovered from sponges, corals, other coelenterates (Portuguese man-of-war), snails, and various poisonous fishes.

A few years ago, it was my working hypothesis that the reason freshwater pollution bacteria died upon entering seawater was due to a marine "antibiotic" of this type. Other explanations for the killing effect of seawater for freshwater bacteria existed such as seasonal variations in the seawater, the destructive action of the ultraviolet rays of sunlight, the adsorption and sedimentation of contaminating microorganisms with particles in suspension, the lack of essential nutrients, the presence of destructive bacterial viruses (bacteriophage), the utilization of microbes as food by protozoa and filter-feeding predatory animals, and the effect of change in salinity on the freshwater bacterial cells. After several years of work on this problem, an entirely different conclusion was reached: the small amounts of toxic heavy metals in seawater such as copper, zinc, lead, and nickel were sufficient to poison these freshwater bacteria unless they were complexed with metal-binding (chelating) agents. At any given place in the sea, some of the other factors may also be playing a part, but heavy metal toxicity is a lethal factor for the unadopted microorganisms.

Marine microorganisms are at home in the sea and require its complex constituents to survive when first isolated from their natural environment. We know that these marine microorganisms grow better on proteins than carbohydrates or fats, that many can tolerate wide ranges of oxygen tensions, that many prefer relatively low temperatures (below 20° C.), and that many are pigmented.

A young science

A large number of fundamental questions remain to be answered: Where should most marine microorganisms be classified? Do they differ from terrestrial bacteria in any fundamental physiological way (cell wall composition, enzymatic activity, ash content, overall composition, etc.)? How important are marine microorganisms to biogeochemical phenomena? What is their distribution and total biomass? How much intimate contact is there between microorganisms and marine plants and animals? How important are the bacterial transformations of nitrogen to the living economy of the sea? Are microorganisms a significant source of food for marine animals in the abyss below the zone of light penetration and above the bottom in open ocean areas? How are cell permeability and enzymatic activity affected by high hydrostatic pressures equivalent to those in the deep ocean? What are the basic requirements for marine microbes—such as sodium, which Robert MacLeod of McGill University has shown is essential for all of the marine bacteria he has tested? How important is the bacteria flora in the intestinal tracts of fish and invertebrate animals? What byproducts of commercial importance, such as antibiotics, vitamins, special pigments, organic acids, and alcohols, may be derived from marine microorganisms. How important are marine microorganisms to corrosion in the sea?

Questions such as these are being asked. Answers are being obtained which raise new questions. The marine microbiologists of the world are small in number but enthusiastic. We have a pioneering opportunity to contribute to an important, young area of science.

Human Water Needs
and Water Use in America

CHARLES C. BRADLEY*

The current rapid rise in population poses many problems, among them the question, Where are the limits, if any? More carefully stated for America, the question seems to be, how many people can we sustain at what standard of living?

My purpose in this article is to examine one vital resource, water—(i) to show the minimum amount necessary to sustain human life, (ii) to show the amount we are now using in the United States to maintain our standard of living, and (iii) to indicate from these figures when we may expect to find certain ceilings imposed on the crop of human beings in this country.

While water economics is admittedly important in the complex problem of water supply, no discussion of this aspect of the problem is attempted in this article.

Water needs of man

The 2 quarts or so of water which a man needs daily for drinking is a requirement obvious to anyone. Less obvious is the equally vital but much larger volume of water needed to sustain a man's food chain from soil to stomach. This is the water necessary to raise the wheat for his daily bread and the vegetables that fill his salad bowl. This is also the still larger volume required to raise alfalfa to feed a steer from which a man may get his daily slice of meat. All this water represents a rather rigid requirement for human life, and it is water which is consumed, in the sense that it is removed from the hydrosphere and returned to the atmosphere.

An adult human has a daily food requirement of about 2½ pounds, dry weight. If he is strictly a vegetarian, an illustrative approximation of the water

* Dean of the division of letters and science, Montana State College, Bozeman.

requirements for his food chain can be made by assuming man *can* "live by bread alone."

Wheat has a transpiration ratio of 500 (1); that is, ideally it takes 500 pounds of water circulating through the wheat plant from the soil to the air to bring 1 pound (dry weight) of wheat plant to maturity. If grain to be milled represents half the weight of the wheat plant, we can say that it takes 1000 pounds of water to make 1 pound of milling wheat, or (simplifying again) 1000 pounds of water to make 1 pound of bread. Therefore, it takes 2500 pounds of water, or approximately 300 gallons, to make 2½ pounds of bread. Three hundred gallons per day per person is, therefore, probably not far from the theoretical minimum water requirement to sustain human life.

The introduction of animal protein to a man's diet lengthens the food chain, thereby greatly increasing the water requirement. To illustrate, let us assume what might be called a simplified but generous American diet of 1 pound of animal fat and protein (beef) and 2 pounds of vegetable foods (bread) per day. It takes about 2 years to raise a steer. If butchered when it is 2 years old, the animal may yield 700 pounds of meat. Distributed over the 2 years, this is about 1 pound of meat per day. It may be seen, therefore, that this diet requires a steady-state situation of about one steer per person.

A mature steer consumes between 25 and 35 pounds of alfalfa a day and drinks about 12 gallons of water (2). Alfalfa has a transpiration ratio of 800 (1), hence 20,000 pounds of water are required to bring 25 pounds of alfalfa to maturity. In other words, a little over 2300 gallons per day per man are required to introduce 1 pound of beef protein and fat into a person's diet. Add to this the 200 gallons necessary to round out his diet with 2 pounds of vegetable matter and we have a total water requirement of about 2500 gallons per day per person for a substantial American diet.

It should be remembered that these are conservative figures, because transpiration ratios are derived from carefully controlled laboratory experiments and not from data collected in the field, where perhaps half the total rainfall is lost directly by evaporation and does not pass through the plant body. It should be noted, too, that the water cost of a pound of meat is about 25 times that of a pound of vegetable. We should anticipate a similar ratio for the water cost of wool to that of cotton or for the water cost of butter to that of margarine. In any case, somewhere between 300 and 2500 gallons per day is the bare subsistence water cost for one naked human being.

Water use in the United States

When we talk about "use" we have to add to the foregoing figures the water requirements for all our fibers, lumber, and newsprint, as well as the water needed to process steel, to run the washing machine, to flush the toilet, and to operate our air conditioning and our local laundries, and especially that required to sweep our sewage to the sea. It is therefore pertinent, at this point, to digress slightly in order to clarify our concept of the American standard of living, or at least that portion sustained by water use. The American standard of living is not a wholly unmixed blessing. In achieving such luxuries as the flush toilet, synthetic detergents, cheap newspapers, and atomic power we find ourselves also achieving polluted streams, sudsy well-water, radioactive milk, and poisoned oysters.

Underlying and supporting our standard of living are powerful industrial centers and a mass production scheme which creates inexpensive commodities. This scheme rests firmly upon certain prodigal wastes, polluted streams being a prime example. To clean up the streams would take a tremendous amount of money which might otherwise be spent on cheap commodities. On the basis of some standards of values, this could be construed as a lowering of the standard of living.

To illustrate the magnitude of the practical problems we have created for ourselves, we note that if river-disposal of waste were suddenly denied the city of St. Louis, the city fathers would have to decide what else to do with the daily discharge of 200,000 gallons of urine and 400 tons of solid body-wastes, to say nothing of all the industrial wastes. River disposal of human waste, though cheap, involves a double loss of resources. On the one hand there is the polluted river; on the other, the depleted soil. So long as these losses are deemed less important than the production of inexpensive commodities which they support, we will have to accept our befouled streams and depleted soil as part of the cost of our standard of living. In addition to waste disposal we can see that water power, river transportation, fisheries, and water recreation are all well-established items in our standard of living. Therefore, as we move into a discussion of water use, especially future use of surface waters, we must remember that most of our runoff is already committed to our living standard and is working hard to support it.

A figure for water use in the United States can be obtained by subtracting that water which we are *not* using from the total water available.

Thirty inches of annual rainfall on the surface area of the United States (exclusive of Alaska and Hawaii) gives us theoretically nearly 5000 billion gallons per day, a figure which represents the total water available for our use (3). Of this 5000 billion gallons, about 1300 billion gallons a day, or about one-fourth of the rainfall, is discharged by our rivers (4). It may also be said that this discharge figure contains the groundwater increment, since stream flow is largely maintained by effluent seepage from the ground.

It can be seen that 75 percent of our rainfall is returned to the atmosphere through evaporation and transpiration. It is difficult to assess the relative contributions of these two factors. A ratio of 50:50 is probably not far from the truth. From a utilitarian standpoint, evaporation constitutes pure waste, and it may be that here some significant gains in water conservation can be made. But until this is done, we have to reckon this loss, too, as part of the price being paid for our standard of living.

Very little of the area of the United States which could produce crops for man is not actually doing so. The largest nonproducing area is, of course, our desert, and even here we are irrigating, using stream water exported from regions of water surplus. Additionally, we are forcing the desert to raise crops through the use of ground water. But in many such areas we have considerable evidence that the annual draft from the ground-water reservoir exceeds the annual recharge. Consequently, some of these operations will be short-lived and perhaps socially and economically catastrophic for the people involved.

About 2 percent or more of the surface of the United States is "paved" with cities and roads and will probably remain agriculturally unproductive until some far-sighted city planners provide for extensive roof gardens. Another 2 to 3 percent of the land in this country is devoted to wilderness and national parks. While these do not directly produce crops for man, we do include them and their waters in our standard of living. Finally, we can say that bad agricultural management has reduced the productivity of a fraction of our arable land, and that this percentage must be added to our total for unproductive lands. Let us make a quasi-educated guess and say that as much as 10 percent of our land in areas of abundant rainfall is, at the moment, non-productive.

Three-fourths of the nation's rain (3700 billion gallons per day) falls on about half the nation's area, and it is this three-fourths, largely unmetered, that does the big job of raising crops for America. As concluded previously, perhaps one-tenth of this rain falls on unproductive areas. Hence we may say that 3300 billion gallons per day are productive of crops or surplus water. Of this, about one-fourth is unconsumed runoff, giving a remainder of about 2500 billion gallons per day which we are *consuming*, though perhaps wastefully, to raise our crops. In a population of 180 million people, this amounts to approximately 13,800 gallons per day per person. In addition, 240 billion gallons per day are metered out of our streams, lakes, and ground-water reservoirs to serve industry, municipalities, and rural areas (4); over half of it is consumed in irrigation and other processes. This 240 billion gallons per day is almost 1400 gallons per day per person, a figure which now must be added to the 13,800 gallons for a grand total of 15,200 gallons per day per person. Thus we find that the per capita daily use of water in the United States is in excess of 15,000 gallons, 95 percent of which is consumed.

Some population limits in the United States

How many people could we feed if all the rainfall in the United States were completely utilized? Since 300 gallons per person per day is needed for a vegetarian diet, we could, in theory, sustain about 17 billion people, or approximately 8 times the present world population. If, on the other hand, we decided to feed people on the "generous American" diet, we discover, by the same sort of calculation, that we could feed about 2 billion people, or somewhat less than the present world population. If we admit that loss of water through evaporation is unavoidable, as discussed earlier in this article, we must cut these figures to 8 billion and 1 billion respectively.

Assuming a population of 180 million and a rainfall of 5000 billion gallons per day, we discover that each person today theoretically has about 28,000 gallons per day for his use. We are now using 15,000 gallons per day per person, 95 percent of it consumptively. We might, therefore, conclude that if we could use every drop of rain that falls we could almost double our population with no decrease in the standard of living. But this is far from possible because there would then be no surface water to generate power, float ships, raise fish, and carry away the national sewage and waste.

The extent to which we can consume our runoff before our standard of living suffers is difficult to foresee. Involved are not only the waste-disposal and commercial uses of rivers but the fact that river water is generally most abundant and most available where it is least needed for agriculture.

Let us guess that we might safely and profitably use one-third of our remaining river water, or 400 billion gallons per day, for future development without expecting a resultant drop in our standard of living. Add to this figure the amount of water that falls on unproductive areas which might rather easily be made productive. We now have a total of about 750 billion gallons per day for future development. At 15,000 gallons per day per person we seemingly can accommodate 50 million more people, or a total population of 230 million, before our standard of living starts to suffer. There is little doubt that America will have reached that population figure well before the year 2000. The evidence of the moment suggests, then, that young Americans alive today will see a significant deterioration in their standard of living before they are much past middle age. Improved cropping, mulching, and other conservation practices could, of course, extend the grace period by a few years.

How far deterioration in the American standard of living will progress depends, of course, upon what action Americans choose to take on their own numbers problem—upon *what* action, and especially upon *when* they take it. Fortunately we have at our disposal human intelligence and considerable time in which intelligence can function. At present rates of rainfall and of population growth we should have almost 200 years before the American standard of living drops to subsistence level and Malthusian controls eliminate the necessity for intelligent action.

REFERENCES AND NOTES

1. N. A. MAXIMOV, *The Plant in Relation to Water* (Macmillan, New York, 1929).
2. F. W. WOLL, *Productive Feeding of Farm Animals* (Lippincott, New York, 1921).
3. It is doubtful whether artificial conversion of salt water will ever make a significant difference in this total, although it may be of great significance to certain communities.
4. L. B. LEOPOLD and W. B. LANGBEIN, *A Primer on Water* (U.S. Government Printing Office, Washington, D.C., 1960).

Ecology and Nutritional Stress in Man

MARSHALL T. NEWMAN*

Beyond the quite considerable metabolic tolerance of man to dietary inadequacies lie extreme conditions of nutritional stress where health and physical status may be affected from prenatal life onward. Through either starvation or acute shortage of essential nutrients, severe nutritional stress may result in death, especially in the young. When less severe, it retards physical development, reduces vitality, and increases susceptibility to most infectious diseases. Nutritional stresses in man are clearly a reflection of his ecology, culture, and biology. The ecological factors of particular importance in this regard are the direct effect of climate upon dietary needs, the disease environment that must be endured, and the food producing potential of the living area. Cultural factors are reflected principally in food producing technologies, food preparation, differential distribution to the people, and food habits. Biological factors of major import are population dynamics and the degree of acclimatization and adaptation to stress conditions. All these factors focus upon man's food intake, which in fair measure determine who thrives and propagates and who does not in this rapidly changing world.

Climate and nutritional requirements

Quite apart from matters of food supply, the climate where humans reside has a direct bearing on their nutritional requirements. In cold climates, as Mitchell and Edman (1951:17–20) have shown, caloric needs are increased to help keep the body warm and allow for extra energy expenditures such as imposed by the hobbling effect of heavy clothing. In man there is a linear increase of resting metabolic rates below the critical level 78°–81° F. air temperature, although this

* Department of Anthropology, University of Washington.

is partly mitigated by well-designed clothing and built-in biological adaptations. There is, nevertheless, a highly significant average increase in basal metabolic rates with decreasing ambient temperatures, as Roberts (1952:174) has shown. In addition to enhanced caloric needs in cold climates, an increase in fat intake is also advantageous in helping preserve body temperatures at tolerable levels. The clinical consequences of inadequate fat intake in the Arctic is the sort of "rabbit hunger" described by Stefansson (1956:31).

Vitamin-wise there is incomplete evidence, drawn partly from animal experiments, that cold climates slightly decrease the need for niacin and increase it for ascorbic acid (Mitchell and Edman 1951:32–33); Dugal and Fortier 1952:146). Increased requirements for dietary vitamin D also characterize cold climate living, since clothing and cloudy skies reduce the amount of ultraviolet radiation received by the body.

Caloric needs decrease in warm climates, partly because of the smaller body mass that must be sustained and partly because extra dietary calories are not needed for body heating. There is, however, a slight increase in protein needs in the heat, possibly 5–10 gm. per day (Mitchell and Edman 1951:94). This may be wholly cancelled by smaller body mass and other adjustments to a hypoprotein intake. There are usually small vitamin losses through sweating in hot climate people, but these losses are mostly inconsequential except in the face of decidedly low intake for a particular vitamin. There is, of course, an increase in water needs and a great increase in salt requirements, although fully adapted or acclimated peoples possess special physiological mechanisms fostering water and salt economy. Increased sweat and fecal losses in hot climate peoples also call for increased iron and, less certainly, calcium needs. Increased fat intakes in hot dry climates and other areas of marked atmospheric aridity may also be indicated.

Nutrition and disease

The bearing of disease upon nutritional status is summed up in the historic relationship of famine and pestilence. The diet-and-disease experiments on man and other animals clearly show that inadequate food intake increases the frequency and severity of most infections (Scrimshaw et al. 1959). There are only a few diseases such as malaria where inadequate diets serve some alleviative function (Scrimshaw et al. 1959:380–82). As Allison (n.d.) has indicated, malarial parasites do not thrive in human systems when hemoglobin levels are low because of grossly inadequate iron intake. Yet in such deficient hosts even a low parasite count may result in active malaria. But since dietary deficiencies are synergistic to many diseases in man, the actual cause of death in a poorly nourished individual may be in doubt. Unless special studies are made of the usual mortality records, credit is often given to some respiratory or gastroenteric disease that may in fact have only administered the coup de grâce.

Agriculture and food producing potentials

The food producing potential of a living area depends basically upon the fertility of its soils, whether used for cultivation or pasturage. Soil fertility depends upon the available macro- and micro-nutrient elements and their interbalances, interacting with the climatic factors of rainfall, temperature, and their seasonal qualities. It is quite impossible to make broad generalizations by world zone on soil fertility. Large-scale detailed maps are needed to show nutritionally meaningful differences in soils. Phillips (1960) was only able to reduce the soils of subsaharan Africa to some 40 type-regions on the basis of climate and vegetation associations. Each type-region has its own particular problem in agricultural technology.

In general, however, the vast tropical zone with the 64° F. coldest month isotherm and the <30″ annual rainfall isohyet has the poorest agricultural soils. Due to extensive leaching by heavy rainfall the tropics has many areas of very poor soils, although some more fortunate areas have very fertile soils. The best agricultural lands, on the other hand, are in the middle latitudes of temperate climate. In this broad zone the soils of only moderate development by a medium and seasonally well distributed rainfall are superior. Other temperate zone soils are less satisfactory, being either drought-prone as in the mineral-rich prairie areas or overdeveloped as in the formerly heavily forested areas. Drought-prone areas are susceptible to crop failure and famine; areas of overdeveloped soils have problems akin to those in the extremely leached tropical soils.

It seems likely that within the broad framework of agricultural land use, proper solutions of the technological problems are more important to human welfare than soil fertility per se. In terms of technology, many of the New World and African cultivators in the tropics practice the extensive methods of shifting agriculture that exploit but a small portion of the arable land. These practices have low output in terms of harvest per unit area and low productivity viewed as yield per man-day. As Gourou (1956:343) indicates, these techniques limit slash-and-burn cultivators to the poorer lands such as the lighter soils of terraces and plateaus. Although he urges use of the swampy and heavy soils of the valley bottoms, they may have been avoided by shifting cultivators for epidemiological as well as technological reasons. In contrast, the Asian cultivators in the tropics use intensive methods on even the poorest soils and achieve a quite high proportion of land use, a high output, but a low productivity that is prodigal of human labor. Many of the temperate zone countries cultivate a high 40 to 60 percent of their total arable land, much more than in most of the tropics. Output is mostly high as well. Excepting the special hand techniques such as required in wet rice culture, productivity in the temperate zone is only high where advanced mechanized technologies are used.

Nutrition and human adaptation

It is clear that the bulk of the world's population today is principally dependent upon agriculture for its sustenance, and that this dependence came only with the

Neolithic Revolution less than 8,000 years ago. Thus, agricultural man anywhere has had only 150 to 400 generations to adapt himself to new dietaries, principally the grain and root crops that now support the world. Moreover, man has also been faced with adapting to different varieties of the same crop that have quite distinct nutritional properties and, indeed, have their own evolution. In this regard, Scrimshaw (1953) has emphasized that the variation is great enough in corn consumed in Central America to have important nutritional consequences. Increased yield and disease resistance in these corns may do damage to protein and oil content, and the amount of protein may bear no direct relationship to the content of tryptophan, methionine, and lysine.

In the long evolutionary view, 150 to 400 generations have been insufficient time for man wholly to adapt himself to new and changing foods. The degree of adaptation to shortages of different nutrients may vary considerably in human populations. Some of these differences may be regional and could reflect the length of time that adaptations to specific nutrient deficiencies have been necessary. For example, there is a possibility that the generally salutary adaptations of Negro Africans to a low calcium and ascorbic acid intake (Scientific Council for Africa 1956:79) reflect a longer evolution than do their manifest and clinically expressed difficulties with protein and niacin shortages. The study of human responses to changing dietaries engendered by ecological and technological alterations is, in my opinion, equal in importance to researches on man's reactions to changing disease environments. Adjustments to dietary and disease hazards, themselves closely related, are rarely adequate over the present-day world except with the intervention of advanced food technologies and costly public health services. Neither biological nor cultural evolution has fully kept pace with rapidly shifting total environments. Yet in the fairly immediate past, the major racial blocks of mankind—Whites, Mongoloids, and Negroes—achieved salutary enough adaptations to their separate and distinct environments to undergo population explosions (cf. Hulse 1955:190).

Nutrition and population

In terms of the numbers of mankind, the world areas where intensive agricultural technologies are practiced are also the areas of the greatest population densities. Indeed, man's reproductive success can be seen to be pressing his food supply in almost all populous areas of the world. Food surpluses are a rarity among nations. Population increases move at such a rate that strong outmovement, such as from Italy to the United States around the turn of the century, only offers temporary relief before the gap is closed again. It would appear that man's biological success vis-à-vis reproduction is fully sufficient to strain his food resources and thus create a nutritional stress situation. As Spengler (1960:1499) recently put it, "Much of Asia, Africa, and Latin America—perhaps two-thirds of the world's population—is caught in a Malthusian trap, in a quasi-stable equilibrium system in which forces making for increase in income evoke counter-balancing income-depressing forces, among them a high rate of population growth."

Undernutrition in man

It is the nutritional consequences of this stress situation that are to be examined here. The observable aspects of nutritional stress lie in diet-connected mortality and morbidity rates, and in the residues of the latter. These residues are most readily observable in the altered growth and maturation rates of the children surviving these dietary crises, their disease susceptibilities, and in the vitality of the adults.

On a gross world basis the American Geographical Society (1953) maps show that the areas of undernutrition and malnutrition closely coincide with the tropical and warmer temperate regions of backward food producing technologies. Undernutrition in a hypocaloric sense and malnutrition in terms of vitamin and mineral deficiencies usually go along together, aiding and abetting each other, as it were, in creating human misery. The effects of famine and qualitative deficiencies in diet are therefore hard to separate. Where famine strikes, as in war disasters, the civilian mortality is quite selective, bearing down as it does on the very young and the old as well as the lower socioeconomic strata. The effect of severe maternal undernutrition on the developing fetus is buffered to a considerable extent by a sort of homeostasis. In experiments where maternal nutrition has been carefully measured, intakes were never low enough to influence significantly the condition of the newborn. In the less well controlled war-time food crises, striking diminutions in birth size have been observed. For example, the undernutrition in northwest Holland during the war winter of 1944–45 was severe enough to interfere with the prenatal growth of infants born during that period (Smith 1954). Congenital malformations, which appear irregularly in normal times, were so slightly increased as to be inconclusive in the few conceptions occurring at the worst stage of the undernutrition. With this degree of famine the frequent intervention of amenorrhea, as a protective device, makes it virtually impossible to collect useful data on fetal anomalies.

When severely undernourished women go into labor, it may be prolonged by as much as five hours. This constitutes a well recognized hazard for both mother and newborn. Very poor nutrition can also affect lactation and cause sharp rises in infant mortality. This is especially the case in societies having no ready milk substitutes and no inter-family cooperation in wet nursing. Such was the case among Okinawans after the 1945 invasion of their island (see Emory 1946:616).

There is a vast literature on the influence of dietary deprivations on child growth. One of the most interesting of these reports concerns Howe and Schiller's (1952) unique 40-year record spanning the two World Wars for statures and weights of school children in Stuttgart, Germany. These cross-sectionally presented data show extreme sensitivity to economic conditions bearing upon nutritional status. Thus, there were dips in the stature and weight curves during World War I, the 1922–23 inflation, the 1932 unemployment crisis, World War II, and the 1946–47 food shortage due to drought. For these German children, as well as those from Belgium, France, England, and Japan, Howe (n.d.) believes that, unless the undernutrition is of long duration, growth simply slows down and, as it were, waits for better times. When they arrive, growth takes place with unusual rapidity until the bulk of the children approach their genetically-determined growth tracks, along which they proceed as before. Viewing Howe's thesis critically, one significant consequence of a belated recuperative cycle lies in the timing of growth and its allometric effect upon somatotype. Another consequence of chronic undernutrition is reduced resistance to disease. Both consequences are well illustrated in Lewit's (1947) study of 4,000 Czech children at the end of World War II. In these children the pre-pubertal growth spurt in leg length was stated to be greater than the trunk height increases, resulting in a thin ectomorphic body build with weak musculature. Some 10 to 15 percent of the children were tested as tuberculin-positive, with the percentage increasing in each succeeding age-grade. Telltale enlargement of cervical glands was found in almost every child.

Another consequence of chronic undernutrition is the delay in skeletal maturation, which not only involves belated appearance of ossification centers and their slow subsequent development, but also a noteworthy increase in osseous anomalies (Snodgrasse et al. 1955; Dreizen et al. 1958). Studies thus far on non-Western children show them to average one to four years behind Greulich-Pyle (1959) and other standards for skeletal maturation, and for the gap to widen with increasing age. And there may also be, as Keys (1950:372) has suggested, far more critical residues of undernutrition and malnutrition expressed in lowered work capacities, reduced disease resistance, and various psychological traumata.

The classic study on the effect of famine upon physique was done by Ivanovsky (1923) during the long starvation period in post-Revolutionary Russia. In 16 populations of varying ethnic origins within the Soviet, adult statures decreased on average 3.8–6.6 cm. in men, 3.6–4.8 cm. in women, on a longitudinal basis. Weight losses of 30 percent occurred in a great number, and other bodily measures showed gross decreases. Organic and psychological traumata were common. A milder laboratory version of Ivanovsky's study was carried out on 34 U.S. white volunteers who were put on a semi-starvation diet for 24 weeks (Lasker 1947). They averaged a 24 percent weight loss and showed a 66 percent increase in ectomorphy.

The biological and psychological effects of seasonal shortages in food supply constitute another aspect of undernutrition. The effect of the "hungry months" from January to March upon social interactions is one of Richard's (1939) principal cultural themes for the Bemba of northeastern Rhodesia. Brock and Autret (1952:48) indicate that seasonal fluctuations in food supply are marked in subsaharan Africa, and the birth weights of infants are significantly less there during the "hungry months." Vitamin-deficiency states and kwashiorkor are also more prevalent during these lean times. These lean times occur elsewhere in the world. For the Vicos Quechua in the northern Peruvian Sierra, the rainy season from December to February or March includes a period of food shortages for families without emergency stores. Kuczynski-Godard (1945:35–38) indicates that among the Aymará of Ichu the diet is particularly low in energy producing foods at just the time that the hardest harvesting labor is needed.

Malnutrition in man

To a considerable extent the nutritional deficiency diseases are distributed by climate zones, are often worse at certain seasons, and are sometimes related to specific food crops. When these deficiency diseases reach epidemic proportions, they appear to represent the worst lags in man's adaptations to his nutritional environment. Rickets and osteomalacia are typically the nutritional deficiency diseases of cold climates. In the higher latitudes with more cloud cover, ultraviolet radiation is reduced, especially in the winter. In the United States wintertime, the percentage of total possible sunshine varies from 20 to 40 percent around the Great Lakes and the Pacific Northwest to 70 to 90 percent in the Southwest. Moreover, use of heavy clothing as a protection against cold blocks out most of the solar radiation reaching near-ground level. Bodily absorption of ultraviolet radiation makes possible the production of irradiated ergosterol which goes through a series of reactions to form vitamin D (Clark 1953:23). But where solar radiation is slight and blocked off, dietary vitamin D must take its place or deficiency diseases will result. It is in the dietarily acculturated cold climate peoples that rickets and osteomalacia are the greatest problems. Among the Labrador Eskimo who have largely abandoned their native dietary, rickets, scurvy, and combinations of these two deficiency diseases are said to be universal (Anonymous 1943:207). In Swedish Lapps who had also shifted their diet, almost one-half of the children had rickets. The severity of rickets was notably greater during the winter. Rickets and osteomalacia are also prevalent in the poorest socio-economic classes in the colder urbanized areas where intake of the so-called protective foods is very low. Neither rickets nor osteomalacia are likely to be killers of the very young, but they retard and deform and in so doing affect work capacity and disease resistance.

The present world distribution of scurvy shows no strong distributional patterning. Two centuries or more ago, however, it was a wide-spread disease throughout the northern part of the Western World and in other regions where antiscorbutic vitamin C was largely omitted from the dietary. Thus, we may think of scurvy as a wind sailor's disease and associate its ravages with Stefansson's (1956) "Pemmican War" between the Hudson Bay and the Northwest Companies. But scurvy used to be so common during the English winter months that it was known as the "London Disease." Lack of fruits and lightly cooked vegetables in the diets of all people at that time rendered all socio-economic classes scurvy-prone. Infantile scurvy can be a real killer, and very low vitamin C intake at any age can bring on the classic symptoms of joint pain, hemorrhage, gum softening, and tooth loss.

The iodine deficiency disease of goiter has an interrupted distribution in the mountainous parts of the world as well as the northern continental segment of North America (Amer. Geogr. Soc., 1953:map 1). While more unsightly than serious in moderate form, strong iodine deficiencies in combination with other shortages can lead to severe degenerative syndromes such as D. C. Gajdusek (personal communication) found in the Mulia of the Central Highlands of Netherlands New Guinea.

Pellagra, due principally to niacin deficiency, is much more prevalent in the world's temperate zones than elsewhere and is more severe during the warmer months' maxima of solar radiation (Gillman and Gillman 1951:33). Moreover, pellagra is likely to be endemic in those areas where maize is a principal food crop, although the nature of this association is in some dispute (Gillman and Gillman 1951:40–41). Pellagra reached epidemic proportions during the 19th century in European countries such as France, Italy, and Rumania. After ameliorative measures reduced its morbidity and mortality rates in Europe, pellagra became the scourge of the southern part of the United States. Between 1890 and 1909, some 22 percent of those afflicted with pellagra in the South did not survive (Thompson-McFadden Commission 1913), and since that time the death rate has risen to 40 to 60 percent during epidemics. After an intensive campaign of agrarian and industrial reforms in the Southern States, pellagra became a much less serious public health problem. But in South Africa Gillman and Gillman (1951:64) tell us that the steep increase in pellagra ". . . is a reflection of economic deterioration of the African. While at the moment [over 10 years ago] the disease in South Africa is not virulent, the history of pellagra in other countries has shown that the mortality rate can become very great, claiming as much as 60 percent of the afflicted." Pellagra is quite variable in the forms it takes, but often involves severe dermatoses, hepatic derangements, and severe alimentary and neurological disorders. It is a killer at all ages, from prenatal life onward. The growth and maturational disturbances and loss of vitality residual in the survivors is such that Africans recruited from pellagroid areas for work in the mines are said to be routinely "fed up" before they are expected to do the full day's work required of them.

What pellagra is to maize consumers, so is beri-beri to the eaters of rice. The thiamine deficiency associated with diets based largely upon milled rice is the undeniable cause of beri-beri. Accordingly, this deficiency disease is largely restricted to Southeast Asia, but it is also present to some extent in Venezuela, the Minas Gerais area of Brazil, the former Cameroons, and Madagascar (Amer. Geogr. Soc. 1953). Beri-beri takes various forms in which a polyneuritis strongly affecting the lower extremities is an almost constant feature. This is "dry" beri-beri. "Wet" beri-beri also involves edema and the collecting of fluid in the body cavities. "Cardiac" beri-beri has the obvious association with heart failure. Infantile beri-beri can be a real killer. This used to be the case among lower class Burmese in Mandalay, where food restrictions imposed upon pregnant and lactating women and upon their ailing offspring caused high mortality in the latter (D. C. Sharma, personal communication). The East Indians and Chinese then resident in Mandalay imposed no such deprivations of thiamine-rich foods and had little infantile beri-beri. This is but one of the many instances where nutritional stresses are both class-structured and culture-conditioned.

The protein deficiency syndrome known as kwashiorkor has a broad distributional sweep of the lower latitudes from Mexico south to many parts of northern South America, throughout subsaharan Africa except for the cattle-raising eastern portion, and in India and much of China. Notably these are the countries of low agricultural productivity in terms of yield per man-day. Kwashiorkor, which means "red boy," is most serious in infants but also leaves perceptible residues in the children and adults who survive. The trouble may start with a poor prenatal and immediately postnatal nutritional environment. In Central America, Scrimshaw et al. (1957) found that partial starvation during the first year of life from insufficient maternal milk is more likely to result in marasmus (progressive wasting of the body) than kwashiorkor. For most children, however, the critical time for onset of kwashiorkor is toward the end of the first year when maternal milk fails to supply enough protein, and supplementary foods—if given at all—are principally carbohydrates. The clinical changes involved in active kwashiorkor include grossly retarded growth and maturation, apathy and anorexia, edema, depigmentation and other changes in the hair (hence "red boy"), diarrhea, and anemia. According to researches cited by Brock and Autret (1952:56–58) for subsaharan Africa, protein requirements per given caloric intake are perceptibly higher in children under five years of age than they are later on in life. The progressive decline in body weight for large numbers of Kampala infants and children, as viewed cross-sectionally in comparison with European standards, is but one of the observable symptoms of kwashiorkor in that area.

The mortality rate attributable to kwashiorkor is impossible to determine without special studies. Such studies were made, however, by Scrimshaw and his colleagues (1957) in four Guatemalan towns totaling 7,000 in population. In Guatemala as a whole the leading cause of death in children is listed as "gastroenteritis and diarrheal disease," yet a careful study of the four towns indicated that at least one-quarter of all deaths under five years of age was due to kwashiorkor or some other nutritional deficiency. Excepting the first year of life, at least half the deaths in one- to four-year-olds appeared to be a direct consequence of malnutrition. These death rates are highly class-structured in Guatemala and are race-conditioned as well, since the lowest socio-economic class and the most Indian are usually one and the same.

Even when protein deficiencies were not strongly expressed clinically, Scrimshaw et al. (1957) felt that the poorly nourished Guatemalan children were an easier prey to other diseases and might die as a direct consequence of pneumonia, measles, whooping cough, infectious diarrhea, or tuberculosis. Moreover, extra stresses of any kind could result in the expression of frank clinical symptoms of kwashiorkor. Thus, if a child developed a heavy parasite load, it might lapse into severe kwashiorkor.

In subsaharan Africa, Brock and Autret (1952:24) report that mortality among kwashiorkor sufferers was high, especially in cases with edema. Until the advent of modern treatment the reported mortality rates never went below 30 percent. In the absence of such treatment, death was a 100 percent certainty in kwashiorkor-afflicted Congolese children. Closely associated with kwashiorkor in Africa are apparently irreversible fatty changes in the liver, hence the frequently used synonym of "fatty liver disease." There is a strong seasonal association of kwashiorkor outbreaks in Africa with the "hungry months."

Mention must be made of other nutritional deficiency diseases of less dramatic but nevertheless significant stress in man. There are the pro-vitamin A and vitamin A deficiencies associated with retarded growth rates in experimental animals and perhaps man (Clark 1953:12–13), as well as with dermal hyperkeratosis and impaired night vision. Ariboflavinosis is also associated with skin and visual disturbances. Then there are the various minerals that are often deficient in the soils or in the diets selected from them. Of the so-called macronutrients, calcium and phosphorus appear to be the most important to human welfare, but in part this is because they have been the best studied. Marett (1936:226–27) claims a strong ecological correlation between tropical rainforests and soils deficient in calcium and phosphorus and hypothecated that pygmy body size represented an advantageous economy in these macronutrient elements. There is fair evidence that other human populations have successfully adapted themselves to low calcium intakes by slow growth and maturation and small adult body size (Nichols and Nimalasuriya 1939; Schraer and Newman 1958). In the micronutrient group—iron, copper, zinc, and manganese—iron-deficiency anemias are widespread in man and have clear ecological and epidemiological correlates. One rather curious ecological association in Alaskan Eskimos is the widespread but usually mild anemia (Scott et al. 1955) with heavy consumption of fish (Margaret Lantis, personal communication). Comparable anemias are not found in the caribou and sea mammal hunters.

Conclusions

Undernutrition and malnutrition often go together in man to provide gross and general stressing of a nutritional nature. Qualitative deficiencies are often multiple because of the metabolic interactions of the various nutrients. Where deficiency diseases principally attributable to a single nutrient are apparent, these diseases have strong ecological associations—rickets and osteomalacia with cold climates; scurvy and pellagra with, respectively, the more northerly and more southerly portions of the world's temperate zones; and beri-beri and kwashiorkor with warmer temperate and hot climates. Moreover, pellagra is associated in some way with maize cultivation, while beri-beri has a more direct relationship to heavy dietary use of milled rice. Most of these deficiency diseases have strong seasonal associations—rickets, osteomalacia, and scurvy with the winter months, pellagra with the summer months, and kwashiorkor with the "hungry months" whenever they occur.

Mortality attributable to dietary shortages is therefore frequently differential in its effect upon human populations, by region, socio-economic class, and age-grade. So are the biological and psychological residues in those who survive these diseases. In terms of mortality and morbidity rates, the greatest nutritional stresses are present in the underdeveloped countries of the world, especially where agricultural output and/or productivity are low. These are principally the countries of the tropics and warmer temperate zone, where the vectors of disease seem to be most strongly entrenched. Disease often goes along with poor nutrition, and the two are largely synergistic in relationship.

In terms of the histories of diseases, the underdeveloped countries are currently plagued by many of the nutritional deficiency and other diseases common less than several centuries ago in the more advanced countries. As Gordon's (1952:49) data suggest, the technologically more advanced countries have proceeded apace to develop new mortality patterns, with the degenerative diseases such as atherosclerosis and cancer now high on the list of killers. Atherosclerosis, for example, has a quite clear association with high intake of saturated fat and with reduced physical exercise, and hence has very obvious ecological and cultural connotations.

As a whole, then, nutritional stress in man has very strong ecological and cultural correlates. It should be equally apparent that the nutritional stresses that play such a potent role in human malaise must also impose their stamp upon the forms and functions of many aspects of man's culture as well.

REFERENCES

ALLISON, A. C. 1960. Genetic factors in resistance to malaria. Annals of the New York Academy of Sciences. N.Y. 91:(3):710–29.

AMERICAN GEOGRAPHICAL SOCIETY OF NEW YORK. 1953. Study in human starvation (two sets of annotated maps).

ANONYMOUS. 1943. Food and health of Eskimo and Lapps. British Medical Journal ii:207.

BROCK, J. F. and M. AUTRET. 1952. Kwashiorkor in Africa. World Health Organization Monograph Series No. 8.

CLARK, G. W. 1953. A vitamin digest. Springfield, Charles C Thomas.

DREIZEN, S., R. M. SNODGRASSE, H. WEBB-PEPLOE, and T. D. SPIES. 1958. The retarding effect of protracted undernutrition on the appearance of the postnatal ossification centers in the hand and wrist. Human Biology 30:253–64.

DUGAL, L-P. and G. FORTIER. 1952. Ascorbic acid and acclimatization to cold in monkeys. Journal of Applied Physiology 5:(3):143–46.

EMORY, H. L. 1946. Soybean milk-substitute as used on Okinawa. U.S. Navy Medical Bulletin 46:(4):616–18.

GILMAN, J. and T. GILMAN. 1951. Perspectives in human malnutrition. New York, Grune and Stratton.

GORDON, J. E. 1952. Ecological investigation of disease. New York, Milbank Memorial Fund.

GOUROU, P. 1956. The quality of land use by tropical cultivators. *In* Man's role in changing the face of the earth, W. L. Thomas, ed. University Chicago Press.

GREULICH, W. W. and S. I. PYLE. 1959. Radiographic atlas of skeletal development of the hand and wrist. Stanford University Press.

HOWE, P. E. n.d. Growth of the adolescent child as affected by restricted nutrition (Manuscript).

HOWE, P. E. and M. SCHILLER. 1952. Growth responses of the school child to changes in diet and environmental factors. Journal of Applied Physiology 5(2): 51–61.

HULSE, F. S. 1955. Technological advance and major racial stocks. Human Biology, 27:(3):184–92.

IVANOVSKY, A. 1923. Physical modifications of the population of Russia under famine. American Journal of Physical Anthropology 6:(4):331–53.

KEYS, A. 1950. The residues of malnutrition and starvation. Science 112:2909, pp. 371–73.

KUCZYNSKI GODARD, M. H. 1945. Estudio familiar demografico-ecologico en estancias Indias de la Altiplano del Titicaca (Ichupampa). Lima, Peru, Ministerio de Sálud Publica.

LASKER, G. W. 1947. The effects of partial starvation on somatotype. An analysis of material from the Minnesota Starvation Experiment. American Journal of Physical Anthropology 5:(3):323–33.

LEWIT, E. 1947. A preliminary report on a study of 4,000 Czechoslovakian children. Medical Women's International Journal, London. 54:(1):41–44.

MARETT, J. DE LA R. 1936. Race, sex, and environment. London, Hutchinson's Scientific and Technical Publications.

MITCHELL, H. H. and E. EDMAN. 1951. Nutrition and climatic stress. Springfield, Charles C Thomas.

NICHOLS, L. and A. NIMALASURIYA. 1939. Adaptation to a low calcium intake in reference to the calcium requirements of a tropical population. Journal of Nutrition 18:(6):563–77.

PHILLIPS, J. 1960. Agriculture and ecology in Africa. New York, Praeger.

RICHARDS, A. I. 1939. Land, labour, and diet in Northern Rhodesia. Oxford University Press.

ROBERTS, D. F. 1952. An ecological approach to physical anthropology: environmental temperatures and physiological features. Actes du IVᵉ Congrés International des Sciences Anthropologiques et Ethnologiques, Vienne, Tome I: 145–48.

SCHRAER, H. and M. T. NEWMAN. 1958. Quantitative roentgenography of skeletal mineralization in malnourished Quechua Indian boys. Science 128:3322, pp. 476–77.

SCIENTIFIC COUNCIL FOR AFRICA SOUTH OF THE SAHARA (CSA). 1956. Nutritional research in Africa south of the Sahara. London, CCTZ/CSA Pub. No. 19.

SCRIMSHAW, N. S. 1953. Excerpt from address published in Proceedings Food and Nutrition Board, 12:24 (May), 1952, Journal American Dietetic Association 29:(2):133 (Feb.).

SCRIMSHAW, N. W., M. BÉHAR, F. VITERI, G. ARROYAVE, and C. TEJADA. 1957. Epidemiology and prevention of severe protein malnutrition (kwashiorkor) in Central America. American Journal of Public Health 47:(1):53–62.

SCRIMSHAW, N. S., C. E. TAYLOR, and J. E. GORDON. 1959. Interactions of nutrition and infection. American Journal of the Medical Sciences 237:(3):367–403.

SCOTT, E. M., R. C. WEIGHT, and B. T. HANAN. 1955. Anemia in Alaskan Eskimo. Journal of Nutrition 55:(1):137–49.

SMITH, C. A. 1954. Effects of maternal undernutrition upon the newborn infant in Holland (1944–45). Journal of Pediatrics 30:229–43.

SNODGRASSE, R. M., S. DREIZEN, C. CURRIE, G. S. PARKER, and T. D. SPIES. 1955. The association between anomalous ossification centers in the hand and wrist, nutritional status and rate of skeletal maturation in children five to fourteen years of age. American Journal of Roentgenology, Radium Therapy, and Nuclear Medicine 74:1037–48.

SPENGLER, J. L. 1960. Population and world economic development. Science 131, 3412, 20 May, pp. 1497–1502.

STEFANSSON, V. 1956. The fat of the land. New York, The Macmillan Co.

THOMPSON-MCFADDEN PELLAGRA COMMISSION. 1913. First progress report. American Journal of the Medical Sciences 191.

REPRODUCTION

The environment may affect human reproduction at three critical stages: (a) the production of sperm, (b) the production of the egg, or (c) during the uterine environment. It has long been known that high temperatures decrease the production of sperm. The paper by Glover and Young summarizes many studies on this subject. This phenomenon is not unique for humans or even for primates. Studies in comparative anatomy in the vertebrates show that the testes are frequently found outside of the body where it is cooler or, if inside the body, in a cooler position. Present preliminary evidence from Hong Kong (see Appendix C) would indicate that conception rates are significantly decreased during the summer months in contrast to the winter months.

The selection on the response of spermatozoa to increased temperature found on page 123 may be regarded as an optional reading.

For many years there existed the "old wives' tale" that the uterus was the safest place possible for a human fetus. Recently, research would indicate that the uterus is one of the severest, if not the most severe environment to which human life is exposed. Although we do not have critical data on the conception rate in humans, it would appear that at least 25% of human life which is conceived, fails to survive the uterine ecological period. The paper by Monie surveys many of the problems involved with uterine environment. Recent studies have shown that the developing fetus can be adversely affected by an excess of "good" factors. Notice in Table 1 (p. 131) that a proper amount of Vitamin A is necessary for a well-formed child but that malformations may be brought on

117

by an excess or a deficiency of this vitamin. The section on page 135 entitled, "Testing for Teratogenicity" may be regarded as an optional reading.

The study by Bresler would indicate that the "uterine cavity" presents certain anatomical or spatial restrictions to the developing fetus. Presumably a fetus may fail to develop into a full-term live child because of this restriction.

In time, techniques will be developed whereby a human fetus need not be left in the female uterus for its development. It could be removed surgically and placed into fetal tanks for further development. This inevitable scientific and technological advance will raise great moral and social issues.

Temperature
and the Production
of Spermatozoa*

T. D. GLOVER
AND D. H. YOUNG

A number of factors well known to seminologists prevent a well-planned and clear-cut experiment from being carried out on the fertility of the human male. Largely for this reason, it would seem, a lot of data on male fertility have been obtained from experiments on animals, and many aspects of function in the human testis have necessarily involved considerable speculation. The question of temperature and its effect on male fertility is outstanding in this connection, for experimental results have been obtained on only a limited number of subjects, while other data have been derived from clinical observations where adequate control measures are often difficult to ensure. However, it is well recognized that in a wide variety of mammals, including man, the testes function at a temperature which is lower than that of the abdominal viscera. Furthermore, many experiments with animals have revealed that the production of male gametes is extremely susceptible to any increase in the temperature of the testes. It would therefore seem worthwhile to review some of the experiments and examine the situation as it applies to human problems. The present paper is an attempt to do this, and it is hoped that it might provide some perspective upon which future experiments with the human subject could be based.

Experiments on the importance of testicular temperatures

Harrison listed differences between abdominal and testicular temperatures in several mammals and pointed out that it was greatest in the rat and mouse (mean

* From the Department of Veterinary Anatomy, University of Liverpool, and the Male Infertility Clinic, The Royal Infirmary, Liverpool, England.

values being 8.3 and 8.5°C., respectively), intermediate in the rabbit and ram (6.2 and 7.1°C.) and least in the macaque monkey (2.0°C.). In man, this temperature difference is between 2.0 and 2.5°C. While the delicacy of thermoregulation in the human testis has never been firmly established, it is recognized in laboratory animals that spermatogenesis is sensitive to relatively small increases in environmental temperature.[43, 44, 50] By means of artificial cryptorchidism in guinea pigs, these workers induced testicular degeneration and established the thermoregulatory role of the scrotum. Under these circumstances the temperature of the testes would, according to Harrison's data, be raised only 4.0°C. above normal. These findings were confirmed by Moore and Oslund,[48, 49] and already similar effects had been observed in dogs by Griffiths. More direct evidence of the susceptibility of the testes to heat was provided by Fukui,[12, 13] who found that application of heat rays to the testes of rabbits resulted in defective spermatogenesis. Moore and Chase also reported this result from the direct application of heat to the scrotum.

Cunningham and Osborn sterilized rats with 5-min. treatments of infrared radiation at 48°C., and Fukui[12, 13] showed that bathing the scrotum in hot water at this temperature destroyed the spermatogenic epithelium of rabbits within 1 hr. These results are not really surprising, since physiologic mechanisms, such as enzyme systems, are likely to be impaired if not inhibited by temperatures approaching 50°C. By contrast, it appears from Fukui's work that at 40°C. very long periods of exposure are needed to produce complete degeneration of spermatogenic tissue. He gave 180–200 hr. of continuous exposure as examples. Yet Asdell and Salisbury reported damage in the rabbit testis after only 24 hr. of experimental cryptorchidism, but in comparing the two results, the degree of spermatogenic interference must be taken into account. In addition, it would seem incautious on existing evidence to regard the effects of cryptorchidism as exclusively due to increased testicular temperature. This is particularly so in clinical cases of the disorder, and this point was emphasized by Klein and Mayer. Nevertheless, it is clear that spermatogenic activity is sensitive to localized increase in temperature irrespective of its mode of induction. Guieyesse-Pellisier, for example, claimed a sterilizing effect of hot steam when applied to the scrotum of dogs, and insulation of the scrotum in bulls and rams, where an increase in the temperature of the testes is unquestionable, results in characteristically deficient sperm production;[16, 24, 35, 39] similar effects have also been produced by artificial cryptorchidism in rabbits.[18] In man, subfertility is sometimes reported in association with varicocele,[57–60, 66, 67] and it has been suggested that this may be a reflection of a localized temperature effect.[26] Apparently hydroceles act similarly, and it is also likely that increased temperature plays a part in the manifestations of orchitis. In rams, for instance, Gunn et al. reported defective sperm production due to inflammation caused by blowfly maggot on the scrotum.

The detrimental effects of increased temperature on the function of the testes are not confined to local applications, however, for exposure of animals to high environmental temperatures also induces degeneration in the quality of ejaculated semen.[4, 39] In the human being MacLeod and Hotchkiss showed, too, that by increasing body temperature experimentally the concentration of spermatozoa in ejaculated semen could be reduced. It has been claimed also that in clinical cases involving pyrexia, the normal function of the human testis can be impaired, and pneumonia and typhoid have been mentioned in this connection.[27, 42] Further evidence of the effects of pneumonia was produced by MacLeod, who also showed that chicken pox can cause a temporary disturbance of sperm production. Gunn *et al.* demonstrated seminal degeneration in rams as a result of the intraperitoneal injection of pus from acute abscesses. The purpose of this procedure was simply to produce an experimental pyrexia.

It therefore seems clear that elevation of temperature, whether local or general, affects spermatogenic tissue adversely in mammals whose testes are normally resident in a scrotum.

Possible causes of "heat degeneration"

Fukui[12, 13] suggested that damage to the testes incurred by increased temperature was due to the thermolability of certain "spermatogenous" proteins. The contention has never been confirmed or refuted in subsequent work, but it is more often held that circulatory changes are involved. Barron believed that "heat degeneration" could be due to hyperemia resulting from vasodilatation, while Moore[11] gave vascular stagnation and oxygen lack as a possible explanation. If heat is applied to an exposed testicle, a hyperemia is apparent, as would be expected, but in the rabbit a characteristic cyanosis ensues. It would seem possible that when the temperature is elevated, blood flow to the testes might be slowed because of back pressure, and an alteration in the capillary-reduction curve might follow,[36] but Cross and Silver (1962) have shown that oxygen tension in the testis of rabbits increases when the scrotum is warmed. Circulatory factors, therefore, need more study—but certainly even slight changes in the circulation of the testes can affect spermatogenesis.[30] A relationship between circulatory and temperature effects has been demonstrated by Moule and Knapp, who showed that in the ram, ligation of the external pudendal artery causes a rise in the temperature of the testes.

An entirely different suggestion as to the mechanism of "heat degeneration" was put forward by Meschaks, who showed that seminal degeneration in bulls following insulation of the scrotum is closely related to the excretion of neutral steroids in the urine; he suggested that abnormal function of the testes under these conditions might be due to excessive production of testicular and adrenal cortical hormones.

The matter remains unsettled, but as far as the effects of circulation are concerned, quantitative data on blood flow such as those recently provided by Waites and Moule[63, 64] are the most helpful contribution. With regard to hormonal effects, consideration of the problem makes painfully clear the dearth of precise information on the endocrine control of the testes. It is perhaps for this reason that results obtained on the hormonal activity of the testes in conditions of increased temperature are difficult to interpret.

Endocrine function of the testes during "heat degeneration"

Moore and Gallagher reported that in guinea pigs 8 months of artificial cryptorchidism produced no apparent effect on the secretion of testicular hormone, and Jeffries, using the cytology of the accessory organs as an indicator, made a similar claim for the rat. Nelson,[52] however, observed changes in the seminal vesicles of rats after 240 days of experimental cryptorchidism. Moore[45] also used rats as experimental animals and took the weight of the seminal vesicles as an indicator of male-sex-hormone activity. He found that confinement of the testes in the abdomen reduced hormonal activity, although, if the condition was continued, the hormone output appeared to attain some constancy after 20–80 days. Pfeiffer showed a reduction in the size of the seminal vesicles of the rat following an increase in environmental temperature, and Elfving obtained similar results in the guinea pig with direct application of heat to the scrotum.

All these experiments relied on the weight or cytology of the accessory glands as indicators of the male sex hormone. More recently Clegg[6] used levels of seminal fructose and citric acid as indicators of male sex hormone activity in artificial cryptorchidism in rats. This was based on the work of Mann et al., who had shown these levels to be accurate indicators of circulating androgen. By using these technics, Clegg was able to show that reduction in androgenic activity during cryptorchidism was preceded by a sharp rise. The finding was later confirmed[7] by means of a detailed histologic examination of the interstitial cells of the testes. Earlier, increase in seminal fructose during insulation of the scrotum in rams had been demonstrated,[17] and a similar increase in excretion of 17-ketosteroids was shown by Meschaks in bulls. This apparent increase in androgenic activity during the early stages of artificial cryptorchidism doubtless explains the findings of Bouin and Ancel, Hanes and Hooker, and others that the interstitial tissue of the testes increases in amount in cryptorchidism. Nevertheless, Engberg claimed in the human being that bilateral cryptorchidism reduced androgenic activity by half, and explanation of the cause of these fluctuations must remain speculative at present.

Possible differences in effect between naturally occurring and artificial cryptorchidism should be borne in mind, however, since in the former condition the testes have generally been exposed to an abnormal environment for a longer period of time.

The response of spermatozoa to increased temperature

Since it is necessary for spermatozoa to traverse the epididymis before they are ejaculated, it is of obvious importance to consider the effects of high temperature upon the spermatozoa themselves during their prolonged sojourn in the excurrent ducts. It might be emphasized in this regard that spermatozoa spend much of their adolescence and often their entire adult life in the epididymis. This structure is permanently packed with spermatozoa, and its length in many mammals is striking, being more than 70 M. in the stallion, at least 40 M. in bulls,[14] and roughly 6 M. in man.[62]

If spermatozoa in the epididymis were unaffected by variations in temperature, the adverse effects of cryptorchidism or insulation of the scrotum would not be revealed in ejaculated semen for some time, because the epididymis would first have to be emptied of its contents (normal spermatozoa) unless defective spermatozoa could squeeze their way through the main sperm mass. This would necessitate an extra impetus to the passage of abnormal spermatozoa, and on present evidence it would seem highly unlikely. However, during insulation of the scrotum in rams, degenerated (decapitate) spermatozoa do not appear in ejaculates for about 1–2 weeks,[16, 56] so it is relevant to ask whether this delay represents the time of migration through the epididymis. If it does, the assumption must be made that decapitation occurs only in the testes. This would not be justified for rabbits, where it has been shown that artificial cryptorchidism exerts a profound effect on spermatozoa already in the epididymis.[19, 20] In this species, however, the effect appears to vary according to the level of the epididymis at which the spermatozoa are located. Decapitation of so-called mature spermatozoa from the tail of the epididymis is not seen in artificial cryptorchidism for 7–11 days while it appears to occur more rapidly in spermatozoa situated in the head of the epididymis.[21] It thus appears that the action of increased temperature on the morphology of mature spermatozoa in the tail of the epididymis is cumulative. Nevertheless Knaus showed that rabbits become infertile after only three days of experimental cryptorchidism, and thus it seems that their fertilizing capacity is lost before decapitation occurs, and that a cumulative action of increased temperature relates only to the morphology of spermatozoa. This important possibility requires further investigation, especially since Young[68] showed that in vitro, sperms from the tail of the epididymis were most susceptible to high temperatures. This would seem to be the exact converse of the situation in vivo.

Decapitate spermatozoa can be produced in rams by a short 24-hour period of insulation of the scrotum[15] where accumulation of effect could hardly occur, but in these cases, abnormal sperms are not ejaculated for some 17–24 days, which closely resembles the time of migration of spermatozoa through the epididymis.[54] It thus seems possible that in the ram also, spermatozoa in the testes and upper regions of the epididymis react more readily to the effects of elevated temperature.

The effect of low temperature on the production of spermatozoa

Harris and Harrison demonstrated, by surrounding the exposed rat testis with a mixture of ice and salt, that application of a temperature of $-5°C$. for 1 hr. caused some destruction of spermatogenic epithelium. A temperature of $-11°C$. was needed, however, to bring about severe spermatogenic damage. These workers suggested that the effects were related to induced ischemia, presumably due to vascular spasm, and the results Cross and Silver (1962) obtained following the application of ethyl chloride to the scrotum of the rabbit appear to confirm this, since marked reduction in testicular oxygen tension was recorded. But it is again important to have some knowledge of the response of spermatozoa in the epididymis to such variations in temperature, and Chang showed that the application of ice to the scrotum of rabbits caused rapid decapitation of spermatozoa in the tail of the epididymis. Excessively low temperature therefore seems to have rapid effects on sperm production, but the effects of minor decreases in temperature need to be studied more critically.

It would seem important indeed to establish more precisely the range of temperature in which testes situated in a scrotum normally function, for the peculiar vascular pattern of the mammalian testis, the cremaster muscles, and the dartos muscle indicate in themselves that efficient thermoregulation of the testes is vital.

Conclusions

From relatively limited information on temperature and testicular function in man, together with more abundant data in animals, it is justifiable to conclude that increasing the temperature of the human testis is likely to reduce fertility. But the "population explosion" detracts from attaching too much importance to this as far as the average man is concerned. Nevertheless, it might well be profitable for the subfertile male to keep his testes "cool" for perhaps they might be especially prone to damage from high temperatures. Some reports,[9] in fact, have indicated that subfertility has been overcome by bathing the scrotum in cold water or casting away close-fitting underclothes. The evidence is, however, by no means conclusive, and a controlled experiment on the subject is strongly indicated.

A vital question today is, could a human male be *temporarily* sterilized by insulation of his scrotum, or by taking frequent hot baths? The answer would seem to be in the affirmative, provided that the insulation was adequate, the baths sufficiently frequent, and the water hot enough. An interpretation of these nebulous terms must, however, await the results of further experiments, of which some are in progress and others might usefully be undertaken in the future. Little progress can be made until more quantitative data are available and since fertility trials on the human being cannot easily be planned, particularly when background knowledge is scanty, conventional semen tests could afford valuable information as an initial approach. It would be worthwhile to establish conclusively the effects of local applications of heat to the human scrotum on the motility, morphology, and metabolic activity of ejaculated spermatozoa.

An accurate appraisal of semen samples in mammals must take into account the differences in the structure of the male organs of reproduction in different species, as well as possible specificity in function.

Perhaps the testes of various mammalian species differ in their response to body temperature. The fact that Montremata, Cetacea, Proboscidea, Xenarthra, Hyracoidea and some of the Insectivora retain their testes permanently in the abdomen lends support to the possibility. This is particularly so where there appears to be no close correlation between body temperature and the position of the testes.[65]

That the length of the ductus epididymidis also differs between species might be of additional importance, since wide variations in the number of contained spermatozoa must occur. The time at which testicular abnormalities are revealed in ejaculated semen in different species might thus vary considerably. Figure 1 illustrates, as an example, differences in basic structure between the epididymis of the ram and that of man. Apart from over-all size differences, the tail of the epididymis of the ram is extensive when compared with that of the human being. Therefore, if spermatozoa are damaged in the testes or upper regions of the epididymis only (as, for instance, after short periods of temperature elevation), it seems likely that they might appear in human ejaculates sooner than they would in those of the ram. It could be, of course, that the response of human spermatozoa to elevated temperature is entirely different from that of

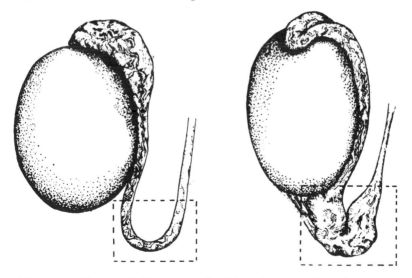

FIG. 1. Diagrams of human (*left*) and ram (*right*) testis and epididymis, illustrating form of tail of epididymis relative to rest of epididymis. (See text.)

spermatozoa in experimental animals, and also, the time of migration of spermatozoa through the human epididymis needs to be established beyond all doubt.

From this survey, we suggest that experiments on the influence of increased testicular temperature on the fertility of the human male are desirable, for it might be significant in certain cases of infertility or subfertility. In addition, application of the effects of increased testicular temperature to the problems of birth control cannot be altogether dismissed. It seems that severe heat treatment is needed in animals before the testes are damaged irreversibly, that spermatozoa in the epididymis readily respond to increased temperature by first losing their fertilizing capacity and then rapidly disintegrating. Furthermore, libido does not appear to be affected by short-term treatments. If sperm production is not completely abolished or the adverse response of spermatozoa is not total, the effects may still be of value in solving a world problem though they may be disappointing in individual cases. Certainly it seems from experiments with animals that local heat treatment of the testes is systemically innocuous, and the possibility of side effects can be disregarded. When a number of noxious agents, some of which might upset general physiologic functions, are being tested, it would seem appropriate also to investigate seriously the applicability of a well-known and apparently harmless phenomenon to the problem of population control.

REFERENCES

1. ASDELL, S. A., and SALISBURY, C. W. *Am. J. Physiol. 132:*791, 1941.
2. BARRON, D. H. *Anat. Rec. 55:* suppl. 6, 1933.
3. BOUIN, P., and ANCEL, P. *Arch. Zool. exp. gen. 1:*437, 1903.
4. CASADY, R. B., MYERS, R. M., and LEGATE, J. E. *J. Dairy Sc. 1:*14, 1953.
5. CHANG, M. C. *J. Exper. Biol. 20:*16, 1943.
6. CLEGG, E. J. *J. Endocrinol. 20:*210, 1960.
7. CLEGG, E. J. *J. Endocrinol. 21:*433, 1961.
7a. CROSS, B. A., and SILVER, I. A. *J. Endocrinol. 3:*377, 1962.
8. CUNNINGHAM, B., and OSBORN, T. I. *Endocrinology 13:*93, 1929.
9. DAVIDSON, H. A. *Practitioner 173:*703, 1954.
10. ELFVING, G. *Effects of the Local Application of Heat on the Physiology of Testis.* T. A. Sahalan Kirjapaino, Oy., Helsinki, 1950.
11. ENGBERG, H. *Proc. Roy. Soc. Med. 42:*652, 1949.
12. FUKUI, N. *Jap. Med. World 3:*27, 1923.
13. FUKUI, N. *Jap. Med. World 3:*160, 1923.
14. GHETIE, E. *Anat. Anz. 87:*369, 1939.
15. GLOVER, T. D. *J. Physiol. 128:*22P, 1955.
16. GLOVER, T. D. *Stud. Fertil. 7:*66, 1955.
17. GLOVER, T. D. *J. Endocrinol. 13:*235, 1956.
18. GLOVER, T. D. *Stud. Fertil. 10:*80, 1959.
19. GLOVER, T. D. *J. Endocrinol. 18:*xi, 1959.

20. GLOVER, T. D. *J. Reprod. Fertil. 1:*121, 1960.
21. GLOVER, T. D. *J. Endocrinol. 23:*317, 1962.
22. GRIFFITHS, J. *J. Anat. Physiol. 27:*482, 1893.
23. GUIEYESSE-PELLISSIER, A. *Arch. d'anat. microscop. 33:*5, 1937.
24. GUNN, R. M. C., SAUNDERS, R. N., and GRANGER, W. *Bull. Counc. Sci. Industr. Res. Australia* No. 148, 1942.
25. HANES, F. M., and HOOKER, C. W., *Proc. Soc. Exper. Biol. & Med. 35:*583, 1937.
26. HANLEY, H. G. *Proc. 2nd World Cong. Fertil. & Steril.,* 1956, p. 93.
27. HANSEMANN, D. *Virchow's Arch. Path. Anat. 142:*538, 1895.
28. HARRIS, R., and HARRISON, R. G. *Stud. Fertil. 7:*23, 1955.
29. HARRISON, R. G., in *Conference on Infertility.* The Family Planning Association, London, 1948, p. 14.
30. HARRISON, R. G., and OETTLE, A. G. *Proc. Soc. Study. Fertil. 2:*6, 1950.
31. JEFFRIES, M. E. *Anat. Rec. 48:*131, 1931.
32. KLEIN, M., and MAYER, G. *Abstracts of xvii Int. Physiol. Congr.* 1947, p. 193.
33. KNAUS, H. *Arch. Gynäk. 151:*302, 1932.
34. KNUDSEN, O. *Acta Path. Microbiol. Scandinav.,* Suppl. Cl, 1954.
35. LAGERLOF, N. *Acta Path. Microbiol. Scandinav.,* Suppl. 19, 1934.
36. LUNSGAARD, C., and VAN SLYKE, D. D. *Cyanosis.* Williams & Wilkins, Baltimore, 1923.
37. MACLEOD, J. *Fertil. & Steril. 2:*523, 1951.
38. MACLEOD, J., and HOTCHKISS, R. S. *Endocrinology 28:*780, 1941.
39. MCKENZIE, F. F., and BERLINER, V. *Res. Bull. Mo. agric. exper. Sta.,* No. 265, 1937.
40. MANN, T., DAVIES, D. V., and HUMPHREY, G. F. *J. Endocrinol. 6:*75, 1949.
41. MESCHAKS, P. *CIBA Symposium on Mammalian Germ Cells.* Churchill, London, 1953.
42. MILLS, R. G. *J. Exper. Zool. 30:*505, 1919.
43. MOORE, C. R. *Anat. Rec. 24:*383, 1923.
44. MOORE, C. R. *Am. J. Anat. 24:*269, 1924.
45. MOORE, C. R. *Yale J. Biol. & Med. 17:*203, 1944.
46. MOORE, C. R., and CHASE, H. D. *Anat. Rec. 26:*344, 1923.
47. MOORE, C. R., and GALLAGHER, T. F. *Am. J. Anat. 45:*39, 1930.
48. MOORE, C. R., and OSLUND, R. *Anat. Rec. 26:*343, 1923.
49. MOORE, C. R., and OSLUND, R. *Am. J. Physiol. 67:*595, 1924.
50. MOORE, C. R., and QUICK, W. J. *Am. J. Physiol. 68:*70, 1924.
51. MOULE, G. R., and KNAPP, B. *Australian J. agric. Res. 1:*456, 1950.
52. NELSON, W. O. *Cold Spring Harb. Symp. quant. Biol. 5:*123, 1937.
53. NELSON, W. O. *J. Urol. 69:*325, 1953.
54. ORTAVANT, R. *C. R. Soc. Biol. 148:*866, 1954.
55. PFEIFFER, G. A. *Endocrinology 21:*260, 1937.
56. PHILLIPS, R. W., and MCKENZIE, F. F. *Res. Bull. Mo. agric. exper. Sta.* No. 217, 1934
57. RUSSELL, J. K. *Brit. M. J. 1:*1231, 1954.
58. RUSSELL, J. K. *Lancet 2:*222, 1957.
59. SCOTT, L. S. *Stud. Fertil. 10:*33, 1958.
60. SCOTT, L. S. *J. Obst. & Gynaec. Brit. Emp. 65:*904, 1958.

61. Scott, L. S., and Young, D. *Fertil. & Steril. 13:*325, 1962.
62. Testut, L. *Traité d'Anatomie humaine,* ed. 18. Paris, 1934.
63. Waites, G. M. H., and Moule, G. R. *J. Reprod. Fertil. 1:*223, 1960.
64. Waites, G. M. H., and Moule, G. R. *J. Reprod. Fertil. 2:*213, 1961.
65. Wislocki, G. B. *Quart. Rev. Biol. 8:*385, 1933.
66. Young, D. H. *Proc. Soc. Study Fertil. 5:*27, 1953.
67. Young, D. H. *Brit. J. Urol. 28:*426, 1956.
68. Young, W. C. *J. Exper. Zool. 49:*459, 1927.

Influence of the Environment on the Unborn*

IAN W. MONIE

Throughout our lives we are constantly reacting to the environment in which we live. Heat, light, atmospheric pressure, terrestial and extraterrestial radiation, gravity, microorganisms and the multitude of chemicals contained in food, water and air are continually acting upon us, determining our constitutions and our destinies. At one time it was felt that the mammalian fetus was relatively sheltered from the effects of such environmental factors but careful clinical and experimental studies have now shown this belief to be untenable.

While the mother does afford protection to the unborn in many ways—for example, by detoxifying noxious substances and by destroying microorganisms which would be harmful were they to reach the young—this is secondary to the preservation of her own organism. Where the agent is not harmful to the mother and protective reactions are absent, the effect on the embryo can be disastrous. Indeed, the majority of teratogenic (malformation-producing) agents or procedures belong to this category and are especially destructive in the early stages of gestation. Thus, rubella, if contracted by the mother during the first trimester, causes little maternal upset but may result in serious eye, ear and cardiovascular malformations in the embryo.[11] Again, maternal ingestion of thalidomide, a glutamic acid imide that once was supposed to be a harmless sedative, has recently been linked with a syndrome of phocomelia, cavernous angioma and duodenal stenosis in the offspring.[17]

---

* Presented as part of the Basic Science Session at the 92nd Annual Meeting of the California Medical Association, Los Angeles, March 23 to 27, 1963. From the Department of Anatomy, University of California Medical Center, San Francisco 94122.

129

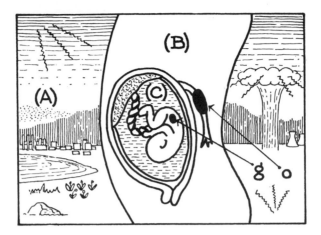

FIG. 1. The maternal and embryonic environments. (A) the *matroenvironment* consisting of the physical and chemical components, and the animal and plant life, in the
surroundings of the mother. Radiation from outer space, the earth, and man-made sources
is indicated by wavy lines; (B) the *macroenvironment* or maternal body; (C) the *microenvironment* composed of the placenta, membranes and amniotic fluid. (B) and (C) constitute the embryonic environment.

The maternal and embryonic environments

The unborn has to contend with three environments. The one with which it is in
immediate contact, consisting of the amniotic fluid, the placenta and membranes,
has been designated the *microenvironment* by Warkany.[7] The maternal body
may be called the *macroenvironment,* and the surroundings of the mother, the
matroenvironment (Figure 1). Substances inhaled or ingested by the mother
from the matroenvironment may reach the embryo unchanged, or may produce
changes in the macroenvironment or microenvironment which are ultimately
experienced by the embryo. It is also possible for substances to pass from the
macroenvironment and accumulate in the microenvironment in large enough
amounts to cause embryonic damage. In the case of radiation the embryo may
be directly affected, or it may be affected by the products of reaction with the
macroenvironment.

Environment and genetic factors

Nineteenth century experimental embryologists clearly showed that environmental change could disturb development both in invertebrates and in lower
vertebrates, and by the beginning of the present century considerable attention
was being directed to abnormal intrauterine conditions as causes of malformation and abortion in man.[2,18] However, the importance of inherited factors in the
normal and abnormal development of mammals was now appreciated and the
significance of the environment gradually became subordinated to that of the
germ-plasm; this concept generally prevailed until the early forties.

TABLE 1. Some factors which produce malformations.

	In Animals	In Man
Physical	Radiation, hypothermia	Radiation
Chemical:		
Hormones	Insulin, cortisone, androgen, estrogen, epinephrine	Sex hormones
Antigrowth factors ...	Nitrogen mustard, chlorambucil, azaserine, 6-mercaptopurine	?
Other	Trypan blue, quinine, hypoxia, salicylate, colchicine, iodine deficiency, antibiotics	Thalidomide
Nutritional:		
Deficiency	Vitamins A, B_{12}, D, E,* folic acid (PGA*), pantothenic acid,* nicotinic acid,* riboflavin*	Aminopterin†
Excess	Vitamin A	....
Other	Starvation	....
Micro-organismal	Hog cholera, influenza A, Newcastle virus	Rubella, syphilis, toxoplasmosis

* Vitamin antagonist employed alone or with deficient diet.
† A folic acid antagonist.

Nevertheless, during the period when genetic factors were considered of primary importance in the causation of congenital abnormalities, reports continued to appear on the influence of the environment on the unborn. It became evident, for example, that x-irradiation[13,14] or radium treatment of the mother during pregnancy could result in fetal death or deformity, and that lack of iodine in pregnant sows resulted in reduced litter size.[27] Cleft palate[3] was frequently seen in whelps of captive lions unless the mothers were fed goat flesh and soft bone during pregnancy, while sows receiving a vitamin A-deficient diet produced piglets with eye defects[12] and other malformations. However, it was not until 1940 and the publication of a study by Warkany and Nelson[28] showing that pregnant rats fed a deficient diet (later shown to be riboflavin deficiency) produced young with skeletal and other abnormalities, that attention was again seriously directed to the influence of the environment on mammalian development. The teratogenic effect of rubella on the human fetus observed soon after this gave further impetus to the renewed interest in environmental factors; since then a host of teratogenic agents or procedures has been discovered (Table 1).

Today, however, it is generally agreed that the majority of congenital abnormalities result from the interplay of *both* genetic and environmental factors[9] although in certain instances one may play a much more important role than the other. Since there is no apparent structural difference between congenital abnormalities produced by genetic and by environmental factors, in many cases it is difficult to determine which is of primary or sole importance.

In addition to malformations resulting from environmental or genetic factors, or to a combination of these, it is now known that abnormality of chromosomal number is responsible for such conditions as Turner's and Klinefelter's syndromes, and for mongolism. What role, if any, environmental or genetic factors play in the determination of such chromosomal disturbance has not yet been determined.

Teratogenic agents—timing and specificity

It would appear that either an excess or an insufficiency of almost any chemical or physical agent can, in certain circumstances, result in defective embryonic development; thus, either maternal insufficiency[31] or excess[5] of vitamin A produces abnormal rat young when occurring at a particular stage of pregnancy.

The time of introduction of a teratogenic agent is especially important, the embryo usually being most sensitive when the principal body systems are being established; in man, this is between the third and eighth week, and in rats during the second week of gestation (parturition occurs on the 22nd or 23rd day). In the later stages of pregnancy the fetus is much less sensitive but by no means immune to environmental influence; thus, in man, toxoplasmosis can produce hydrocephaly, and syphilis a variety of malformations in the later stages of gestation. Also, in rats the giving of 6-aminonicotinamide (6-AN), a nicotinic acid antimetabolite, as late as the 19th day of gestation can produce hydrocephaly in the young.[4]

Generally, when a teratogenic agent is given very early in gestation it either does not disturb the conceptus or it destroys it entirely, while, if given late in pregnancy its effects may be greatly reduced or absent; there is consequently a critical time for each agent during which maximum damage to the conceptors will result, and this varies with the species involved. In the case of thalidomide, for example, it has been observed that the human embryo is most sensitive between the 27th and 43rd days after conception.[17]

While the time of introduction of the agent is undoubtedly of importance, there is generally mounting evidence that certain agents have a predilection for one or more systems or regions of the embryo.[30] This is suggested, for example, by the preponderance of limb damage in human fetuses by thalidomide, and by the frequent absence of the kidney in rat young from chlorambucil.[23] On the other hand, certain teratogenic factors, such as maternal folic or pteroylglutamic acid (PGA) deficiency,[10,25,26] are associated with a broad spectrum of malformations and are considered "universal" teratogens.

The employment of teratogens in experimental animals is exceedingly valuable for studying the pathogenesis of many congenital abnormalities, and different defects can be produced by varying the time of action of the same agent, or

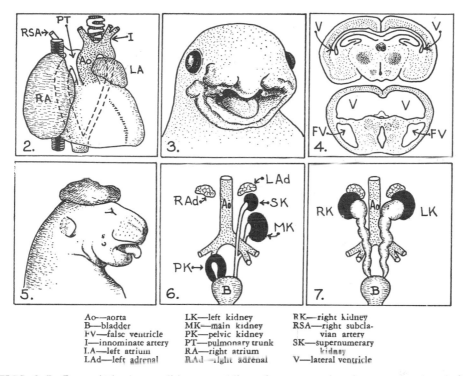

Ao—aorta
B—bladder
FV—false ventricle
I—innominate artery
LA—left atrium
LAd—left adrenal

LK—left kidney
MK—main kidney
PK—pelvic kidney
PT—pulmonary trunk
RA—right atrium
RAd—right adrenal

RK—right kidney
RSA—right subcla-
   vian artery
SK—supernumerary
   kidney
V—lateral ventricle

FIGS. 2 7. Congenital abnormalities resembling those occurring in man produced in rat young as a result of trypan blue (Figure 2), and folic acid (PGA) deficiency (Figures 3 7) during pregnancy; (2) Transposition of the great vessels and double aorta; (3) Facial defects and cleft palate; (4) Control and hydrocephalic brains from three-week-old rats; (5) Exencephaly, micrognathia, and glossoptis; (6) Pelvic and supernumerary kidneys; and (7) Bilateral hydronephrosis.

by using different agents (Figures 2 through 7). Thus, a transitory PGA-deficiency in rats from the 7th to 9th day of gestation produces many abnormalities of the brain and eye; from the 9th to 11th day, mainly cardiovascular abnormalities;[1,21] and from the 10th to 13th days, principally urogenital malformations.[22] However, if it is desired to study dextrocardia or transposition of the great vessels, trypan blue[8] is the agent of choice, as it provides a much higher incidence of these anomalies than maternal PGA-deficiency.

Human teratogens

Of the great number of agents or procedures recognized as teratogenic in mammals, only a few are definitely known to affect humans. Proven teratogenic agents in man are: rubella, sex hormones, aminopterin (4-amino PGA), toxoplasmosis, radiation and thalidomide (Table 1). Many other chemical substances, physical factors and microorganisms are suspect but absolute proof is lacking.

It is sometimes stated that experimentally produced congenital malformations are caused by dosages of teratogenic agents at levels much greater than ever experienced by man. In many instances this is probably true but the effects of combinations of small amounts of teratogens cannot be overlooked and work on this important aspect is now proceeding.[6] Preliminary results indicate that certain combinations of low dosages of teratogenic agents have an adjuvant effect on the production of malformations while others seem to show a protective effect. The problem, however, is complex and requires more detailed study.

Pathogenesis of malformations

The ability to produce abnormal embryos in animals by means of teratogenic agents has made it possible to obtain more accurate information on the genesis of many malformations. Thus, absence of a kidney is not always the result of primary renal agenesis but may be due to degeneration of the metanephros secondary to maldevelopment of the ureter or the Wolffian duct;[23] again, renal ectopia can result from retarded growth of the vertebral column.[22] Further, hydrocephaly may follow from retarded development of the cerebral cortex, and closure of the aqueduct result from secondary compression of the midbrain by the distended cerebral hemispheres.[24]

Any congenital abnormality must spring initially from disturbance of intracellular chemistry. Actively dividing cells are the most sensitive to teratogenic agents, although the phase when such sensitivity is maximal varies. Thus, radiation and radiomimetic substances such as chlorambucil cause fragmentation of chromosomes, the cell being most sensitive during the resting phase; colchicine, on the other hand, interferes with anaphase, so that mitosis is incomplete.

The mode of action of many teratogenic agents is uncertain although seemingly relevant facts are known is some instances. Thus, trypan blue, at one time used to treat mange in animals, is highly teratogenic and when injected into pregnant animals rapidly stains the maternal tissues; no similar coloration occurs in the embryo and it has been suggested that it may cross the placenta in a colorless form. However, when injected into pregnant rabbits, trypan blue alters the serum protein content of the maternal blood[16] and it is possible that this may lead, in turn, to abnormal placental transfer and subsequent fetal abnormality. In the case of PGA-deficiency the formation of nucleoproteins essential for growth and cell-division is probably disturbed; riboflavin deficiency, on the other hand, possibly may interfere with the oxidative processes in both the mother and the embryo.

The site of primary damage by a teratogenic agent conceivably may be either the placenta or the embryo; studies on the effect of maternal PGA-deficiency, however, have shown that embryonic death precedes placental change, and it is probable that this sequence is common to many teratogenic procedures.[15]

The teratogenic effects of antimetabolites generally can be counteracted by simultaneously supplying an adequate amount of the corresponding vitamin, yet in some instances an entirely different substance may also have an alleviating effect. Thus, in maternal vitamin A-deficiency in rats it has been observed that fetal damage can be reduced by thyroxine.[20] Also, recent studies, again in rats, have shown that thalidomide increases the sensitivity of hemoglobin to oxidation by nitrites and that this can be prevented by simultaneously giving pyridoxine and riboflavin.[19] In the future, it is possible that teratogenic side-effects of otherwise useful drugs may be prevented by prescribing with them antidotes to their undesired effects.

Testing for teratogenicity

The fact that thalidomide has produced severe malformations in man when no such effects were found in test animals has drawn attention to the difficulties of screening substances for possible teratogenicity in man. Species, and even strain, differences often result in decidedly different responses to the same agent and this undoubtedly is related to genetic make-up.

Even where a drug is non-teratogenic for the majority of humans, there is always the possibility of teratogenic effect in a few individuals on account of their genetic construction. This, however, is no different from drug sensitivity or post-vaccinal conditions which we are accustomed to anticipate in a small number of cases. New drugs, of course, must be intensively screened in a greater variety and number of test animals than before. This will help to reduce the chance of disaster in man. Also, we should not fail to check the old established drugs, the long-trusted components of the physician's armamentarium. In this regard, the demonstration of teratogenic action by salicylates[29] in rats should be kept in mind. In view of our present knowledge, avoiding all drugs in the early stages of pregnancy unless deemed absolutely necessary by the physician is obvious.

The quest for information on the causation of malformations also requires the detailed study of aborted human embryos. Too often normality or abnormality is determined by external inspection alone and, since a normal-looking embryo can have severe visceral abnormalities within, a diagnosis is of little value unless based on dissection, and possibly on histological and biochemical studies as well. Detailed examination of such material is time-consuming and requires special skills, but it must be undertaken and, wherever possible, the findings related to the maternal history. The establishment of centers to which human abortion material could be sent for special study would doubtless facilitate such an undertaking.

Lastly, while laboratory studies have an important part in the detection of teratogenic agents, an equally significant role is played by the practicing physician, for by astute observation and careful recording he can, as he has so often in the past, draw attention to actual or potential dangers and open the way to appropriate safeguards.

REFERENCES

1. BAIRD, C. D. C., NELSON, M. M., MONIE, I. W., and EVANS, H. M.: Congenital cardiovascular anomalies induced by PGA-deficiency in the rat, Circulation Res., 2:544–554, 1954.
2. BALLANTYNE, J. W.: Manual of Antenatal Pathology, Vol. II, William Wood & Co., New York, 1902.
3. BLAND-SUTTON, J.: The Story of a Surgeon, Methuen, London, 1930.
4. CHAMBERLAIN, J.: Effects of 6-Aminonicotinamide on rat embryogenesis, Ph.D. Thesis, University of California, 1962.
5. COHLAN, S. Q.: Congenital anomalies in the rat produced by excessive intake of vitamin A during pregnancy, Pediatrics, 13:556–567, 1954.
6. CHIN, E.: Combinations of teratogenic procedures in rat embryogenesis, Ph.D. Thesis, University of California, 1963.
7. EBERT, J. D.: First International Conference on Congenital Malformations, J. Chron. Dis., 13:91–132, 1961.
8. FOX, M. H., and GOSS, C. M.: Experimental production of a syndrome of congenital cardiovascular defects in rats, Anat. Rec., 124:189–207, 1956.
9. FRASER, F. C.: Causes of congenital malformations in human beings, J. Chron. Dis., 10:97–110, 1959.
10. GIROUD, A. J., and LEFEBVRES, J.: Anomalies provoquées chez le foetus en l'absence d'acide folique, Arch. franç. pediat., 8:648–656, 1951.
11. GREGG, N. M.: Congenital cataract following German measles in mother, Tr. Ophth. Soc. Australia, 3:35–46, 1942.
12. HALE, F.: Pigs born without eyeballs, J. Hered., 24: 105–106, 1933.
13. HANSON, F. B.: Effects of x-rays on the albino rat, Anat. Rec., 24:415, 1923.
14. JOB, T. T., LEIBOLD, G. J., and FITZMAURICE, H. A.: Biological effects of roentgen rays, Amer. J. Anat., 56:97–117, 1935.
15. JOHNSON, E. M., and NELSON, M. M.: Morphological changes in embryonic development resulting from transitory PGA-deficiency in early pregnancy, Anat. Rec., 133:294, 1959.
16. LANGMAN, J., and VAN DRUNEN, H.: The effect of trypan blue upon maternal protein metabolism and embryonic development, Anat. Rec., 133:513–526, 1959.
17. LENZ, W., and KNAPP, K.: Thalidomide embryopathy, Arch. Envir. Health, 5:100–105, 1962.
18. MALL, F. P.: In Keibel and Mall's Human Embryology, Vol. 1, J. B. Lippincott Co., Philadelphia, 1910.
19. METCALF, W. K.: Thalidomide, the nitrite sensitivity reaction and the vitamin B complex, Proc. Anat. Soc. Gt. Brit. and Ire., February 1963.
20. MILLEN, J. W., and WOOLLAM, D. H. M.: Thyroxine and hypervitaminosis, A. J. Anat., 93:566, 1959.
21. MONIE, I. W., NELSON, M. M., and EVANS, H. M.: Persistent right umbilical vein as a result of vitamin deficiency during gestation, Circulation Res., 2:187–190, 1957.
22. MONIE, I. W., NELSON, M. M., and EVANS, H. M.: Abnormalities of the urinary system of rat embryos resulting from transitory PGA-deficiency during gestation, Anat. Rec., 127:711–724, 1957.

23. MONIE, I. W.: Chlorambucil-induced abnormalities of the urogenital system of rat fetuses, Anat. Rec., 139:145–152, 1961.

24. MONIE, I. W., ARMSTRONG, R. M., and NELSON, M. M.: Hydrocephaly in rat young as a result of PGA-deficiency from the 8th to 10th day of gestation, Anat. Rec., 139:315, 1961.

25. NELSON, M. M., ASLING, C. W., and EVANS, H. M.: Production of multiple congenital abnormalities in young by maternal PGA-deficiency during gestation, J. Nutrition, 48:61–80, 1952.

26. NELSON, M. M., WRIGHT, H. V., ASLING, C. W., EVANS, H. M.: Multiple congenital abnormalities resulting from transitory PGA-deficiency during gestation in the rat, J. Nutrition, 56:349–370, 1955.

27. SMITH, G. E.: Fetal athyrosis. A study of the iodine requirements of the pregnant sow, J. Biol. Chem., 29:215–225, 1917.

28. WARKANY, J., and NELSON, R. C.: Appearance of skeletal abnormalities in the offspring of rats reared on a deficient diet, Science, 92:383–384, 1940.

29. WARKANY, J., and TAKACS, E.: Experimental production of congenital malformations in rats by salicylate poisoning, Am. J. Path., 35:315–331, 1959.

30. WILSON, J. G.: Experimental studies on congenital malformations, J. Chron. Dis., 10:111–130, 1959.

31. WILSON, J. G., and BARCH, S.: Fetal death and maldevelopment resulting from maternal vitamin A deficiency in the rat. Proc. Soc. Exp. Biol. & Med., 72:687–693, 1949.

Maternal Height and
the Prevalence of Stillbirths*

JACK B. BRESLER

In a series of investigations spanning many years, Baird and his co-workers in Aberdeen, Scotland, have developed the thesis that shorter women generally had poorer reproductive histories than taller women (Baird, 1949; Baird, 1952; Baird and Illsley, 1953; Baird, Hytten and Thomson, 1958). In Baird's papers there occur repeatedly a number of important and interrelated themes correlating maternal height with reproduction: (a) where ability to deliver a child through the vagina was taken as an index of poor reproductive performance, it was found that this inability was about four times greater for women under 5'1" than for women over 5'4", (b) the rate of caesarean operations was inversely related to maternal height, (c) premature labor is more common in shorter women, (d) taller women have pelvic brim areas large enough to accommodate a baby of any size, and (e) generally women with larger pelvic areas (correlated with taller maternal height) have better reproductive potentialities for mechanical reasons.

The purpose of this report is to provide data relating maternal height to still-births and abortion rates for an American population.

Methods

The population presented in this report is derived from a larger sample previously described in extensive detail (Bresler, 1961).

A few summary statements pertinent to the accumulation of the present sample are in order, however. The medical records of the Providence Lying-In Hospital, Providence, Rhode Island, were searched for family information on all

---

* This investigation was supported by a research grant RG-9426, Public Health Service.

white, Rh negative women who entered the hospital at least once from 1950 to 1958. The items collected which are of particular importance to the present study included the number of pregnancies, stillbirths, and abortions, age, height, and religion of mother, presence or absence of Anti-Rh titer reading for each trimester of each pregnancy.

Each woman or case met certain criteria before being included in this sample. In general the requirements were established in order to derive a sample of women with optimal capacities for the production of live born offspring. Women who were shown in previous studies to be poorer risks for the production of full-term live offspring were eliminated. At no time was maternal height a cause for the rejection or acceptance of a case. Accordingly, only women who were 18 to 34 years of age and who had not had more than four pregnancies at time of data collection were included. Fetal loss, from reasons still not completely under-stood, rises very rapidly with increasing age after 34 and with more than four pregnancies. Baird's papers provide information on these points. Furthermore the entire case of a woman was eliminated from study if she exhibited a positive Anti-Rh titer reading for any trimester of any pregnancy. These restrictions re-sulted in a sample of non-sensitized, white, urban women who, from the stand-point of age and parity, had excellent advantages for reproduction.

Data will be presented on the reproductive histories of these 272 women. The mean age of the women was 26.9 years and the mean number of pregnancies these women had was 2.44. In none of the classes or categories of Tables 1, 2, or 3 was there any significant divergence from the mean age or mean number of pregnancies.

Data. In Table 1, data are presented relating maternal height to the number of women who have ever had a spontaneous abortion or a stillbirth.

A 2×2 comparison was made for the number of women who had ever aborted with those who had never aborted. The other division was made for women under 5'6" compared with those 5'6" or over. The two-tailed X^2 test was used because there is not available from Baird's papers or other sources any

TABLE 1. Relation of maternal height to number of women who have ever had abortions or stillbirths.

	Height of women					
	Under 5'	5'0" to 5'2"	5'3" to 5'5"	5'6" to 5'8"	5'9" to 5'11"	Total
Number of women	9	65	131	57	10	272
Women ever abortion	1	14	25	11	1	52
Percent women ever abortion	11.1	21.5	19.8	19.3	10.0	19.1
Women ever stillbirth	1	5	6	0	0	12
Percent women ever stillbirth	11.1	7.7	4.6	0.0	0.0	4.4

TABLE 2. Religious distribution of women who have ever had a stillbirth. All women are under 5'6".

Religion of women	No.	Total	Ever stillbirth	Expected— based upon % total
		%		
Catholic	132	64.4	8	7.7
Protestant	58	28.4	3	3.4
Other	15	7.3	1	0.9
Total	205	100.0	12	12.0

TABLE 3. Height distribution for Catholic and Protestant women.

	Under 5'6"		5'6" and over		Total
	No.	%	No.	%	
Catholic	132	69.5	32	50.0	164
Protestant	58	30.5	32	50.0	90
Total	190	100.0	64	100.0	254

Test on distribution: d.f. $= 1$, $X^2 = 7.1$, $P < 0.01$. Correction made for continuity.

statement that maternal height and abortion rate are correlated. The X^2 is .03 and $.90 < P > .80$. It is reasonable to conclude that maternal height is not a factor in the abortion rate.

On the other hand Baird has established the stillbirth rate to be height dependent and it is this foreknowledge which permits the use of the one way Fisher exact probability test. The 2×2 analysis for the stillbirth rate was the same as indicated for the abortion rate. The exact probability is .03. The data on the average stillbirth rate per woman corroborate Baird's findings on average stillbirth rate per pregnancy.

Religion was the only ethnic group datum available and this distribution is indicated in Tables 2 and 3. Although the numbers in Table 2 are small, the observed frequency of women who have ever had a stillbirth is close to the expected values. In Table 3 the relationship of maternal height to religion is not on a random basis. This indicates that Protestant women are generally taller than the Catholic women.

Conclusion

Even after some very stringent limitations were made upon the sample selection, there does appear to be an inverse relationship between maternal height and the rate at which women have had a stillbirth. It is certainly understood that maternal height signifies or represents pelvic area with which it is correlated. Pelvic area data is not available for this investigation but Bernard (1952) has previously presented data correlating maternal height and pelvic brim area.

The findings of Baird's investigation and the present study have a number of ramifications. It will be necessary, for example, for demographers to take careful note of the height of a woman when obtaining stillbirth data. It will never do to compare the stillbirth rate between an hypothetical upper class of a predominantly Protestant population with a lower class of a predominantly Catholic composition without correcting for height differences. Otherwise lower stillbirth rates which will almost certainly be found in the upper class strata may be ascribed exclusively to better environmental factors when in fact this class is significantly taller and inherently predisposed for anatomical reasons to a lower stillbirth rate.

REFERENCES

BAIRD, D. 1949 Social factors in obstetrics, Lancet, *1:* 1079–1083.

———— 1952 The cause and prevention of difficult labour. Amer. J. Obstet. Gynec., *63:* 1200–1212.

BAIRD, D., and R. ILLSLEY 1953 Environment and childbearing. Proc. Roy. Soc. Med., *46:* 53–59.

BAIRD, D., F. E. HYTTEN and A. M. THOMSON 1958 Age and human reproduction. J. Obstet. Gynec. Brit. Emp., *65:* 865–876.

BERNARD, R. M. 1952 The shape and size of the female pelvis. Trans. Edinburgh Obstet. Soc., *59:* 1–16.

BRESLER, J. B. 1961 Effect of ABO-Rh interaction on infant hemoglobin. Hum. Biol., *33:* 11–24.

CYCLES

Recent studies on biological rhythms indicate that man exhibits four identifiable patterns—yearly, monthly, weekly, and daily. The first, second, and fourth patterns have their counterpart in the physical world. It seems appropriate, therefore, to relate these biological rhythms to physical rhythms. The weekly cycle has no demonstrable association with a physical rhythm. We can, therefore, only conclude that the weekly cycle has been developed by man.

Not all the paper by Du Bois is concerned with biological rhythms. The section on population fluctuations may be read in connection with Chapter 9 and the sections on geophysical factors and air conditioning in connection with Chapter 3.

Knobloch and Pasamanick, in a retrospective study, show that a significant portion of mentally defective children admitted to a state school were born in winter months. They suggest that this increase in mental defectives is related to decreased protein intake by the mother during the summer months. Consult the paper by MacMahon and Sowa (Appendix C) for a positive reaction and the paper by Lander, Forssman, and Akesson (Appendix C) for a negative reaction to the study by Knobloch and Pasamanick.

Problems in Bioclimatology

RENÉ J. DUBOS

Ideally, the bioclimatologist should have the characteristics of both the classical and the romantic type of scientist, for he must deal quantitatively with the measurable effects that the known forces of the physical environment exert on biological processes, and he must also cultivate an awareness of the fact that other undefined cosmic factors influence in obscure but profound ways the growth, behavior, and fate of all living things. I must acknowledge immediately that I have never worked in any aspect of bioclimatology, nor have I made a systematic survey of the relevant literature. But as a student of the etiology of disease, both in individuals and in complex populations, I have come to realize, like many others, that bioclimatological mechanisms often condition both the etiology and the manifestations of pathological processes. While this type of experience constitutes no justification for dogmatic statements on bioclimatological problems, it has led to more general questions regarding the effects that environmental forces exert on living things and particularly on man. These questions I shall now try to formulate.

Biological rhythms

As everyone knows, most biological phenomena exhibit rhythms which are linked to those of the physical world. There are many well documented examples of biological cycles characterized by daily, seasonal, annual, or longer periodicities, and some of them have been studied in the laboratory with exquisite precision. For example, the phototactic response of Euglena exhibits a rhythm with a 24 hour period which is independent of temperature, at least between 16°C. and 33°C. The fact that this endogenous rhythm is exhibited by a unicellular organism demonstrates that "biological clocks"* do not require the

---

* A critical review of the concept of "biological clocks" has recently been published by Brown, F. A., Jr., *Am. Scientist,* **47,** 147 (1959).

complexities of nervous organization.[1] Other phenomena like the emergence of insects into activity act as landmarks for the season of the year and may be more complex in their determinism.[2] Our colleague, Dr. Frank L. Horsfall, has told me that he shelters under his Long Island home a colony of termites which regularly emerge between March 15 and March 25 every year, independently of any climatic factor of which he is aware.

Clearly, these rhythms are the manifestations of built-in biological clocks and for this reason they appear at first sight to have no bearing on our symposium. After all, as pointed out by Dr. Konrad J. K. Buettner,[3] nearly all biological and meteorological factors have a yearly and a daily period and, therefore, any correlation between the two groups is but an expression of the fact that weather and life take place on a revolving and rotating earth. Nevertheless, the problem of cycles is one pertinent to our discussion because the biological clocks are not as immutably set as appears; instead, they rapidly change their timing in accordance with changes in the physical environment. Let me illustrate this statement with a specific example taken from a very recent publication.

TABLE 1. Time displacement of potassium urinary excretion.

| | | ⌐——Meq/3 hr. at indicated time*——⌐ | | |
Place	Date	0–3	9–12	21–24
U.S.A.	8/1	3.1	15.8	5.7
Japan	8/5	21.8	6.5	11.4
Korea	10/14	4.5	12.7	4.6

* Time is recorded as local time. (Data from E. B. Flink and R. P. Doe, 1959).

In man, the urinary excretion of 17 hydroxycorticosteroids exhibits a well-defined and fairly stable daily rhythm. Thus, measurements of these adrenal hormones made at very frequent intervals during a thirty-hour shift by air travel from Continental United States (Central Standard Time) to Japan and Korea, revealed that the urinary excretion remained synchronized with C.S.T. even after arrival in Asia.[4] Progressively, however, the timing of excretion changed and after 9 days it had become synchronized with Asian time. The rhythm of excretion of sodium and potassium exhibited a similar pattern. Likewise, other physiological phenomena have cyclical patterns which are under the influence of the environment. Thus, the diurnal temperature rhythm in man was observed to change following airplane flight from Ontario to England. In this case, it took three to four days for the Canadian temperature rhythm to fall in step with the European rhythm.[5] The problem of biological cycles certainly lends itself to experimental analysis since changes in rhythm can be produced at will in laboratory animals. For instance, it has been possible by inverting the light schedule of mice for two weeks to produce shifts in daily rhythm with regard to blood eosinophils, mitoses in pinnal epidermis of liver, hepatic nucleic acid metabolism, and blood levels of corticosterone.[6]

As is well known, the Hippocratic writings repeatedly and forcefully emphasized that the occurrence of many types of disease has a marked seasonal character. In our communities, every one is aware of the winter incidence of acute
respiratory disease and the summer incidence of poliomyelitis among human
beings. And our colleague, Dr. Richard Shope, never tires of discussing the
striking autumn incidence of hog influenza and hog cholera among the swine
herds in the Middle West. Less well known, but almost as pronounced, are the
seasonal ebbs and flows in the clinical manifestation of metabolic disorders, for
example diabetes and circulatory diseases.[7, 8]

A number of well known facts immediately come to mind to suggest mechanisms through which climatological factors could indirectly affect the incidence
or severity of disease. Crowding, physical activity, availability of certain types
of food, prevalence of parasites and their vectors, etc. etc., are all factors in the
causation of disease which are profoundly conditioned by the physical environment. But in addition to these obvious determinants there are others less well
recognized, which are probably more significant. This belief is based on the
fact that the internal environment of man—as well as of animals—is more
variable than was believed a generation ago.[9]

There is no doubt of course that the essential characteristics of the internal
environment must remain within certain limits to be compatible with the maintenance of life. On the other hand, it is also true that some of the biochemical
activities of tissues can undergo profound quantitative variations and that some
of these changes exhibit a marked seasonal pattern. A striking illustration of
these biochemical cycles was discovered by C. and G. Cori some 30 years ago.[10]
In the course of their studies on sugar metabolism, the Coris became aware of a
marked seasonal variation in the ketonuria of rats kept without food for 48 hours.
During the summer months (from May to October) the excretion of acetone

TABLE 2. Seasonal ketonuria in fasting rats.*

| | Mg of acetone bodies per diem | |
Month	per 100 gm. wt.	per rat
Apr.		32
May		67
June	6.2	51
July		36
Sept.		12
Oct.		5
Nov.		7
Dec.	1.9	5
Jan.		12
Feb.		7
March		7

* Data from G. and C. Cori, 1927 (seasonal averages) and from Burn and Ling, 1928
(monthly averages).

bodies brought about by fasting proved consistently to be three times greater than during the winter months. The fact that the excretion of acetone bodies did not rise during the winter when the rats were placed in a room at a temperature comparable to that of the summer provides evidence that factors other than heat were responsible for the greatest fasting ketosis observed during the summer.

These findings have been confirmed and extended in England by Burn and Ling,[11] who found indeed that the difference in fasting ketonuria between the spring-summer season and the fall-winter season was even much greater than that observed by the Coris. With the strain of rats used in England, the difference was of the order of ten-fold. Furthermore, the amount of glycogen in the liver of rats after 24 hours' fat diet also proved to vary according to a seasonal pattern, being much higher in the winter than in the summer.

There have been suggestions that this seasonal change has an evolutionary basis, namely that animal tissues have developed mechanisms which enable them to withstand successfully long periods of starvation in the winter. According to this view, energy requirements during the winter would be more likely to be met by combustion of the fat stores whereas this metabolic mechanism would not play as essential a role during the summer.[9, 11, 12]

While the intimate biochemical processes involved in the shift from summer to winter metabolism need not be discussed here, it is of interest to point out that the summer ketosis was associated with a reduced capacity of the tissues to oxidize glucose, and was probably due to a reduced functional activity of the pancreas. It appears, in other words, that the seasonal patterns of physiological behavior can have their basis in seasonal variations of hormonal activity. There are, of course, many other examples of cycles involving hormonal activity—for example, those associated with menstruation or those resulting in the diurnal variation in output of adrenal corticosteroids mentioned above. What must be emphasized anew at this time is that these built-in cycles are influenced by variable climatologic factors. It has long been known that the size of the thyroid and of the adrenals is normally greater in the winter than in the summer in laboratory animals, and can be altered at will by changing the environmental temperature (for a recent example, see reference 13). We have seen also that the rhythm in secretion of adrenal corticosteroids progressively varies when the geographical environment is changed. In fact, the study of these effects constitutes a rapidly expanding field of animal physiology. Suffice it to mention here as examples the studies of human performance in high mountains[14, 15] and of the nutritional aspects of climatic stress.[16] Professor Alexander von Muralt has kindly provided me for this occasion with a list of papers dealing with the pathological effects of weather on man. From these studies it appears that objective tests are available for quantitative observations as shown by the fact that warm fronts are associated with a decrease, and cold fronts with an increase, in capillary resistance.[17] It can hardly be doubted therefore that disease states—which in final analysis are always the expression of physiological disturbances—can be affected by the complex of physical forces which make up the climatological environment. Moreover, this statement applies not only to metabolic disorders, but just as well to diseases caused by microbial agents.

Population fluctuations

In addition to diurnal and seasonal rhythms which are well documented, there are other biological cycles with longer periodicities. It has long been known, of course, that plant and animal populations in the wild undergo tremendous quantitative changes.[18] For example, the records of the Hudson Bay Company provide fascinating material to document the statement that there have occurred large fluctuations in the numbers of fur animals as well as of the rodents on which they feed.[19, 20] The analysis of historical records and of the findings in recent wild life surveys have led to the belief that many population changes are determined by climatic factors, and furthermore there has been a tendency to accept that some at least of these changes exhibit a cyclic character. While the evidence for a true periodicity is not always convincing, there seems to be little doubt that population fluctuations are often the expression of responses to changes in the physical environment.

Well documented information bearing on this problem has come from the study of tree rings in the North American continent. Comparison of the thickness of tree rings has revealed that marked changes have occurred in the rate of plant growth during the past 2,000 years, probably as a result of variations in temperature and in atmospheric precipitation. There is reason to believe that these changes have also played an important part in the life of the Pueblo Indians— affecting the location of their settlements and the size of their population.[21] It is worth mentioning here that, as repeatedly emphasized by Huntington, climatic changes have probably been influential also in determining the growth and decay of other civilizations all over the world.

Fairly accurate information derived from wild life surveys in our time has provided evidence that the climate conditions both the distribution and the abundance of several animal species—as illustrated by the history of rabbit populations in Australia.[22, 23] The European rabbit *Oryctolagus cuniculus* was introduced into Tasmania at the beginning of the 19th century and spread over much of the island. Very rapidly, color variants became established and they now exist with different frequencies in different areas—the black rabbits reaching a frequency of 20 percent in places of highest rainfall. This particular example is of special interest because it illustrates that climatic factors can operate through genetic mechanisms. A related example is provided by the well-known fact that animals living in colder climates are usually larger than those of related species living in warmer climates. In most situations considered in the present report, however, mechanisms other than genetic must be invoked since the biological responses to climatic changes occur so rapidly that they can hardly be due to genetic alterations.

In certain cases, the explanation appears rather straightforward, for example with regard to plankton which changes continuously in abundance and composition from season to season and from year to year. In 1925 the warm equatorial counter-current off Columbia and Ecuador (El Nino) shifted its course so strongly to the South (as it does once every seven years) that the population of plankton, fish, and water birds normally found off the Peruvian coast fled or died, being replaced by warm water species.[24] When the current from the Atlantic predominates on the English coast, it brings water rich in phosphate which favors one species of glassworm on which the herring feeds. In contrast, current from the Channel brings in water poor in phosphate, resulting in failure of the herring fishery. The "red tide" which swept immense numbers of dead fish into the Florida beaches in 1946 and again in 1952, as it does approximately once a decade, was caused by a microscopic flagellate which is always present in the waters off the Florida coast, but in numbers too small to be harmful: its population reaches toxic levels only when atmospheric circumstances bring about the local stagnation of low-salt brackish water in certain areas.

In contrast to these fairly simple situations, the biological findings remain unexplained in most cases. Over the past three decades Errington[25] has analyzed the wild life surveys in Iowa with regard to populations of the ruffed grouse, the snowshoe hare, and especially the muskrats. The results of his analysis leave no doubt that the numbers of these animals have fluctuated enormously during the period under consideration. Yet there is no indication that heat, humidity, water levels, and other obvious variables can account for population changes, for disease states, or for patterns of behavior of the animals. While the findings are not explainable in terms of the meteorological data customarily recorded by the Weather Bureau, it is not impossible according to Errington that the biological patterns are related to the intensity of ultraviolet or other radiation—perhaps indirectly through some effect on the qualitative characteristics of the food available to the animals.

Decreases in the numbers of wild animals are commonly associated with a variety of disease states—both of metabolic and infectious character.[25, 26] It is therefore of importance to inquire into the evidence that climatological factors can actually affect resistance to disease. In fact, as already mentioned, there is a widespread belief among lay persons and physicians alike that certain types of weather disturbances are associated with particular illnesses.

In this country, Petersen and Mills[7, 8] have long emphasized that the incidence and gravity of each type of pathological disorder can be correlated with either climate or weather. As illustration it will suffice to mention here two types of weather which appear to be potentially harmful to man. One is the frontal or disturbed weather, the other the Föhn or Chinook with descending subtropical air in the whole troposphere, each type apparently bringing in its train a specific set of clinical and physiological events. Most familiar is the conviction expressed in many folklores that pains from scars and from arthritis sharpen during weather of the frontal type. Few are the persons indeed who do not believe that:

> "A coming storm our shooting corns presage,
> Our aches will throb, our hollow tooth will rage."

There are many reports, on the other hand, that periods of Föhn in Switzerland and in Southern Germany are associated with increases in death rates, in automobile accidents, and in circulatory as well as mental disorders.[3]

In these special climatic situations, the pathological disorders seem to occur without any detectable change in any of the known geophysical surface elements. The patients may not even be aware of any bad weather in the usual sense. It would appear, therefore, that these weather disturbances operate through physical factors which are still obscure or even completely unrecognized. A few related observations made with microorganisms are worth mentioning at this time. Whereas the metabolism of bacteria and yeast seems to be attenuated during cyclonic periods, it is intensified during anticyclones. By recording automatically such activities as luminescence, motility, acid production, sporulation, etc., it was found that the changes occurred so rapidly ($\frac{1}{2}$–1 hour) that they could not be correlated with the usual daily weather curves.[27]

Geophysical factors involved in bioclimatology

It would be appropriate at this point to discuss in detail the specific components of climate which are known, or have been claimed, to exert biological effects. However, this aspect of the problem will be treated cursorily because of shortness of time and even more for lack of convincing knowledge.

Temperature and humidity are of course the two climatological factors which are best understood. At their simplest their biological effects are illustrated by the close connection that exists between air temperature and the tempo of a cricket's chirp. It is said that counting the number of chirps in 14 seconds and adding 40 will give the temperature within a couple of degrees. Likewise, the higher the temperature, the faster ants move. As example of more complex effects of temperature, one could quote the discovery by Dr. André Lwoff (reported by Dr. Albert Sabin) that a difference of 2°C. can bring about the selection of virulent or avirulent mutants of polioviruses.[28] On the other hand, temperature and humidity have also less direct consequences by reason of the physiological responses that they elicit in living things. In the case of man, his semitropical origin is reflected in the narrow range of atmospheric environment to which he is adapted in his native biological state. Any departure from this environment is likely to cause physiological disturbances. A temperature of 29.4°C. (85°F.), with moderate humidity and low air movement, seems best for human comfort in the absence of housing and clothing. In practice, these artificial acids supplement several physiological mechanisms which permit a fairly wide range of adaptive heat control. Thus, enormous changes in blood flow through the skin capillaries can occur within a few minutes and regulate heat loss upward or downward as needed. When increased blood flow proves inadequate for rapid cooling, the sweating mechanism comes into play and provides heat loss by evaporation. While the needs for temperature control are more prolonged, for example in cases of passage from one season or one country to another, the body can regulate its own heat production through changes in metabolic rates. Needless to say, these regulatory mechanisms are effective only within a limited range and, furthermore, any excessive demand on them will cause profound physiological disturbances. In fact, as already mentioned, there is an enormous amount of clinical evidence that weather changes are commonly associated with exacerbation of many disease states. As Hippocrates said 2,000 years ago, "It is changes that are chiefly responsible for diseases, especially the greatest changes, the violent alterations both in the seasons and in other things. But seasons which come on gradually are the safest, as are gradual changes of regimen and temperature."

Contrary to common belief, it has not yet been shown that pressure changes *per se* can affect either the comfort or the health of man—except of course in the special cases of life at great depths or high altitudes. It may be worth mentioning at this time, however, that very slight reductions in pressure have been shown to exert profound effects on insect behavior, effects which appear to be independent of oxygen tension. In the laboratory, as well as in the field, the feeding habits, rate of development, and locomotor activity of higher insects are appreciably increased by slightly lowered or falling pressures. These conditions also seem to be associated with the sudden occurrence of mass emergencies.[29]

Needless to say, there is no general statement that can serve to describe the multifarious biological effects of the various types of radiation. Their deleterious effects go from reversible lesions in the skin to the production of lethal hereditary defects. Their beneficial effects range all the way from the synthesis of vitamin D to the orientation provided by polarized light for the motion of insects. The use of artificial light to prolong and increase egg production denotes profound influences on the endocrine system, and this becomes manifest also in bird migrations and in many other complex biological processes.

Recently, experiments with cosmic rays and their secondaries have pointed to the existence of even more profound hormonal effects of radiation. Whereas no clear evidence has been obtained that ordinary cosmic rays have any biological activity, cosmic ray shower electrons (produced by cosmic ray particles that penetrate into heavy matter) were found to increase mutation rates in a fungus, to interfere with normal reproduction in rabbits, and to accelerate the rate of development of cancers in mice pretreated with 20-methylcholantrene.[30]

Among other climatological factors which have been recognized recently are the small ionized molecules of the air and the so-called "sferics" which stem from natural electric discharges. It has been claimed that positive space charges have deleterious effects whereas negative space charges have beneficial effects—as illustrated, for example, by enhancement of proliferation of tissue cells exposed *in vitro* to negative ions.[31] Even human patients have apparently benefitted from such treatment.[3] If these claims can be validated, they point to a neglected aspect of biophysics, namely the space charges of small ions.

Air pollution is a bioclimatological factor of increasing importance in the causation of disease. Air pollutants range in kind from pollens and other allergens to toxic gases and aerosols produced by industrial plants, automobile exhausts, and domestic fires. Free HCl and H_2SO_4, sulfur dioxide, nitrogen dioxide, ozone, hydrocarbons, and pulverized rubber from automobile tires are but a few of the air pollutants known to exert toxic effects on human, animal, plant, and microbial life.[32, 33] The disappearance of lichens from modern cities, and the tremendous toll exacted by chronic bronchitis in certain industrial areas, serve to illustrate the varied aspects and the magnitude of the problem. Ozone deserves to be singled out in this discussion because it is present in large concentration in the smogs over Los Angeles, Phoenix, and Tucson, as well as in the atmosphere reached by high altitude flying. Even short exposure to the concentrations of ozone encountered in these circumstances produces pulmonary oedema and increases the susceptibility of experimental animals to bacterial infections.[34–36] It is worth mentioning in this respect that in Switzerland the Föhn seems to bring down large amounts of ozone from the upper atmosphere, a peculiarity which has been claimed to account for some of the untoward physiological effects of this type of air current.[3]

Air conditioning

It is theoretically possible to control almost any factor of the indoor environment—temperature, humidity, pressure, radiation, space charge, size and composition of aerosol particles, etc. And it is obvious that air conditioning has already greatly contributed to general comfort, relief of allergic symptoms, and increase in working efficiency. At first sight, therefore, it would appear that control of the indoor environment is always desirable and that the only practical problems that it presents are those to be dealt with by architects and engineers. In reality, however, air conditioning has biological implications that transcend comfort and working efficiency, and that are still obscure.

While it is easy to appreciate the immediate direct effects of air conditioning, such as the sense of well-being and renewed vigor, it is difficult to predict its distant and indirect effects. Little is known, for example, concerning the responses of the mucous membranes and of the vascular bed to sudden and repeated shifts from the hot humid atmosphere of the street to the cool and dry environment indoors. Comfort of the moment may have to be paid for in the future in the form of new respiratory and circulatory disorders.

More studies are also needed with regard to the effect of air conditioning on the ability of the body to adapt to unpleasant and even dangerous environmental factors. To illustrate the range of these adaptive processes, it will suffice to mention again the physiological mechanisms used by the body to regulate its temperature, and to refer to the new finding that progressive exposure to low concentrations of ozone increases resistance to the toxic effects of this gas.[37]

Even more important perhaps is the fact that air conditioning may interfere with some of the diurnal and seasonal cycles discussed earlier in this report. One need only recall here the variations in endocrine activities that are brought about by changes in temperature or in exposure to light. Of interest also are the claims that an increased rate of growth appears to result from the removal of certain metabolic stresses.[38] No information is available concerning the effect of air conditioning on processes which are so obviously correlated with seasonal metabolic changes. Yet these problems will certainly become of increasing urgency as man achieves greater control over his physical environment and removes himself from the physicochemical conditions under which he has evolved as a physiological machine.

Conclusions

I have tried to illustrate in this essay some of the effects of climatological factors on different types of biological phenomena: on the regular endogenous rhythms which exhibit diurnal or seasonal periodicities; on the long range fluctuations in size and behavior of populations; on the immediate physiological disturbances which are caused by the vagaries of the weather. I have also tried to emphasize that the biological responses to the environment cannot be described merely in terms of immediate direct effects, but must be regarded as dynamic processes, conditioned by the adaptive powers of the organisms, and often resulting in long range cumulative alterations. More than anyone, I realize the superficiality of my knowledge in these fields. Nevertheless, I cannot help expressing my belief that living things, including man, respond not only to heat, humidity, light and other obvious climatic components which are readily perceived by the senses, but also to many other environmental factors not readily identified, and in part still unknown. Awareness of these complexities may not be helpful in solving practical problems. But it teaches humility to the overconfident biologist. In this spirit I had intended to close this essay with Hamlet's words:

> "There are more things in heaven and earth, Horatio,
> Than are dreamt of in your philosophy."

But the wise remarks of one of my critical colleagues now seem more apropos. In his words: "A lack of correlation with known environmental factors does not prove that unknown factors are operating. Primitive man explains natural phenomena with magic; when we are confronted with the inexplicable we too often fall back on mysticism, in somewhat more sophisticated language. This is a matter of personal taste, and on this point I must confess to being rather more with Horatio than Hamlet. Horatio no doubt was limited in his philosophy, but Hamlet believed in ghosts."

REFERENCES

1. BRUCE, V. G., and C. S. PITTENDRIGH, *Proc. N.A.S.,* **42,** 676 (1956).
2. BROWN, F. A., JR., "Discussion on Biological Rhythms," at Federation of American Societies for Experimental Biology (1959).
3*a*. BUETTNER, K. J. K., "Physical Aspects of Human Bioclimatology," in *Compendium of Meteorology,* ed. T. F. Malone (Boston: American Meteorological Society, 1951), p. 1112.
3*b*. ⸺, *Fed. Proc.,* **16,** 631 (1957).
4. FLINK, E. B., and R. P. DOE, *Proc. Soc. Exp. Biol. and Med.,* **100,** 498 (1959).
5. BURTON, A. C., *Canad. M. A. J.,* **75,** 715 (1956).
6. HALBERG, F., C. P. BARNUM, R. H. SILBER, and J. J. BITTNER, *Proc. Soc. Exp. Biol. and Med.,* **97,** 897 (1958).
7*a*. MILLS, C. A., *Medical Climatology* (Springfield, Ill.: Charles C Thomas, 1939).
7*b*. ⸺, "Climate in Health and Disease," in *The Oxford Medicine,* ed. H. A. Christian (New York: Oxford University Press, 1949), **1,** p. 453.
8. PETERSEN, W. F., *The Patient and the Weather* (Ann Arbor: Edwards Bros., 1937).
9. SARGENT, F., II, *Meteorological Monographs,* **2,** 68 (1954); SARGENT, F., II, *Arch. Met. Geoph. Biokl.,* Serie B: Allgemeine und Biologische Klimatologie, Band II, p. 289.
10. CORI, G. T., and C. F. CORI, *J. Biol. Chem.,* **72,** 615 (1927).
11. BURN, J. H., and H. W. LING, *J. Physiol.,* **65,** 191 (1928).
12. HUGHES, E., *Seasonal Variation in Man* (London: H. K Lewis and Co., Ltd., 1931).
13. MAQUSOOD, M., *Nature,* **167,** 323 (1951).
14. MONGE, M. C., *Meteorological Monographs,* **2,** 50 (1954).
15. VON MURALT, A., *Experimentia Supplementum,* **6,** 86 pp. (1957).
16. MITCHELL, H. H., and M. EDMAN, *Nutrition and Climatic Stress* (Springfield, Ill.: Charles C Thomas, 1951).
17. REGLI, J., and R. STÄMPFLI, *Helv. Physiol. Acta,* **5,** 40 (1947).
18. COLE, L. C., *Cold Spring Harbor Symp. Quant. Biol.,* **22,** 1 (1957).
19. ELTON, C., *Voles, Mice, and Lemmings, Problems in Population Dynamics* (Oxford: Oxford University Press, 1942).
20. PITELKA, F. A., *Cold Spring Harbor Symp. Quant. Biol.,* **22,** 237 (1957).
21. HUNTINGTON, E., *Civilization and Climate,* 3rd edition, (New Haven: Yale University Press, 1924).
22. BIRCH, L. C., *Cold Spring Harbor Symp. Quant. Biol.,* **22,** 203 (1957).
23. BARBER, H. N., *Nature,* **173,** 1227 (1954).
24. WELTY, C., *Sci. American,* **197,** 118 (1957).
25. ERRINGTON, P. L., *Cold Spring Harbor Symp. Quant. Biol.,* **22,** 287 (1957).
26. CHRISTIAN, J. J., *J. Mammal.,* **31,** 247 (1950).
27. BORTELS, H., *Zbl. Bakteriol., II,* **105,** 305 (1942); BORTELS, H., *Zbl. Bakteriol.,* **155,** 160 (1950); BORTELS, H., *Die Naturwissenschaften,* **38,** 165 (1951); BORTELS, H., *I. J. B. B.,* **3,** Part I, Section F (1959).
28. SABIN, A. B., and A. LWOFF, "The Relation between Reproductive Capacity of Polioviruses at Different Temperatures in Tissue Culture and Neurovirulence,"

presented at 96th Annual Meeting of National Academy of Sciences, Washington, D.C., April 1959.

29. WELLINGTON, W. C., *Canad. J. Res.*, **24,** Sect. D, 51 (1946).
30. DUELL, G., and B. DUELL, *Meteorological Monographs,* **2,** 61 (1954).
31. WORDEN, J. L., and J. R. THOMPSON, *Anat. Rec.,* **124,** 500 (1956).
32. HAAGEN-SMIT, A. J., *Science,* **128,** 869 (1958).
33. *Proceedings of National Conference on Air Pollution,* Public Health Service, Washington, D.C., November 18–20, 1958.
34. STOKINGER, H. E., in *Proceedings of the Air Pollution Research Planning Seminar,* Public Health Service, Cincinnati, December, 1956.
35. HEIMANN, H., L. O. EMIK, R. A. PRINDLE, and W. M. FISHER, *Progress in Air Pollution Medical Research,* Public Health Service (1958).
36. MILLER, S., and R. EHRLICH, *J. Inf. Dis.,* **103,** 145 (1958).
37. MENDENHALL, R. N., presented at Ohio Valley Section Society for Experimental Biology and Medicine, Columbus, Ohio, October 31, 1958.
38. HERRINGTON, L. P., *Meteorological Monographs,* **2,** 30 (1954).

Seasonal Variation
in the Births
of the Mentally Deficient

HILDA KNOBLOCH,
AND BENJAMIN PASAMANICK

It is well known that the time at which injury to the developing fetus occurs results in a differential effect on the production of congenital anomalies. The embryonic stage, rather than the specific nature of the prenatal stress, appears to determine the type of malformation that will appear. Defects will manifest themselves in those organ systems that are undergoing the greatest amount of differentiation or organization at the time of the injury.[1] In the central nervous system[2] damage which occurs prior to the eighth week of fetal life usually results in gross anomalies, many of which are incompatible with life. During the eighth to twelfth week the cerebral cortex is undergoing its organization into the various molecular layers, and this period would be the critical time during which maternal stress would be apt to lead to those neuropsychiatric disabilities which result from cortical disorganization.

Infectious diseases play prominent roles in the production of central nervous system damage. Congenital lues in the past was one of the major conditions which acted during fetal life to produce remote as well as immediate damage to the brain. In the more recent past reports have appeared about the effect of rubella in the first trimester of pregnancy in the production of several central nervous system defects. Viral infections operate in the postnatal period to damage the brain and their effects are easily observed. The influence of similar infections in the mother during pregnancy is not as easily subjected to investigation, but it may be equally if not more important.

As a starting point, one of a series of neuropsychiatric disabilities—mental deficiency—was selected and a study designed to test the hypothesis that, because of the variation in the prevalence of viral infection, differences in the incidence of mental deficiency would occur which would be dependent on the season of birth. Infants conceived in the winter months it was postulated would have an increased incidence of mental deficiency when compared to infants conceived in the summer months, because of the increase in the prevalence of these infections during the colder seasons.

Materials and method of study

The birth dates of all individuals who had ever been admitted to the Columbus State School were supplied by the Statistical Bureau of the Division of Mental Hygiene; patients who were born between 1860 and 1949 were included. The number of admissions in the years before the turn of the century and even well into the twentieth century was obviously small, either because of the incompleteness of the records or because of the limited facilities available. Likewise, because of the policy of the school of not admitting children under the age of six years, less than a dozen were born after 1948 at the time that the list was compiled. Since a minimum of 100 individuals per year was admitted from 1913 through 1948, the analysis was made on patients born in those years.

The number of births in each month was supplied by the Ohio State Health Department. These data were available for all of the years during which adequate numbers of admissions occurred with the exception of 1946, and this year was consequently eliminated from consideration. A rate which can be considered a "first admission rate" was then calculated according to the month of birth for those years already delineated above. This rate would express the seasonal variation in births of the mentally deficient. It is obviously not a precise expression of the differential incidence of mental deficiency, but is sufficiently analogous to permit substitution of the single word "incidence" for the more cumbersome phraseology.

It was recognized that, at the very most, only 10 percent of all of the mental defectives born in the state were admitted to the Columbus State School. Admissions are allocated to the 88 counties of the state strictly on the basis of county population, some counties having 24 admissions per year and some many times that number. Since the children are six years of age by the time that they are admitted, month of birth is not likely to be a factor taken into consideration in any decision to admit a child. It was also recognized that neither could account be taken of the precise amount of in- and out-migration; we do not believe that a decision to move is influenced by the month in which a child is born, however. There is no reason to believe, therefore, that bias would be introduced by either of these factors because of season of birth.

Findings and discussion

There is variation in the "first admission rate" for mental deficiency and the rate per 1,000 live births by month of birth is shown in Table 1. Contrary to what was predicted by the hypothesis, however, the greatest incidence occurs not in the late summer and early fall months but rather in the winter months,

TABLE 1. Mental deficiency first admission rates by month of birth, Columbus State School, 1913–1948 (excluding 1946).

Months	No. of Births	No. of Admissions	Rate/1,000
January	358,848	503	1.402
February	339,704	512	1.507
March	365,631	520	1.422
April	342,624	475	1.386
May	350,131	485	1.385
June	349,894	472	1.349
July	373,853	494	1.321
August	377,085	489	1.297
September	361,995	484	1.337
October	354,558	463	1.306
November	334,113	473	1.416
December	342,881	485	1.414
Total	4,251,317	5,855	1.377

the peak being found in February. This highest rate of 1.507 per 1,000 births for February is significantly higher than the rate of 1.297 for its seasonal counterpart for August (C.R. $= 2.36$; $P < 0.02$). Likewise, the rate of 1.442 for the first three months of the year is significantly higher than the rate of 1.318 for the contrasting months of July, August, and September (C.R. $= 2.43$; $P < 0.02$). These data are shown in Table 2. For the infants born in February the critical eighth to twelfth week of the gestation period would be the month of July.

Several possible explanations for this finding immediately come to mind. Since there is a higher admission rate to the Columbus State School from the lower socioeconomic groups and also a higher incidence of mental deficiency in

TABLE 2. "First admission rates" for mental deficiency by season of birth, Columbus State School, 1913–1948 (excluding 1946).

Season	No. of Births	No. of Admissions	Rate/1,000	
February	339,704	512	1.507	
				C.R. $= 2.3$
				$P < 0.02$
August	377,085	489	1.297	
January, February, and March	1,064,183	1535	1.442	
				C.R. $= 2.4$
				$P < 0.02$
July, August, and September	1,112,933	1467	1.318	

these groups, any differential between upper and lower socioeconomic groups in the planning of pregnancies would be reflected in the number of patients born in each of the different seasons. The assumption would be, then, that the upper economic groups planned their pregnancies so that their babies were delivered in July and August. This explanation has already been suggested by Goodenough[3] as the explanation for her observation of a slight superiority in IQ's of school children born in the summer months. It would not seem logical to plan to have children in the two hottest months of the year, but fortunately data are available and it is possible to examine the facts without having to inquire into motives.

There is a significant difference in the number of births by month. Analysis of some four million births in Ohio in the period from 1910 to 1955 indicates that the highest birth rates occur in July, August, and September. There is, curiously enough, another peak in February. Data on over 160,000 births in New York City in 1956 show a similar pattern. Data on approximately 23,000 births in Baltimore were used in comparing the upper and lower socioeconomic groups. Census tract of residence was the criterion for placing a birth into a given economic 10th of the population. The peak number of births for the smaller series tends to be in September, October, and November. There are, however, no significant differences according to socioeconomic status; if anything, there appears to be a somewhat higher birth rate for the upper socioeconomic groups for the winter period when compared to the lower socioeconomic groups. Differential planning of birth appears, therefore, to be an inadequate explanation for the seasonal variations in the births of the mentally deficient.

Mills has written extensively on the effects of climate on health and disease in man and animals. He indicates,[4] for instance, that in the rat thiamin requirement doubles as the temperature changes from 65°F. to 90°F. Members of the vitamin B complex act as catalysts at specific stages in glucose combustion and there has been much speculation about the effects of the alteration in the metabolism of glucose on the functioning of the central nervous system. In rats there are also many differences in learning and retention when litter mates kept on uniform diets for three months are reared in temperatures of 55°F., 75°F., and 90°F.[5] This effect apparently carries over to human beings as well. As only one example, students taking college entrance examinations during the summer achieve only about 60 percent of the ratings obtained on the same examination given in the winter.

More important than performance under diverse environmental conditions, perhaps, is the relation of the month of conception to certain later functions. Mills reports that children in the Cincinnati latitudes who are conceived in the summer months have just half the chance of entering college as those conceived in the winter months. There is a low likelihood of being included in "Who's Who" if there is a summer conception and only four out of the 33 presidents were conceived in the third quarter of the year. Peterson[6] has shown findings similar to those of our own, namely that feeble-minded children are more frequently conceived in the summer months. Mills[7] tends to attribute all of these findings to the beneficial effects of atmospheric instability and environmental stimulation, and the consequent greater metabolic potential of the germ cells.

Mills[5] also mentions that it has been shown, in animals at least, that it is possible to control the depressing effects of heat by adequate diet, particularly in respect to the vitamins and protein, and he points out that it is probably necessary to have proportionately more protein to meet the minimum requirements during the summer months when the total caloric intake is reduced.

In a study of a group of New Haven Negro infants born during the years of World War II[8] we demonstrated that white physical and behavioral developmental norms were followed. The only intragroup correlation was the significant superiority of those infants who were above weight at birth, as well as at the time of examination, over the infants who were below the median in weight at both times. It was felt that these findings could be explained on the basis of adequate prenatal care and adequate nutrition during pregnancy consequent to increased employment and wartime rationing.

On the basis of these findings it was postulated that the relationship between temperature and intellectual performance might, perhaps, be greatly influenced by the fact that the diet of the mothers may be poor in the hotter months of the year, and that this lowered dietary intake exerts its greatest effect during the eighth to twelfth week of gestation. If this were true, then it should be possible to demonstrate a difference in the incidence of mental deficiency on the basis of variations in temperature from one year to another.

Accordingly, the monthly mean temperatures for the six largest Ohio cities for which data were available were averaged. The temperatures during June, July, and August were those considered, since these were the months in which the eighth to twelfth week of gestation corresponded to those months of the year with the highest incidence of mental deficiency. The years in which the mean temperature was above the median were then contrasted with those years in which the temperature was below the median. These data were also based on the years from 1913 to 1948.

The differences in the "first admission rates" for mental deficiency, according to whether the mean temperature for the month was above or below the median, are shown in Table 3. When the eighth to twelfth week of pregnancy occurred in June, there are no significant differences in the incidence of mental deficiency between those years with temperatures below and above the median. For July and August the differences are highly significant. The rates in those years where the average temperature was above the median were 1.658 per 1,000 births for July and 1.519 for August, compared to rates of 1.276 and 1.206, respectively, in those years when the average temperature was below the median. Likewise, the differences for the total three-month period of June, July, and August were highly significant, being 1.524 for those years where the weather

TABLE 3. "First admission rates" for mental deficiency by month of birth according to mean temperature during the 8th to 12th week of pregnancy, Columbus State School, 1913–1948 (excluding 1946).

		8th to 12th Week of Pregnancy			
		June	July	August	Total
Mean Temperature		70.19	74.30	72.73	. . . .
Temperature Below Median	No. of Births	170,788	175,522	186,494	532,804
	Admission Rate/1,000 Births	1.411	1.276	1.206	1.295
Temperature Above Median	No. of Births	181,126	171,293	187,598	540,017
	Admission Rate/1,000 Births	1.402	1.658	1.519	1.524

$X^2 = 10.02$
$P < 0.001$

was hot compared to 1.295 for the cooler years ($X^2 = 10.02$; $P < 0.001$). These differences between the warmer and cooler summers are greater than the differences observed between babies born in the first three months of the year and those born in the third quarter. The difference for the month of July on the basis of mean temperature is actually three times as great as the difference between the first and third quarters of all of the years under investigation. These highly significant differences would tend to support the hypothesis that inadequate dietary intake in early pregnancy during the hot summer months has an adverse effect on the development of the child. The number of cases was too small to permit analysis of variations from one season to another from year to year. Before combining all of the years together, however, variation in rates from one year to the next was examined. It was immediately obvious that in the depression years the rates were very much higher than in the nondepression years in both the post-World War I depression and the depression of the 1930's. However, the temperature differences for the so-called "boom years" and for the "depression years" were the same as for the total. Within each group the hotter summers were followed by a higher incidence of mental deficiency in the winter months, regardless of whether the over-all rate for the block of years was high, as in the depression years, or low, as in the boom group.

These findings appear to form one more link in the chain of events demonstrated by our previous studies of the association of prenatal and paranatal factors with the development of neuropsychiatric disabilities and the hypothesis of a continuum of reproductive casualty. These previous studies indicated that the complications of pre- and paranatal periods, particularly the chronic anoxia producing ones, such as toxemia and bleeding, and prematurity, were associated with an increased incidence of a series of clinical conditions ranging from cerebral palsy[9] through epilepsy,[10] mental deficiency,[11] behavior disturbances,[12] reading disturbances,[13] and tics.[14] A higher incidence of these complications of pregnancy was demonstrated in the lower socioeconomic groups[15,16] where dietary factors might be of considerable importance. Some authors[17] have demonstrated that toxemia of pregnancy can be prevented by supplying a diet adequate in protein and vitamins to the mother during gestation and at this time probably the most widely accepted theory of the cause of the toxemias of pregnancy is inadequate protein intake. There may, of course, also be a direct effect of protein deprivation on the production of mental deficiency per se without the necessity of the intermediary influence of toxemia. There have been many reports on a number of differences in infants whose mothers' diets have varied during pregnancy.

Under these theoretical assumptions one would expect to find differences similar to those in mental deficiency in the incidence of complications of pregnancy, and obstetricians are aware of a seasonal variation in toxemia. The New York City Health Department supplied data on the proportion of live birth certificates reporting one or more pathological conditions during pregnancy in 1956. Findings to be reported elsewhere indicate that all of the complications of pregnancy predicted by the hypothesis are significantly higher in the winter months.

These findings do not invalidate the infection hypothesis or preclude other explanations for the differences found. Infectious diseases probably play an important role prenatally. Since it is more likely that they act to a larger extent in the winter months rather than in the summer, these findings are only strengthened. As a matter of fact, the incidence of summer encephalitis was examined in an attempt to correlate it with the rates of admissions for mental deficiency and it was found that the rates were lower in the years when encephalitis was high in the summer months, although not significantly so. Another factor that immediately comes to mind as being associated with hot summer weather is salt depletion and this may very well play a role, the exact nature of which is not immediately clear at the present time.

There are, undoubtedly, complex interactions of many environmental influences which alter susceptibilities and change the manifestations of central nervous system damage. We are engaged in further investigations which may elucidate the etiologic factors and open up greater possibilities for prevention. A host of additional epidemiologic studies immediately comes to mind—an investigation of all the neuropsychiatric disabilities and complications of pregnancy by seasonal and temperature variation; the effect of geographic location on the production of differences in incidence; the influence of hyperemesis gravidarum on the development of the child. Intensification of dietary and behavioral experimentation with laboratory animals, where the experimenter can vary conditions at will, also appears indicated.

These findings also add to the mounting body of evidence, based on studies done by others as well as ourselves, that the characteristics of a human being are far from being immutably determined by the genes at the moment of conception. Environmental factors act continuously on the fetus from this moment, if they have not already significantly affected the parents also, to determine the anatomical structure as well as behavioral functioning. Except for a comparatively few and rare hereditary disorders, life experiences, rather than inherited characteristics, may be the primary factors making one individual significantly different from the next.

It does not appear necessary, however, to wait until the last iota of evidence is in, proving the association of diet and disability. Present knowledge, exclusive of the results of this study, would appear sufficient to demand that public health workers turn their attention more directly to this problem. We are well beyond the stage of paying lip service to the importance of the chronic diseases; possible avenues for prevention should be seized upon—and action taken. In a field as complex as behavioral functioning, prevention of dysfunction is often the only method of demonstrating etiology.

The possibility of dietary control in the prevention of disability need not be confined to efforts in this country, even though we recognize the tremendous cost of the neuropsychiatric disabilities in terms of chronicity, loss of productivity, family dislocation, and the need for provision of care.

There may be much more to gain in the developing countries which are, by and large, the tropical ones. The inability to improve productivity to support their increase in population, which is largely a result of public health measures in controlling acute infectious diseases, may well hinge on the long-term effects of diets which we know to be suboptimal. It seems likely that this damaging influence is acting not only on the present generation, but also on future individuals yet unborn to produce a whole series of neuropsychiatric disabilities. Breaking the vicious cycle by a concerted attack at one point, namely, women in the child-bearing period, could be extremely rewarding.

Summary

In studying the admissions of mentally defective children, born in the years 1913–1948, to the Columbus State School, it was found that significantly more had been born in the winter months, January, February, and March. Since the third month after conception is known to be the period during pregnancy when the cerebral cortex of the unborn child is becoming organized, any damage which occurred at that time could affect intellectual functioning. The months when this might happen would be June, July, and August, the hot summer months, when pregnant women might decrease their food intake, particularly protein, to dangerously low levels and consequently damage their developing babies. If this were so, one would expect that hotter summers would result in significantly more mental defectives born than following cooler summers. This was exactly what was found to a highly significant degree. Possible explanations of the above findings were sought in the occurrence of summer encephalitis and an increased birth rate in the lower socioeconomic group, but these were not confirmed.

These findings have wide public health implications, since the writers have shown previously not only that physical growth is affected by what happens to the unborn child but also that cerebral palsy, epilepsy, and even behavior and reading disorders may follow damage during this period. There is a growing body of evidence which indicates that it is very important for women in the child-bearing age to have good diets if they are to produce healthy, normally developing children. Inadequate dietary intake during pregnancy, because of heat as well as substandard economic conditions, may be an important link in the vicious cycle that results in poor physical and mental growth.

REFERENCES

1. INGALLS, THEODORE H. The Epidemiology of Congenital Malformations. In Mechanisms of Congenital Malformation. Proc. Second Conference of the Association for the Aid of Crippled Children. New York, N.Y.: Watkins 1954, pp. 10–20.
2. OSTERTAG, B. Die Einzelformen der Verbildung. In Handbuch der Speziellen Pathologischen Anatomie und Histologie. Berlin, Germany: Springer-Verlag, 1956, Vol. 13, Part IV, pp. 362–601.
3. GOODENOUGH, FLORENCE. Intelligence and Month of Birth. Psychological Bull. 37: 442, 1940.
4. MILLS, CLARENCE A. Influence of Environmental Temperature on Warm-Blooded Animals. Ann. New York Acad. Sc. XLVI: 97–105, 1945.
5. ―――. Temperature Dominance Over Human Life. Science 110, 267–271, 1949.
6. PETERSEN, WILLIAM F. The Patient and the Weather. Vol. III. Mental and Nervous Diseases. Ann Arbor, Mich.: Edwards Bros., 1934.
7. MILLS, CLARENCE A. Mental and Physical Development as Influenced by Season of Conception. Human Biol. 13, 3: 378–389, 1941.
8. PASAMANICK, BENJAMIN. A Comparative Study of the Behavioral Development of Negro Infants. J. Gen. Psychol. 59: 3–44, 1946.
9. LILIENFELD, ABRAHAM M., and PASAMANICK, BENJAMIN. The Association of Prenatal and Paranatal Factors with the Development of Cerebral Palsy and Epilepsy. Am. J. Obst. & Gynec. 70: 93–101, 1955.
10. LILIENFELD, ABRAHAM M., and PASAMANICK, BENJAMIN. Association of Maternal and Fetal Factors with the Development of Epilepsy. Abnormalities in the Prenatal and Paranatal Periods. J.A.M.A. 155: 719–724, 1954.
11. PASAMANICK, BENJAMIN, and LILIENFELD, ABRAHAM M. Association of Maternal and Fetal Factors with the Development of Mental Deficiency. I. Abnormalities in the Prenatal and Paranatal Periods. Ibid. 159: 155–160, 1955.
12. PASAMANICK, BENJAMIN; ROGERS, MARTHA E.; and LILIENFELD, ABRAHAM M. Pregnancy Experience and the Development of Childhood Behavior Disorder. Am. J. Psychiat. 112: 613–618, 1956.

13. KAWI, ALI A., and PASAMANICK, BENJAMIN. The Association of Factors of Pregnancy with the Development of Reading Disorders in Childhood. J.A.M.A. (In press.)
14. PASAMANICK, BENJAMIN, and KAWI, ALI A. A Study of the Association of Prenatal and Paranatal Factors with the Development of Tics in Children: A Preliminary Investigation. J. Pediat. **48:** 596–601, 1956.
15. RIDER, ROWLAND V.; TABACK, MATTHEW; and KNOBLOCH, HILDA. Association Between Premature Birth and Socioeconomic Status. A.J.P.H. **45:** 1022–1028, 1955.
16. PASAMANICK, BENJAMIN; KNOBLOCH, HILDA; and LILIENFELD, ABRAHAⅠ M. Socioeconomic Status and Some Precursors of Neuropsychiatric Disorders. Am. J. Orthopsychiat. **26:** 594–601, 1956.
17. TOMPKINS, W. T., and WIEHL, D. G. Nutritional Deficiencies as Causal Factor in Toxemia and Premature Labor. Am. J. Obst. & Gynec. **62:** 898–919 (Oct.), 1951.

ECOLOGY AND GENETICS

The genetic potentialities of the human organism may be modified consider-
ably by the environment. The series of letters to the Editor of Science *represents*
an excellent summary of views on hairlessness in man involving the interactions
between ecology and genetics.

Glass, in an article entitled, "The Ethical Basis of Science" (Science,
Vol. 150, p. 1254), wrote:

> "Man's own values grew out of his evolutionary origins and his struggle against a
> hostile environment for survival. His loss of certain unnecessary structures, such
> as bodily hair once clothing was invented . . ."

This statement was a signal for an exchange in letters on hairlessness, its
evolution, and a discussion of lamarckian overtones. It is important, therefore,
to consider a few comments about Jean Baptiste de Lamarck, a Frenchman
living from 1744 to 1828. In the year that Charles Darwin was born, Lamarck
published his most famous book, Philosophie Zoologique (*Zoological Philoso-*
phy). *This book by Lamarck is generally regarded as the first attempt to organize*
many factors which suggested an evolutionary trend. It was audacious at the time
for him to suggest that higher forms of life came from lower forms. He conceived
that evolution was brought about by wants or strivings on the part of the living
organism itself. Central to this whole idea was the understanding that any
part of the body could change, develop, disappear, or even become useless. The
change, believed Lamarck, was caused by use or disuse of that part of the body
as required by the way the animal had to adjust to its particular way of life.

167

The term "acquired habits" has been given to the changes which were made in living things. Lamarck generally believed that acquired habits were inherited by the offspring. For a long time, it was assumed that these views and the more generally accepted Darwinian hypothesis of evolution were strongly opposed to one another. Recent evaluations have tended to minimize some of the differences existing between the views of Lamarck and Darwin. Twenty years ago, the term "lamarckianism" could be used to discredit many arguments in biology. This is not so much the case today.

The comments by Glass on hairlessness along with other matters in the original paper, cited above, were discussed in three letters to the editor in the issue of February 25. The excerpts which follow pertain only to the question of hairlessness and not to the other points brought up by Glass. Accordingly, there is reproduced a short paragraph by Baker, a number of paragraphs by Fentress, but no material by Kraft who discussed matters other than hairlessness. These three letters were, in turn, answered by Glass in the issue of April 15th. Once again in this anthology, his excerpts are limited to the problem of hairlessness in man and the genetic and ecological roles involved.

This letter by Glass was further discussed by five other individuals in the issue of July 22. In these letters, a number of alternative theories on hairlessness and how it came to be are presented. Brace suggests an interaction between external temperature and tropical hunting behavior, Hershkovitz discusses sexual selection, Hailman has a preference for a metabolic energy theory, Kennington presents a thesis involving nutrition, and Olson offers a mechanism involving ticks and body lice. All these excellent arguments ought not to obscure the common point that natural selection resulting in hairlessness involves a factor in the environment.

An Exchange of Views

Some anthropologists may wish to debate some of Bentley Glass's premises, in his article "The ethical basis of science," concerning the evolution of human values. Indeed, the biologist part of my make-up twinges at his rather Lamarckian statement connecting the "loss of certain unnecessary structures, such as bodily hair once clothing was invented." The survival value of such a depilation is questionable; the evidence directly connecting human adoption of clothing with hair loss probably still more so. . . .

JEFFREY J. W. BAKER

69 High Street
Middletown, Connecticut

. . . Some questions, such as whether the blue we see is "really" blue, or the logical possibility of causal sequences operating in reverse order, remain forever in scientific never-never land. From the business end of things, these can usually be ignored. Other deceptively similar assumptions, however, may creep into the very tactics of research and thus be of considerable import. Evolutionary theory, upon which Glass dwells, provides a valuable illustration of certain potential problems. "Survival of the fittest" is a tautology, not an explanation per se, for it is through the operation of survival that "fittest" is defined. More important, perhaps, are unanalyzable statements which may follow, such as that man today acts (or should act) thus-and-so because of such-and-such in the past. Fossil records of behavior and individual struggles are difficult to obtain, much less evaluate in such a context. Statements of necessary and proper biological function often reflect little but uncritical assumptions as to adaptive value and overgeneralizations from limited data. Premature confidence that the answer is at hand, with perhaps subliminal fear that it is not, can lead to the arrogance of dogma and its potentially severe consequences.

The espousal of the theory of inheritance of acquired characters is a good example, cited by Glass, of such dangers. Certainly there is extremely strong evidence to suggest the validity of our own current concepts of heredity, from mathematical models of dispersion and repeatable segregation of discrete characters to the occurrence of such behavioral phenomena as imprinting, in which each generation must learn anew to follow particular objects. The main issue, however, is whether such debates should now be closed to further inquiry. Let us take a few particulars: Does it necessarily follow from the failure to transmit experimental mutilations (such as cutting tails off mice) that certain adaptive tendencies cannot be so transmitted? Can failure to transmit demonstrable altered morphological or physiological states be assumed to generalize to all other modes of action, for example, learning and behavior? Could failure to transmit specific tendencies necessarily disprove the possibility of the transfer of more generalized functions, such as timidity or fear in the presence of new stimuli? Can failure to demonstrate transmission of functions through nuclear mechanisms be safely generalized to eliminate change via other biological mechanisms? The possibility of cytoplasmic "holding" functions to carry a species through until a "chance" mutation arises, for example, does not appear to be experimentally discounted. (The day after I drafted this letter the report by J. Brun on "Genetic adaptation . . ." appeared in *Science* [10 Dec., p. 1467]. Whatever the conclusion of parapsychologists, the scientific results are encouraging!) Or, given the importance of mutation, can it definitely be said that environmental circumstances, for example stress, will not alter the rate of "random" change? The point to be made is that such inferences do not necessarily follow from the data at hand, and similar careless generalizations with their hidden assumptions may but replace one dogma with another. . . . The difficulty of evaluating scientific proposals comes in trying to balance the apparent probability of success with the conceptual importance of success if it does occur. To rate only the former is, and I think Glass would agree, "bad." Here indeed ethics and pragmatics merge.

JOHN C. FENTRESS

Center for Brain Research
University of Rochester
Rochester, New York

Most of the remarks made by Baker, Kraft, and Fentress (Letters, 25 Feb., p. 935) seem to me to be interesting extensions of various lines of thought suggested by my essay on "The ethical basis of science" (3 Dec., p. 1254). The unabridged essay contained in the book from which the article derived may offer other extensions and possibly clarification of some moot points.

I must take exception, however, to Baker's comment on my "rather Lamarckian statement connecting the 'loss of certain unnecessary structures, such as bodily hair, once clothing was invented.' " There is nothing whatever Lamarckian about the statement. It would be "Lamarckian" only if I had said or implied that the needs or desires of the human being had led to the inheritance of a trait. Natural selection is required to maintain every functioning, necessary feature at a functioning level. Whenever, by change of environment, a once useful structure becomes useless, the prevalent nature of mutation will lead progressively to its reduction or deterioration. That is to say, it is by *mutation in the absence of natural selection* that functionless structures become reduced, then vestigial, and finally disappear altogther. No geneticist or evolutionist to my knowledge would propose any Lamarckian explanation for the disappearance of useless structures. The wings of all the now wingless insects of Kerguelen have presumably been lost solely by natural selection in an environment where wings were not only useless but a positive handicap. Eyes in cave fish and salamanders are presumably no detriment, but they have lost significance and the animals have evolved to a blind or even eyeless condition.

The situation is similar with respect to human hair. All other primate species, whether living in the tropics or in temperate regions, whether arboreal or ground-dwelling, are hairy. Man, too, still possesses all his hair follicles, but the hair itself, over most of the body, is reduced and vestigial. In this respect he is comparable to the elephants or the cetaceans. Evolutionists suppose that the relative hairlessness of these mammals arose from a change in selection pressure, and it is reasonable to suppose the same is true of the human species. What was this change in selection pressure? One may postulate a positive advantage in being hairless, a disadvantage in hairiness; or one may postulate that hairiness simply became inconsequential to man. The first hypothesis does not seem very probable, because the human species, evolving in East Africa or wherever else, was in the company of other primates who did not become hairless, to judge from their modern descendants. Although the matter must of course remain without conclusive proof, it seems far more reasonable to suppose that man very early in his separate existence as a species (or genus) began wearing clothing (in the form of skins) and later using fire to warm himself. Thus he changed his environment sufficiently to make hairiness an inconsequential feature, except on the more exposed parts of his anatomy.

It is highly significant, as a support of this theory, that head hair, so clearly a protection from sun, wind, and rain, has been retained. Mutations eliminating only body hair have not been removed from the population by natural selection, while those that eliminate head hair have been extinguished. I would go so far as to propose seriously that baldness, like myopia, is largely a genetic trait that has only become widespread and common in human populations since man became civilized and keen vision and a good head of hair were no longer so important to survival. In fact, baldness is still limited almost entirely to males who have passed the age at which most males, in primitive times, would have died of various causes. Thus the apparent extension of baldness as a common human trait is largely a matter of the extension of the life span. That cannot be the case for general body hairlessness.

BENTLEY GLASS

State University of New York
Stony Brook

Like Bentley Glass ("Evolution of hairlessness in man," Letters, 15 April), I object to the implication by Baker and Fentress (Letters, 25 Feb.) that attributing the reduction of biological structures to their loss of function has Lamarckian overtones. Glass has presented the theoretical basis for his views with admirable clarity. But, as an anthropologist, I must question his application.

Human hairlessness does demand an explanation, but from the evidence available it would seem that the development of clothing is probably not involved. Among the living human populations, those that are most dependent upon clothing are also those that have retained the greatest amount of body hair. And there is archeological evidence that a concern for the preparation of hides, and presumably clothing, was first developed by the ancestors of these populations. On the other hand, those populations that wear little or no clothing, and whose ancestors presumably did the same, are just those that retain a minimum of body hair. Since these inhabit the hotter parts of the world, it is quite possible that human body hair was eliminated by natural selection when the problem of dissipating metabolically generated heat became important to human survival. Man's hairless skin, richly endowed with sweat glands, is an admirable heat dissipater.

Throughout most of the last half million years, man subsisted by hunting and gathering. Among hunting mammals, man's heat-dissipating mechanism is unique, and one may suggest that it is a reflection of the fact that man alone has engaged in maximum hunting activities through the heat of a tropical day. South African bushmen have capitalized on this facet of their physiology in their hunting practices right up to the present day.

Correlating human hairlessness with tropical hunting behavior, one can guess that selection reduced the hairy coat at the time when regular and effective hunting techniques were developed. The fossil and archeological record shows that this occurred at the beginning of the Middle Pleistocene, more than half a million years ago. If we can infer it from the sudden proliferation of scrapers and leather working tools, the regular preparation of skins for clothing began with the onset of the last glacial advance about 100,000 years ago. This means that clothing was developed long after man's hairy coat had been lost. But 100,000 years is long enough to have some effect, and it is interesting to note that it is in just those populations whose ancestors first used clothing that skin pigmentation occurs in its most reduced form. Depigmentation, rather than hairlessness, may have been the result of the development of clothing for just the reasons Glass suggests. Reduction in visual acuity and baldness probably have occurred as he has stated. These and other facets of human physical characteristics are treated in greater detail in Brace and Montagu's recent text in physical anthropology (*Man's Evolution,* Macmillan, New York, 1965).

C. LORING BRACE

Department of Anthropology
University of California, Santa Barbara

. . . Glass finds it "highly significant, as a support of [his] theory, that head hair, so clearly a protection from sun, wind, and rain, has been retained." Head hair does protect the crown, but it is far easier for man to guard his pate from exposure with his arms, a leaf, or any sort of cover than to protect the rest of his body with a garment or by warming it near a fire. If the Glass theory were true in this context, then man's head should have become bare first. In another context, nose, ears, and digits, being more exposed and sensitive to cold than the head, should be furred; instead, these organs are nearly or quite glabrous. The Glass theory is further confounded by man's retention of abundant tufts in the axillae and pubic regions, where exposure and need for cover are minimal. Even more perplexing in the light of the theory is the fact that the near-term fetus is furred from head to toe while sheltered in the womb but is born unclad into the inclement world.

Glass goes on "to propose seriously that baldness, like myopia, is largely a genetic trait that has only become widespread and common in human populations since man became relatively civilized and keen vision and a good head of hair were no longer important to survival." The species of mammals which have become quite or nearly bareheaded without awaiting civilization are too numerous to list. The pied marmoset, the uakari, and many individuals of chimpanzees are examples among the primates. Many mammals—whales, elephants, rhinoceroses, hippopotami, naked mole rats (*Heterocephalus glaber*), some species of armadillos, certain strains of laboratory mice—even combine nearsightedness with near-hairlessness. Man has no monopoly on alopecia. Any mammal, whether through age, disease, or mutation, can become bald or bare on the head or any other part of the body. Witness the baboon.

Man's long tresses and relatively thinly haired body and limbs are almost certainly the result of sexual selection, with the male selecting for these traits in the female. In all probability, man was exposed to a cold environment *after* losing most of his body hair; he survived the changing climate because he could adapt physiologically, apart from having the wit to use fire and clothing for greater comfort. Axillary and pubic hairs, which appear in the least exposed parts of the body, are secondary sexual characteristics peculiar to man.

PHILIP HERSHKOVITZ

Field Museum of Natural History
Chicago, Illinois

. . . Glass postulates a selectively neutral character (body hairiness), which disappears through swamping by mutation. Mayr considers it "exceedingly unlikely that any gene will remain selectively neutral for any length of time" (E. Mayr, *Animal Species and Evolution,* Harvard Univ. Press, Cambridge, 1963, p. 207.) an opinion that has been expressed by other authorities (for example, R. A. Fisher, *Genetical Theory of Natural Selection,* Clarendon, Oxford, 1929; T. Dobzhansky, *Evolution, Genetics, and Man,* Wiley, New York, 1955, p. 152ff.). Even if we assume a long period in human evolution during which there is no differential selective pressure affecting hairiness, the latter portion of Glass's assertion is still difficult, for we must postulate a high mutation rate to account for the effective elimination of body hair. But many genetic loci with high mutation probabilities have the high probabilities in both directions; that is, we ought frequently to see very hairy mutants in the present-day population.

An alternative explanation of the loss of inessential characters may be that every character requires metabolic energy to develop and maintain it, and elimination of a useless character diverts this energy to uses that promote survival, so that individuals without the character survive and reproduce at higher rates than individuals who have it.

Glass hypothesizes that baldness is a product of civilization (and hats), since "baldness is still limited almost entirely to males who have passed the age at which most males, in primitive times, would have died of various causes." The real criterion is whether baldness (and the selective disadvantage which it brings to the individual) occurs prior to *reproduction* (not death). Since baldness only rarely, even today, occurs prior to reproduction, there is no reason to suppose that primitive man lacked the baldness genes, unless complicating pleiotropic effects are postulated.

JACK P. HAILMAN

Institute of Animal Behavior
Newark College of Arts and Sciences
Rutgers University, Newark, New Jersey

In arguing that by adopting clothing man "changed his environment sufficiently to make hairiness an inconsequential feature except on the more exposed parts of his anatomy," and further that "head hair, so clearly a protection from sun, wind, and rain has been retained," Glass states the conventional view of the role of hair in man. Evidence is accumulating that this is an unnecessarily limited view of the part hair plays in human and mammalian physiology, indeed that protection from the elements is probably a minor function. Work done in our laboratory and others indicates that hair, as an appendage of the integument, acts with the integument in the management of certain physiological processes, one of which is the highly selective excretion of trace elements. This appears to be true not only of hair in mammals but of feathers in birds and the cast skins of reptiles, amphibians, and arthropods.

Patterns of hairiness in man may follow evolutionary changes in diet or other factors. Baldness itself seems to be associated with increased hairiness over other parts of the body. Hairiness and feather dress is only poorly correlated with severity of climate; tropical mammals and birds have luxuriant hair and feathers. Hence it is reasonably clear that one must be cautious in assigning simple evolutionary roles to hair and similar integumentary derivatives.

GARTH S. KENNINGTON

Department of Zoology and Physiology
University of Wyoming, Laramie

. . . Hair was developed by our earliest mammalian ancestors, probably in the Triassic period, about 200 million years ago. It was part of the temperature regulating mechanism which differentiates mammals from cold-blooded animals and which also includes such components as sweat glands, vasoconstriction and vasodilation, hair erection, panting, shivering, and temperature sensors in various parts of the body. Loss of fur or body hair in man can only be interpreted as due to a mutation involving a defective gene, similar to that responsible for albinism, for example. Because all living men, of all races, now carry this defective gene, we are forced to assume that its introduction into our makeup occurred further back than the development of the genes which serve to distinguish the Caucasian, Negro, Mongoloid, and Pygmy races from each other. The introduction of the gene could hardly have taken place later than the first great dispersion of paleolithic man, which is assumed to have taken place during the great interglacial stage (Yarmouth or Riss-Mindel) about 200,000 years ago. The carriers of the defective gene could hardly have survived except in a highly favorable environment where exposure to cold, mosquitos, sunburn, and spiny vegetation was not too severe a handicap. It is likely, for example, that the Neanderthal race had a heavy coat of fur, because they lived in, and seemed to prefer, an arctic or subarctic environment, which would be fatal to modern man without specialized clothing.

Unless there were some compelling advantage in not having body hair, it would be very unlikely for the defective gene to propagate rapidly throughout a population. The fact that it did, and that all nonbearers of the gene were eliminated completely, requires an explanation. One such possibility will occur to those who have read *Rats, Lice, and History* by Hans Zinsser. Body hair offers exceptional shelter for such insects as ticks and body lice, which have evolved in company with man and other mammals. The nonhairy members of the population probably took great pains to rid themselves of these unwelcome guests, as they still do. Their furry cousins probably never could delouse or detick themselves (as anyone can appreciate who has tried to rid a long-haired dog of ticks). Thus an outbreak of typhus, spotted fever, Black Death, or any similar plague could have wiped out the entire fur-bearing segment of the human population. This could have occurred in a small, compact group of our ancestral humans, while nonancestral groups like the Neanderthalers remained unaffected.

Lack of body hair was unquestionably a compelling incentive for inventing clothing, building shelters, and using fire. The need to compensate for a defective gene may thus have been one of nature's most powerful stimulants for the advancement of mankind.

WALTER S. OLSON

4 Claremont Road
Scarsdale, New York

POPULATION
AND SOCIETY

It is now commonplace to read in the newspaper about problems of population and overpopulation. However, discussions in a newspaper which present the problem areas on a day-to-day basis are not able to report the genesis of over-population and its consequences. Accordingly, the three papers in this section are selected with specific purposes in mind. The paper by Dorn summarizes the demographic aspects of the world and its background, while Deevy and Guhl discuss the behavioral consequences of overpopulation.

Dorn is correct in saying that up to recent times, the world of population has been held in check by high mortality which tended to balance high fertility. In recent times, the mortality rates have dropped significantly, while the fertility rates have dropped only minimally. Therefore, if we choose to reduce the mortality rate, we must reduce the fertility rate as a check upon world popu-lation.

The delightful and humorous essay by Deevy contains an excellent review of modern biological principles on the consequences of overpopulation. The diagram in Fig. 1 (p. 210) may be useful in understanding the various inter-relationships of the factors that Deevy is discussing.

A few ecologists are prepared to accept the behavioral sequelae of overpopu-lation in lower organisms under laboratory conditions but feel that these phenomena have not been shown to exist under natural conditions. The applicability to human populations is also under serious discussion. Many

177

*researchers do accept the findings of the laboratory experiments on lower orga-
nisms as theoretical models for current studies of human behavior.*

*How one person relates to another and how one nation relates to another is
also an important concern to the human ecologist. Guhl points out that observations on the behavioral patterns of the lower vertebrates may represent a theoretical model of "basic" human behavior.*

World Population Growth: An International Dilemma

HAROLD F. DORN*

During all but the most recent years of the centuries of his existence man must have lived, reproduced, and died as other animals do. His increase in number was governed by the three great regulators of the increase of all species of plants and animals—predators, disease, and starvation—or, in terms more applicable to human populations—war, pestilence, and famine. One of the most significant developments for the future of mankind during the first half of the 20th century has been his increasing ability to control pestilence and famine. Although he has not freed himself entirely from the force of these two regulators of population increase, he has gained sufficient control of them so that they no longer effectively govern his increase in number.

Simultaneously he has developed methods of increasing the effectiveness of war as a regulator of population increase, to the extent that he almost certainly could quickly wipe out a large proportion, if not all, of the human race. At the same time he has learned how to separate sexual gratification from reproduction by means of contraception and telegenesis (that is, reproduction by artificial insemination, particularly with spermatozoa preserved for relatively long periods of time), so that he can regulate population increase by voluntary control of fertility. Truly it can be said that man has the knowledge and the power to direct, at least in part, the course of his evolution.

This newly gained knowledge and power has not freed man from the inexorable effect of the biological laws that govern all living organisms. The evolutionary process has endowed most species with a reproductive potential that,

* The author is affiliated with the National Institutes of Health, Bethesda, Md., in the Biometrics Research Branch, National Heart Institute.

179

unchecked, would overpopulate the entire globe within a few generations. It has been estimated that the tapeworm, *Taenia,* may lay 120,000 eggs per day; an adult cod can lay as many as 4 million eggs per year; a frog may produce 10,000 eggs per spawning. Human ovaries are thought to contain approximately 200,000 ova at puberty, while a single ejaculation of human semen may contain 200 million spermatozoa.

This excessive reproductive potential is kept in check for species other than man by interspecies competition in the struggle for existence, by disease, and by limitation of the available food supply. The fact that man has learned how to control, to a large extent, the operation of these biological checks upon unrestrained increase in number has not freed him from the necessity of substituting for them less harsh but equally effective checks. The demonstration of his ability to do this cannot be long delayed.

Only fragmentary data are available to indicate the past rate of growth of the population of the world. Even today, the number of inhabitants is known only approximately. Regular censuses of populations did not exist prior to 1800, although registers were maintained for small population groups prior to that time. As late as a century ago, around 1860, only about one-fifth of the estimated population of the world was covered by a census enumeration once in a 10-year

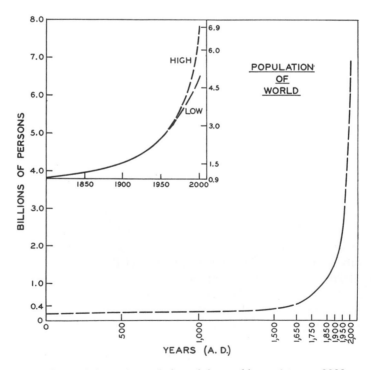

FIG. 1. Estimated population of the world, A.D. 1 to A.D. 2000.

period (*1*). The commonly accepted estimates of the population of the world prior to 1800 are only informed guesses. Nevertheless, it is possible to piece together a consistent series of estimates of the world's population during the past two centuries, supplemented by a few rough guesses of the number of persons alive at selected earlier periods. The most generally accepted estimates are presented in Figure 1.

These reveal a spectacular spurt during recent decades in the increase of the world's population that must be unparalleled during the preceding millennia of human existence. Furthermore, the rate of increase shows no sign of diminishing (Table 1). The period of time required for the population of the world to double has sharply decreased during the past three centuries and now is about 35 years.

TABLE 1. The number of years required to double the population of the world. [From United Nations data (*9, 14*)]

Year (A.D.)	Population (billions)	Number of years to double
1	0.25(?)	1650(?)
1650	0.50	200
1850	1.1	80
1930	2.0	45
1975	4.0	35
2010	8.0*	?

* A projection of United Nations estimates.

Only a very rough approximation can be made of the length of time required for the population of the world to reach one-quarter of a billion persons, the estimated number at the beginning of the Christian era. The present subgroups of *Homo sapiens* may have existed for as long as 100,000 years. The exact date is not necessary, since for present purposes the evidence is sufficient to indicate that probably 50,000 to 100,000 years were required for *Homo sapiens* to increase in number until he reached a global total of one-quarter of a billion persons. This number was reached approximately 2000 years ago.

By 1620, the year the Pilgrims landed on Plymouth Rock, the population of the world had doubled in number. Two hundred years later, shortly before the Civil War, another 500 million persons had been added. Since that time, additional half billions of persons have been added during increasingly shorter intervals of time. The sixth half billion, just added, required slightly less than 11 years, as compared to 200 years for the second half billion. The present rate of growth implies that only 6 to 7 years will be required to add the eighth half billion to the world's population. The change in rate of growth just described has taken place since the first settlers came to New England.

Implications

The accelerating rate of increase in the growth of the population of the world has come about so unobtrusively that most persons are unaware of its implications. There is a small group who are so aroused by this indifference that, like modern Paul Reveres, they attempt to awaken the public with cries of "the population bomb!" or "the population explosion!"

These persons are called alarmists by those who counter with the assertion that similar warnings, such as "standing-room only" and "mankind at the cross-roads," have been issued periodically since Malthus wrote his essay on population, about 200 years ago. Nevertheless, says this group, the level of living and the health of the average person has continued to improve, and there is no reason to believe that advances in technology will not be able to make possible a slowly rising level of living for an increasing world population for the indefinite future. Furthermore, the rate of population increase almost certainly will slow down as the standard of education and living rises and as urbanization increases.

A third group of persons has attempted to estimate the maximum population that could be supported by the world's physical resources provided existing technological knowledge is fully utilized. Many of these calculations have been based on estimates of the quantity of food that could be produced and a hypothetical average daily calorie consumption per person.

As might be expected, the range of the various estimates of the maximum world population that could be supported without a lowering of the present level of living is very wide. One of the lowest, 2.8 billion, made by Pearson and Harper in 1945 on the assumption of an Asiatic standard of consumption, already has been surpassed (2). Several others, ranging from 5 to 7 billion, almost certainly will be exceeded by the end of this century. Perhaps the most carefully prepared estimate as well as the largest—that of 50 billions, prepared by Harrison Brown—would be reached in about 150 years if the present rate of growth should continue (3).

I believe it is worth while to prepare estimates of the maximum population that can be supported and to revise these as new information becomes available, even though most of the estimates made in the past already have been, or soon will be, demonstrated to be incorrect (in most instances too small), since this constitutes a rational effort to comprehend the implications of the increase in population. At the same time it should be recognized that estimates of the world's carrying capacity made in this manner are rather unrealistic and are primarily useful only as very general guidelines.

In the first place, these calculations have assumed that the earth's resources and skills are a single reservoir available to all. In reality this is untrue. The U.S. government attempts to restrict production of certain agricultural crops by paying farmers not to grow them. Simultaneously, in Asia and Africa, large numbers of persons are inadequately fed and poorly clothed. Except in a very general sense there is no world population problem; there are population problems varying in nature and degree among the several nations of the world. No single solution is applicable to all.

Since the world is not a single political unity, the increases in production actually achieved during any period of time tend to be considerably less than those theoretically possible. Knowledge, technical skill, and capital are concentrated in areas with the highest level of living, whereas the most rapid increase in population is taking place in areas where such skills and capital are relatively scarce or practically nonexistent.

Just as the world is not a single unit from the point of view of needs and the availability of resources, skills and knowledge to meet these needs, so it also is not a single unit with respect to population increase. Due to political barriers that now exist throughout the entire world, overpopulation, however defined, will become a serious problem in specific countries long before it would be a world problem if there were no barriers to population redistribution. I shall return to this point later, after discussing briefly existing forecasts or projections of the total population of the world.

Most demographers believe that, under present conditions, the future population of areas such as countries or continents, or even of the entire world, cannot be predicted for more than a few decades with even a moderate degree of certainty. This represents a marked change from the view held by many only 30 years ago.

In 1930 a prominent demographer wrote, "The population of the United States ten, twenty, even fifty years hence, can be predicted with a greater degree of assurance than any other economic or social fact, provided the immigration laws are unchanged" (4). Nineteen years later, a well-known economist replied that "it is disheartening to have to assert that the best population forecasts deserve little credence even for 5 years ahead, and none at all for 20–50 years ahead." (5).

Although both of these statements represent rather extreme views, they do indicate the change that has taken place during the past two decades in the attitude toward the reliability of population forecasts. Some of the reasons for this have been discussed in detail elsewhere and will not be repeated here (6).

It will be sufficient to point out that knowledge of methods of voluntarily controlling fertility now is so widespread, especially among persons of European ancestry, that sharp changes in the spacing, as well as in the number, of children born during the reproductive period may occur in a relatively short period of time. Furthermore, the birth rate may increase as well as decrease.

Forecasting population growth

The two principal methods that have been used in recent years to make population forecasts are (i) the extrapolation of mathematical curves fitted to the past trend of population increase and (ii) the projection of the population by the "component" or "analytical" method, based on specific hypotheses concerning the future trend in fertility, mortality, and migration.

The most frequently used mathematical function has been the logistic curve which was originally suggested by Verhulst in 1838 but which remained unnoticed until it was rediscovered by Pearl and Reed about 40 years ago (7). At first it was thought by some demographers that the logistic curve represented a rational law of population change. However, it has proved to be as unreliable as other methods of preparing population forecasts and is no longer regarded as having any unique value for estimating future population trends.

A recent illustration of the use of mathematical functions to project the future world population is the forecast prepared by von Foerster, Mora, and Amiot (8). In view of the comments that subsequently were published in this journal, an extensive discussion of this article does not seem to be required. It will be sufficient to point out that this forecast probably will set a record, for the entire class of forecasts prepared by the use of mathematical functions, for the short length of time required to demonstrate its unreliability.

The method of projecting or forecasting population growth most frequently used by demographers, whenever the necessary data are available, is the "component" or "analytical" method. Separate estimates are prepared of the future trend of fertility, mortality, and migration. From the total population as distributed by age and sex on a specified date, the future population that would result from the hypothetical combination of fertility, mortality, and migration is computed. Usually, several estimates of the future population are prepared in order to include what the authors believe to be the most likely range of values.

Such estimates generally are claimed by their authors to be not forecasts of the most probable future population but merely indications of the population that would result from the hypothetical assumptions concerning the future trend in fertility, mortality, and migration. However, the projections of fertility, mortality, and migration usually are chosen to include what the authors believe will be the range of likely possibilities. This objective is achieved by making "high," "medium," and "low" assumptions concerning the future trend in population growth. Following the practice of most of the authors of such estimates, I shall refer to these numbers as population projections.

The most authoritative projections of the population of the world are those made by the United Nations (9, 10) (Table 2). Even though the most recent of these projections were published in 1958, only 3 years ago, it now seems likely that the population of the world will exceed the high projection before the year 2000. By the end of 1961 the world's population at least equaled the high projection for that date.

Although the United Nations' projections appear to be too conservative in that even the highest will be an underestimate of the population only 40 years from now, some of the numerical increases in population implied by these projections will create problems that may be beyond the ability of the nations involved to solve. For example, the estimated increase in the population of Asia

TABLE 2. Estimated population of the world for A.D. 1900, 1950, 1975, and 2000. [From United Nations data (9), rounded to three significant digits]

Area	Estimated population (millions)		Projected future population (millions)			
			Low assumptions		High assumptions	
	1900	1950	1975	2000	1975	2000
World	1550	2500	3590	4880	3860	6900
Africa	120	199	295	420	331	663
North America	81	168	232	274	240	326
Latin America	63	163	282	445	304	651
Asia	857	1380	2040	2890	2210	4250
Europe including U.S.S.R.	423	574	724	824	751	987
Oceania	6	13	20	27	21	30

from A.D. 1950 to 2000 will be roughly equal to the population of the entire world in 1958! The population of Latin America 40 years hence may very likely be four times that in 1950. The absolute increase in population in Latin America during the last half of the century may equal the total increase in the population of *Homo sapiens* during all the millennia from his origin until about 1650, when the first colonists were settling New England.

Increases in population of this magnitude stagger the imagination. Present trends indicate that they may be succeeded by even larger increases during comparable periods of time. The increase in the rate of growth of the world's population, shown by the data in Table 1, is still continuing. This rate is now estimated to be about 2 percent per year, sufficient to double the world's population every 35 years. It requires only very simple arithmetic to show that a continuation of this rate of growth for even 10 or 15 decades would result in an increase in population that would make the globe resemble an anthill.

But as was pointed out above, the world is not a single unit economically, politically, or demographically. Long before the population of the entire world reaches a size that could not be supported at current levels of living, the increase in population in specific nations and regions will give rise to problems that will affect the health and welfare of the rest of the world. The events of the past few years have graphically demonstrated the rapidity with which the political and economic problems of even a small and weak nation can directly affect the welfare of the largest and most powerful nations. Rather than speculate about the maximum population the world can support and the length of time before this number will be reached, it will be more instructive to examine the demographic changes that are taking place in different regions of the world and to comment briefly on their implications.

Decline in mortality

The major cause of the recent spurt in population increase is a world-wide decline in mortality. Although the birth rate increased in some countries—for example, the United States—during and after World War II, such increases have not been sufficiently widespread to account for more than a small part of the increase in the total population of the world. Moreover, the increase in population prior to World War II occurred in spite of a widespread decline in the birth rate among persons of European origin.

Accurate statistics do not exist, but the best available estimates suggest that the expectation of life at birth in Greece, Rome, Egypt, and the Eastern Mediterranean region probably did not exceed 30 years at the beginning of the Christian era. By 1900 it had increased to about 40 to 50 years in North America and in

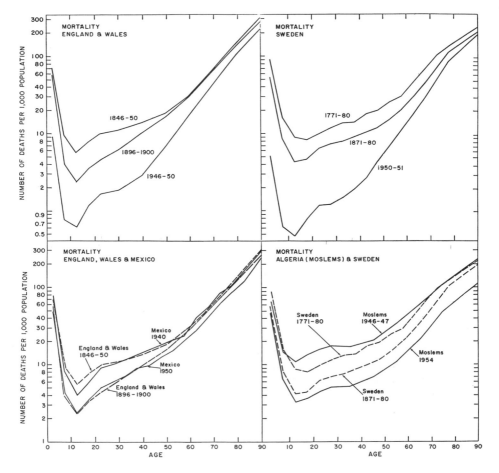

FIG. 2. Age-specific death rates per 1000 per year for Sweden, England and Wales, Mexico, and the Moslem population of Algeria for various time periods from 1771 to 1954.

most countries of northwestern Europe. At present, it has reached 68 to 70 years in many of these countries.

By 1940, only a small minority of the world's population had achieved an expectation of life at birth comparable to that of the population of North America and northwest Europe. Most of the population of the world had an expectation of life no greater than that which prevailed in western Europe during the Middle Ages. Within the past two decades, the possibility of achieving a 20th-century death rate has been opened to these masses of the world's population. An indication of the result can be seen from the data in Fig. 2.

In 1940, the death rate in Mexico was similar to that in England and Wales nearly 100 years earlier. It decreased as much during the following decade as did the death rate in England and Wales during the 50-year period from 1850 to 1900.

In 1946–47 the death rate of the Moslem population of Algeria was higher than that of the population of Sweden in the period 1771–80, the earliest date for which reliable mortality statistics are available for an entire nation. During the following 8 years, the drop in the death rate in Algeria considerably exceeded that in Sweden during the century from 1771 to 1871 (*11*).

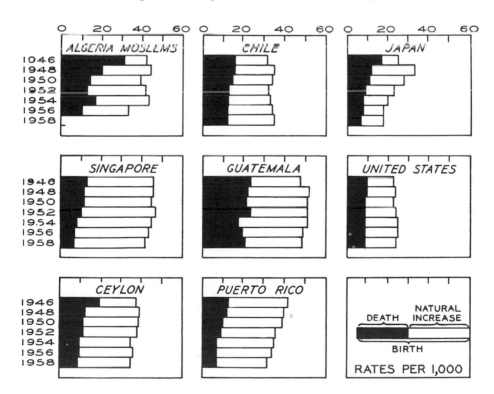

FIG. 3. Birth rate, death rate, and rate of natural increase per 1000 for selected countries for the period 1946–58.

The precipitous decline in mortality in Mexico and in the Moslem population of Algeria is illustrative of what has taken place during the past 15 years in Latin America, Africa, and Asia, where nearly three out of every four persons in the world now live. Throughout most of this area the birth rate has changed very little, remaining near a level of 40 per 1000 per year, as can be seen from Fig. 3, which shows the birth rate, death rate, and rate of natural increase for selected countries.

Even in countries such as Puerto Rico and Japan where the birth rate has declined substantially, the rate of natural increase has changed very little, owing to the sharp decrease in mortality. A more typical situation is represented by Singapore, Ceylon, Guatemala, and Chile, where the crude rate of natural increase has risen. There has been a general tendency for death rates to decline universally and for high birth rates to remain high, with the result that those countries with the highest rates of increase are experiencing an acceleration in their rates of growth.

Regional levels

The absolute level of fertility and mortality and the effect of changes in them upon the increase of population in different regions of the world can be only approximately indicated. The United Nations estimates that only about 33 percent of the deaths and 42 percent of the births are registered (*12*). The percentage

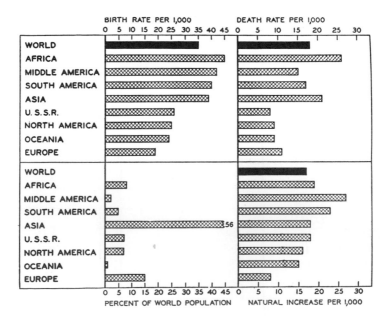

FIG. 4. Percentage of the 1958 world population, birth rate, death rate, and rate of natural increase, per 1000, for the period 1954–58 for various regions of the world.

registered ranges from about 8 to 10 percent in tropical and southern Africa and Eastern Asia to 98 to 100 percent in North America and Europe. Nevertheless, the statistical staff of the United Nations, by a judicious combination of the available fragmentary data, has been able to prepare estimates of fertility and mortality for different regions of the world that are generally accepted as a reasonably correct representation of the actual but unknown figures. The estimated birth rate, death rate, and crude rate of natural increase (the birth rate minus the death rate) for eight regions of the world for the period 1954–58 are shown in Fig. 4.

The birth rates of the countries of Africa, Asia, Middle America, and South America average nearly 40 per 1000 and probably are as high as they were 500 to 1000 years ago. In the rest of the world—Europe, North America, Oceania, and the Soviet Union—the birth rate is slightly more than half as high, or about 20 to 25 per 1000. The death rate for the former regions, although still definitely higher, is rapidly approaching that for people of European origin, with the result that the highest rates of natural increase are found in the regions with the highest birth rates. The most rapid rate of population growth at present is taking place in Middle and South America, where the population will double about every 26 years if the present rate continues.

These regional differences in fertility and mortality are intensifying the existing imbalance of population with land area and natural resources. No matter how this imbalance is measured, that it exists is readily apparent. Two rather crude measures are presented in Figs. 4 and 5, which show the percentage distribution of the world's population living in each region and the number of persons per square kilometer.

An important effect of the decline in mortality rates often is overlooked— namely, the increase in effective fertility. An estimated 97 out of every 100

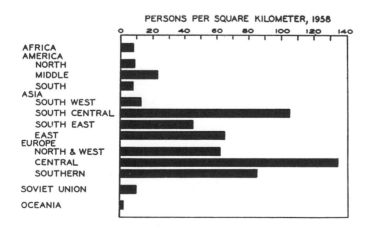

FIG. 5. Number of persons per square kilometer in various regions of the world in 1958.

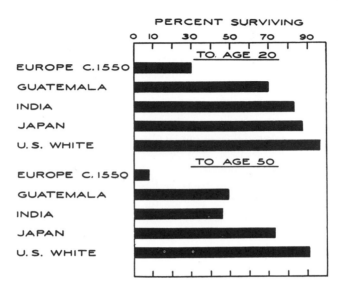

FIG. 6. Percentage of newborn females who would survive to the end of the reproductive period according to mortality rates in Europe around A.D. 1500 and in selected countries around 1950.

newborn white females subject to the mortality rates prevailing in the United States during 1950 would survive to age 20, slightly past the beginning of the usual childbearing age, and 91 would survive to the end of the childbearing period (Fig. 6). These estimates are more than 3 and 11 times, respectively, the corresponding estimated proportions for white females that survived to these ages about four centuries ago.

In contrast, about 70 percent of the newborn females in Guatemala would survive to age 20, and only half would live to the end of the childbearing period if subject to the death rates prevailing in that country in 1950. If the death rate in Guatemala should fall to the level of that in the United States in 1950—a realistic possibility—the number of newborn females who would survive to the beginning of the childbearing period would increase by 36 percent; the number surviving to the end of the childbearing period would increase by 85 percent. A corresponding decrease in the birth rate would be required to prevent this increase in survivorship from resulting in a rapid acceleration in the existing rate of population growth, which already is excessive. In other words, this decrease in the death rate would require a decrease in the birth rate of more than 40 percent merely to maintain the status quo.

As can be seen from Fig. 3, the birth rate in countries with high fertility has shown little or no tendency to decrease in recent years. Japan is the exception. There, the birth rate dropped by 46 percent from 1948 to 1958—an amount more than enough to counterbalance the decrease in the death rate, with the result that there was a decrease in the absolute number of births. As yet there

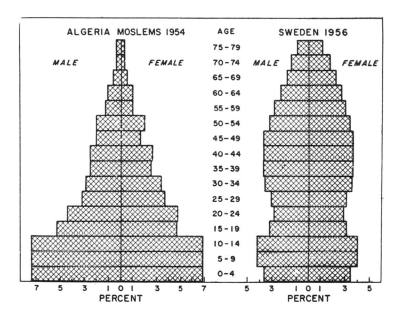

FIG. 7. Percentage distribution by age of the population of Sweden in 1956 and the Moslem population of Algeria in 1954.

is very little evidence that other countries with a correspondingly high birth rate are likely to duplicate this in the near future.

Another effect of a rapid rate of natural increase is demonstrated by Fig. 7. About 43 percent of the Moslem population of Algeria is under 15 years of age; the corresponding percentage in Sweden is 24, or slightly more than half this number. Percentages in the neighborhood of 40 percent are characteristic of the populations of the countries of Africa, Latin America, and Asia.

This high proportion of young people constitutes a huge fertility potential for 30 years into the future that can be counterbalanced only by a sharp decline in the birth rate, gives rise to serious educational problems, and causes a heavy drain on the capital formation that is necessary to improve the level of living of the entire population. A graphic illustration of this may be found in the recently published 5-year plan for India for 1961–66, which estimates that it will be necessary to provide educational facilities and teachers for 20 million additional children during this 5-year period (*13*).

Historical pattern in western Europe

Some persons, although agreeing that the current rate of increase of the majority of the world's population cannot continue indefinitely without giving rise to grave political, social, and economic problems, point out that a similar situation existed in northwestern and central Europe during the 18th and 19th centuries.

Increasing industrialization and urbanization, coupled with a rising standard of living, led to a decline in the birth rate, with a consequent drop in the rate of increase of the population. Why should not the rest of the world follow this pattern?

There is small likelihood that the two-thirds of the world's population which has not yet passed through the demographic revolution from high fertility and mortality rates to low fertility and mortality rates can repeat the history of western European peoples prior to the development of serious political and economic problems. A brief review of the circumstances that led to the virtual domination of the world at the end of the 19th century by persons of European origin will indicate some of the reasons for this opinion.

Around A.D. 1500 the population of Europe probably did not exceed 100 million persons (perhaps 15 to 20 percent of the population of the world) and occupied about 7 percent of the land area of the earth. Four hundred years later, around 1900, the descendants of this population numbered nearly 550 million, constituted about one-third of the world's population, and occupied or controlled five-sixths of the land area of the world. They had seized and peopled two great continents, North and South America, and one smaller continent, Australia, with its adjacent islands; had partially peopled and entirely controlled a third great continent, Africa; and dominated southern Asia and the neighboring islands.

The English-, French-, and Spanish-speaking peoples were the leaders in this expansion, with lesser roles being played by the Dutch and Portuguese. The Belgians and Germans participated only toward the end of this period of expansion. Among these, the English-speaking people held the dominant position at the end of the era, around 1900.

The number of English-speaking persons around 1500, at the start of this period of expansion, is not known, but it probably did not exceed 4 or 5 million. By 1900 these people numbered about 129 million and occupied and controlled one-third of the land area of the earth and, with the non-English-speaking inhabitants of this territory, they made up some 30 percent of the population of the world.

This period was characterized by an unprecedented increase in population, a several-fold expansion of the land base for this population, and a hitherto undreamed of multiplication of capital in the form of precious metals, goods, and commodities. Most important of all, the augmentation in capital and usable land took place more rapidly than the growth in population.

A situation equally favorable for a rapid improvement in the level of living associated with a sharp increase in population does not appear likely to arise for the people who now inhabit Latin America, Africa, and Asia. The last great frontier of the world has been closed. Although there are many thinly populated areas in the world, their existence is testimony to the fact that, until now, these have been regarded as undesirable living places. The expansion of population to the remaining open areas would require large expenditures of capital for irrigation, drainage, transportation facilities, control of insects and parasites, and other purposes—capital that the rapidly increasing populations which will need these areas do not possess.

In addition, this land is not freely available for settlement. The entire land surface of the world is crisscrossed by national boundaries. International migration now is controlled by political considerations; for the majority of the population of the world, migration, both in and out of a country, is restricted.

The horn of plenty, formerly filled with free natural resources, has been emptied. No rapid accumulation of capital in the form of precious metals, goods, and commodities, such as characterized the great 400-year boom enjoyed by the peoples of western-European origin, is possible for the people of Africa, Asia, and Latin America.

Last, but not least, is the sheer arithmetic of the current increase in population. The number of persons in the world is so large that even a small rate of natural increase will result in an almost astronomical increment over a period of time of infinitesimal duration compared to the duration of the past history of the human race. As was pointed out above, continuation of the present rate of increase would result in a population of 50 billion persons in another 150 years. A population of this magnitude is so foreign to our experience that it is difficult to comprehend its implications.

Just as Thomas Malthus, at the end of the 18th century, could not foresee the effect upon the peoples of western Europe of the exploration of the last great frontier of this earth, so we today cannot clearly foresee the final effect of an unprecedented rapid increase of population within closed frontiers. What seems to be least uncertain in a future full of uncertainty is that the demographic history of the next 400 years will not be like that of the past 400 years.

World problem

The results of human reproduction are no longer solely the concern of the two individuals involved, or of the larger family, or even of the nation of which they are citizens. A stage has been reached in the demographic development of the world when the rate of human reproduction in any part of the globe may directly or indirectly affect the health and welfare of the rest of the human race. It is in this sense that there is a world population problem.

One or two illustrations may make this point more clear. During the past decade, six out of every ten persons added to the population of the world live in Asia; another two out of every ten live in Latin America and Africa. It seems inevitable that the breaking up of the world domination by northwest Europeans and their descendants, which already is well advanced, will continue, and that the center of power and influence will shift toward the demographic center of the world.

The present distribution of population increase enhances the existing imbalance between the distribution of the world's population and the distribution of wealth, available and utilized resources, and the use of nonhuman energy. Probably for the first time in human history there is a universal aspiration for a rapid improvement in the standard of living and a growing impatience with conditions that appear to stand in the way of its attainment. Millions of persons in Asia, Africa, and Latin America now are aware of the standard of living enjoyed by Europeans and North Americans. They are demanding the opportunity to attain the same standard, and they resist the idea that they must be permanently content with less.

A continuation of the present high rate of human multiplication will act as a brake on the already painfully slow improvement in the level of living, thus increasing political unrest and possibly bringing about eventual changes in government. As recent events have graphically demonstrated, such political changes may greatly affect the welfare of even the wealthiest nations.

The capital and technological skills that many of the nations of Africa, Asia, and Latin America require to produce enough food for a rapidly growing population and simultaneously to perceptibly raise per capita income exceed their existing national resources and ability. An immediate supply of capital in the amounts required is available only from the wealthier nations. The principle of public support for social welfare plans is now widely accepted in national affairs. The desirability of extending this principle to the international level for the primary purpose of supporting the economic development of the less advanced nations has not yet been generally accepted by the wealthier and more advanced countries. Even if this principle should be accepted, it is not as yet clear how long the wealthier nations would be willing to support the uncontrolled breeding of the populations receiving this assistance. The general acceptance of a foreign-aid program of the extent required by the countries with a rapidly growing population will only postpone for a few decades the inevitable reckoning with the results of uncontrolled human multiplication.

The future may witness a dramatic increase in man's ability to control his environment, provided he rapidly develops cultural substitutes for those harsh but effective governors of his high reproductive potential—disease and famine— that he has so recently learned to control. Man has been able to modify or control many natural phenomena, but he has not yet discovered how to evade the consequences of biological laws. No species has ever been able to multiply without limit. There are two biological checks upon a rapid increase in number—a high mortality and a low fertility. Unlike other biological organisms, man can choose which of these checks shall be applied, but one of them must be. Whether man can use his scientific knowledge to guide his future evolution more wisely than the blind forces of nature, only the future can reveal. The answer will not be long postponed.

REFERENCES

1. *Demographic Yearbook* (United Nations, New York, 1955), p. 1.
2. F. A. PEARSON and F. A. HARPER, *The World's Hunger* (Cornell Univ. Press, Ithaca, N.Y., 1945).
3. H. BROWN, *The Challenge of Man's Future* (Viking, New York, 1954).
4. O. E. BAKER, "Population trends in relation to land utilization," *Proc. Intern. Conf. Agr. Economists, 2nd Conf.* (1930), p. 284.
5. J. S. DAVIS, *J. Farm Economics* (Nov. 1949).
6. H. F. DORN, *J. Am. Statist. Assoc.* **45,** 311 (1950).
7. R. PEARL and L. J. REED, *Proc. Natl. Acad. Sci. U.S.* **6,** 275 (1920).
8. H. VON FOERSTER, P. M. MORA, L. W. AMIOT, *Science* **132,** 1291 (1960).
9. "The future growth of world population," *U.N. Publ. No. ST/SOA/Ser. A/28* (1958).
10. "The past and future growth of world population—a long-range view," *U.N. Population Bull. No. 1* (1951), pp. 1–12.
11. Although registration of deaths among the Moslem population of Algeria is incomplete, it is believed that the general impression conveyed by Fig. 2 is essentially correct.
12. *Demographic Yearbook* (United Nations, New York, 1956), p. 14.
13. New York *Times* (5 Aug. 1961).
14. "The determinants and consequences of population trends," *U.N. Publ. No. ST/SOA/Ser. A/17* (1953).

The Hare and the Haruspex:
A Cautionary Tale.*

EDWARD S. DEEVEY

Fifteen thousand years ago, when some of our more sensible ancestors had retired to paint pictures in caves in the south of France, the Scandinavian peninsula lay buried under a glacier. Even as recently as the seventh millennium B.C., when the arts and vices of civilization were already flourishing in the towns of Mesopotamia, the part of the earth's crust that is now Scandinavia was still depressed by the weight of half a mile of ice. Although the country has been rebounding at a great rate ever since, many Scandinavians remain depressed today. One reason may be that the Ice Age, as any Eskimo knows, is not yet over. The Scandinavian Airlines tourist who comes and goes like a swallow in the opalescent summer rarely glimpses the wintry or Pleistocene side of Nordic character, which accounts for its toughness, but which also results in some of the world's highest rates of alcoholism and suicide.

Perhaps because it was colonized so recently, the land the Norse called *Midgard* has always been treated as such—as middle ground, that is—by some of its inhabitants; as a good place to be *from,* on the way to some such place as *Asgard,* the abode of the gods. Rome, Byzantium, Normandy, and Britain were all chosen in their turn as earthly versions of *Asgard*. For a while, in the later Stone Age, the earliest emigrants could simply retrace their fathers' footsteps back to Europe, for the Danish Sounds were dry then, and dry land in the southern North Sea made Britain a peninsula before Scandinavia became one. By Roman and Viking times, given access to long ships, emigration continued to be almost as easy as it was fashionable. If one looks at a map of the land of the midnight sun (and remembers what happens when the sun goes

* This article was first published in The Yale Review for Winter 1960, copyright Yale University Press. It is reprinted here with permission.

down), it is easy to picture history as a series of glacial pulsations, or Gothic spurts, extruding adventurous Northmen toward successive seats of power, and milder winters. Nowadays, possibly because the northern weather is improving, the emigrants are less warlike than they used to be, and Visigoths and Vikings have tended to give way to movie actresses and physicists. The last of the great landwasters, Gustavus Adolphus, died more than three hundred years ago. It was only a few years before his time—in 1579 to be exact—that the animal kingdom seems to have caught the idea and carried it on, for that is the first year in which the now-famous lemmings are known to have been on the march.

Biologists, of whom I am one, have been taking a lively interest in lemmings lately. These rat-sized hyperborean field mice were unknown in the ancient world, and even the sagas are strangely silent about them. They really began to draw attention only in Queen Victoria's time, and especially in England, when the notion somehow got about that Plato's Atlantis lay on the Dogger Bank, under the North Sea. The lemmings' efforts to emigrate from Norway were then explained as vain attempts to recover a lost homeland, now occupied by such thoroughly English creatures as the haddock and the sprat. The fact that Swedish lemmings march in the wrong direction, toward the Baltic, tends to undermine this theory, but science has not come up with a better explanation until very recently. Biologists always hesitate to impute human motives to animals, but they are beginning to learn from psychologists, for whom attributing animal motives to humans is part of the day's work. What is now suspected is that the lemmings are driven by some of the same Scandinavian compulsions that drove the Goths. At home, according to this view, they become depressed and irritable during the long, dark winters under the snow. When home becomes intolerable, they emigrate, and their behavior is then described by the old Norse word, *berserk*.

A lemming migration is one of the great eruptions of nature, and its reverberations, like fallout, are of more than local concern. Biologists like to picture nature in the abstract as a sort of irregular lattice, or Mondrian construction, composed of feeding relations, whose seemingly random placement is actually so tightly organized that every strut depends on all the others. The lemmings' place in this picture is that of a strut more easily fretted than most, because, like other vegetarians that nourish a variety of carnivores, they are more fed upon than feeding. As Caruso's vocal cords, suitably vibrated, could shatter glassware, the whole of animate creation sometimes seems to pulsate with the supply of lemmings. In normal years they live obscurely, if dangerously, in the mountains of Scandinavia, and on the Arctic tundra generally. Periodically, despite the efficient efforts of their enemies—which include such mainstays of the fur industry as the marten and the white fox—their reproductive prowess gets the upper hand, and the tundra fairly teems with them. At such times, about every four years somewhere in Norway, though any given district is afflicted less frequently, the balance of nature goes entirely awry, and the Mondrian composition seems to degenerate into parody. Sea birds give up fishing and flock far inland to gorge on lemmings, while the more local hawks and owls hatch and feed families that are several times larger than usual. Foxes, on the shores of the Arctic Ocean, have been known to hunt for lemmings fifty miles out on the pack ice. The reindeer, which ordinarily subsist on reindeer moss, acquire a taste for lemmings just as cattle use salt. Eventually, faced with such troubles (but not necessarily *because* of them—I'm coming to that), lemmings are seized with the classic, or rather Gothic, obsession, and millions of them desert the tundra for the lowlands.

The repercussions then begin in earnest. As the clumsy animals attempt to swim the lakes and rivers, the predatory circle widens to include the trout and salmon, which understandably lose interest in dry flies. The forested lowlands, already occupied by other kinds of rodents as well as by farmers and their dogs and cats, are not good lemming country—the winters are too warm, for one thing—but while the lemmings press on as though aware of this, they show no sign of losing their disastrous appetites. When the crops are gone, though seldom before, exorcism by a Latin formula is said to have some slight effect in abating the plague. Finally, the vanguard may actually reach the sea, and, having nowhere else to go, plunge in—sometimes meeting another army trying to come ashore from a nearby island. A steamer, coming up Trondheim Fjord in November 1868, took fifteen minutes to pass through a shoal of them, but they were swimming *across* the fjord, not down it to the sea. The landward part of their wake is a path of destruction, strewn with dead lemmings, and an epidemic focus of lemming fever—which is not something the lemmings *have,* but a kind of tularemia that people get from handling the carcasses. As the Norwegians take up this unenviable chore their thoughts rarely turn to Mondrian or any other artist; the better-read among them may wonder, however, who buried the six hundred members of the Light Brigade.

American lemmings migrate too, but their outbreaks are observed less often, because no cities lie in their path. Knowledgeable bird-watchers are kept posted, nevertheless, by invasions of snowy owls, which leave the tundra when the lemming tide has passed its flood, and appear in such unlikely places as Charleston, the Azores, and Yugoslavia. Every four years or so, therefore, the lemmings affect the practice of taxidermy, and the economics of the glass-eye industry, as the handsome but unhappy birds fall trophy to amateur marksmen while vainly quartering the fields of France and New England. Closer to the center of the disturbance, the cities of western Norway see lemmings before they see owls, and they are not unknown as far away from the mountains as Stockholm, though spring fever is reported to be commoner than lemming fever along the Baltic beaches of Sweden. Oslo is ordinarily too far south, but was visited in 1862, in 1876, in 1890, and again in 1910. The 1862 migration, coinciding with the Battle of Antietam, may have been the greatest of the century, and one of its episodes was touching, if not prophetic. The Norwegian naturalist Robert

Collett saw them, he said, "running up the high granite stairs in the vestibule of the University" (of Oslo). Evidently they were begging to be investigated by professors. The Norwegian savants were busy, however, and scorned the impertinent intrusion. In 1862 the discoverer of the death wish, Sigmund Freud, was a six-year-old boy in far-away Freiburg, and if he ever saw a lemming or shot a snowy owl his biographers have repressed it.

That the lemmings are neurotically sick animals, at least during migration, has not escaped the notice of close, or even of casual, observers. For one thing, they wander abroad in the daytime, as small mammals rarely do. For another, when crossed or cornered they show a most unmouselike degree of fight; as Collett said, "they viciously drive their sharp teeth into the foot, or the stick advanced toward them, and allow themselves to be lifted high up by their teeth." Descriptions of the last snarling stages of the march to the sea recall the South Ferry terminal at rush hour, or a hundred-car smashup on a California turnpike. In his authoritative and starkly titled book, *Voles, Mice, and Lemmings*, the English biologist, Charles Elton, summed up "this great cosmic oscillation" as "a rather tragic procession of refugees, with all the obsessed behaviour of the unwanted stranger in a populous land, going blindly on to various deaths." Offhand, however, neurosis does not seem to explain very much of this, any more than shellshock is a cause of war, and, in trying to understand the upheaval, the experts have tended to set the psychopathic symptoms to one side while looking for something more basic.

That something, presumably, would be some property of the lemmings' environment—food, predators, disease, or weather, or perhaps all working together that periodically relaxes its hold on the mournful numbers. Find the cause of the overcrowding, so the thinking has run, and you will find why the lemmings leave home. But this thinking, though doubtless correct, has been slow to answer the question, because it tends to divert attention from the actors to the scenery. The oldest Norse references to lemmings confuse them with locusts, and the farmer whose fields are devastated can hardly be expected to count the pests' legs and divide by four. More detached students know that mammals do not drop from the sky, but in their own way they too have been misled by the locust analogy, supposing that lemmings swarm, as locusts do, because of something done *to* them by their surroundings. The discovery that the migrations are cyclical, made only a few years ago by Elton, strengthened the assumption that some environmental regularity, probably a weather cycle, must set the tune, to which the lemmings, their predators, and their diseases respond in harmonics. Close listeners to nature's symphony soon reported, however, that it sounded atonal to them, more like Berg's opera *Wozzeck,* say, than like Beethoven's Sixth. Cycles of heavenly conjunctions were also looked into, but while the tides are pulled by the sun and moon, and the seasons are undeniably correlated with the zodiac, nothing in astrology reasonably corresponds to a four-year cycle.

If the lemmings' quadrennial fault lies, not in their stars, but in themselves, it is easy to see why the fact has been missed for so long. One reason, of course, is that most of their home life takes place under several feet of snow, in uncomfortable regions where even Scandinavians pass little time outdoors. The main trouble has been, though, as a quick review of thirty years' work will show, that the lemmings' path is thickly sown with false clues. Among these the snowy owls and white foxes rank as the reddest of herrings. The idea that the abundance of prey is controlled by the abundance of predators is a piece of folklore that is hard to uproot, because, like other superstitions, it is sometimes true. The farmers and gamekeepers of Norway have acted on it with sublime confidence for more than a hundred years, backed by a state system of bounty payments, and hawks, foxes, and other predators are now much scarcer there than they are in primeval Westchester County, for example. The result has been that while the grouse-shooting is no better than it used to be, the lemmings (and the field mice in the lowlands, where varmints are persecuted most actively) have continued to fluctuate with unabated vigor. A pile of fox brushes, augmented mainly every fourth year remains as a monument to a mistaken theory, but their owners may take some gloomy pride in having furnished a splendid mass of statistics.

An even more seductive body of data exists in the account books of the Arctic fur trade, some of which go back to Revolutionary days. They give a remarkable picture of feast or famine, most kinds of skins being listed as thousands of times more plentiful in good years than in lean. Those that belonged to the smaller predators, such as the white fox and the ermine, rise and fall in numbers with the hauntingly familiar four-year rhythm, and the trappers' diaries (which make better reading than the bookkeepers' ledgers) show that their authors placed the blame squarely, or cyclically, on lemmings. Farther south there are periodic surges among such forest-dwellers as the marten and the red fox, whose fluctuating food supply is field mice. Lynx pelts, known to the trade under various euphemisms for "cat," show a still more beautiful cycle of ten years' length, which certainly matches the abundance of showshoe hares, the lynxes' principal prey. The ten-year pulse of lynxes was extricated, after a brief but noisy academic scuffle, from the coils of the eleven-year sunspot cycle, and by the mid-'thirties the theory of mammal populations had settled down about like this: the prey begin to increase, and so do their slower-breeding predators; at peak abundance the predators nearly exterminate the prey, and then starve to death, so clearing the way for the prey to start the cycle over again.

The simple elegance of this idea made it enormously appealing, not least to mathematicians, who reduced it to equations and found it to have an astonishing amount of what they call *generality*. In physics, for instance, it is the "theory of coupled oscillations"; as "servomechanism theory" it underlies many triumphs of engineering, such as remote control by radar; in economics, it explains the tendency for the prices of linked products, such as corn and hogs, to chase each other in perpetually balanced imbalance. Regardless of the price of hogs, or furs, however, some killjoys soon declared that the formulae seemed not to apply to rodents. Some populations of snowshoe hares, for example, were found to oscillate on islands where lynxes, or predators of any sort, were scarcer than mathematicians. Besides, the equations require the coupled numbers of predator and prey to rise and fall smoothly, like tides, whereas the normal pattern of mammal cycles is one of gradual crescendo, followed abruptly by a crashing silence. A Russian biologist, G. F. Gause, was therefore led to redesign the theory in more sophisticated form. The predator, he said, need not be a fur-bearing animal; it can be an infectious disease. When the prey is scarce, the chance of infection is small, especially if the prey, or host, has survived an epidemic and is immune. As the hosts become more numerous, the infection spreads faster, or becomes more virulent, until the ensuing epidemic causes the crash.

In this new, agar-plated guise the theory was not only longer, lower, and more powerful; it was testable without recourse to the fur statistics, the study of which had come to resemble numerology. Made newly aware of lemming fever and tularemia, pathologists shed their white coats for parkas, and took their tubes and sterilizers into the field. The first reports were painfully disappointing: wild rodents, including lemmings, harbored no lack of interesting diseases, but the abundance of microbes had no connection with that of their hosts. Worse, the animals seemed to enjoy their ill health, even when their numbers were greatest, and when they died there was no sign of an epidemic. Not of infectious disease, anyway; but there was one malady, prevalent among snowshoe hares, that certainly was not infectious, but that just as certainly caused a lot of hares to drop dead, not only in live-traps, but also in the woods when no one was around. Long and occasionally sad experience with laboratory rabbits suggested a name, shock disease, for this benign but fatal ailment, the symptoms of which were reminiscent of apoplexy, or of insulin shock. The diagnosis, if that is what it was, amounted to saying that the hares were scared to death, not by lynxes (for the bodies hardly ever showed claw-marks), but, presumably, by each other. Having made this unhelpful pronouncement, most of the pathologists went home. The Second World War was on by that time, and for a while no one remembered what Collett had said about the lemmings: "Life quickly leaves them, and they die from the slightest injury . . . It is constantly stated by eyewitnesses, that they can die from their great excitement."

These Delphic remarks turned out to contain a real clue, which had been concealed in plain sight, like the purloined letter. An inquest on Minnesota snowshoe hares was completed in 1939, and its clinical language describes a grievous affliction. In the plainer words of a later writer,

> This syndrome was characterized primarily by fatty degeneration and atrophy of the liver with a coincident striking decrease in liver glycogen and a hypoglycemia preceding death. Petechial or ecchymotic brain hemorrhages, and congestion and

hemorrhage of the adrenals, thyroid, and kidneys were frequent findings in a smaller number of animals. The hares characteristically died in convulsive seizures with sudden onset, running movements, hind-leg extension, retraction of the head and neck, and sudden leaps with clonic seizures upon alighting. Other animals were typically lethargic or comatose.

For connoisseurs of hemorrhages this leaves no doubt that the hares were sick, but it does leave open the question of how they got that way. Well-trained in the school of Pasteur, or perhaps of Paul de Kruif, the investigators had been looking hard for germs, and were slow to take the hint of an atrophied liver, implying that shock might be a social disease, like alcoholism. As such, it could be contagious, like a hair-do, without being infectious. It might, in fact, be contracted in the same way that Chevrolets catch petechial tail fins from Cadillacs, through the virus of galloping, convulsive anxiety. A disorder of this sort, increasing in virulence with the means of mass communication, would be just the coupled oscillator needed to make Gause's theory work. So theatrical an idea had never occurred to Gause, though, and before it could make much progress the shooting outside the windows had to stop. About ten years later, when the news burst on the world that hares are mad in March, it lacked some of the now-it-can-be-told immediacy of the Smyth Report on atomic energy, but it fitted neatly into the bulky dossier on shock disease that had been quietly accumulating in the meantime.

As a matter of fact, for most of those ten years shock disease was a military secret, as ghastly in some of its implications as the Manhattan Project. Armies are not supposed to react like frightened rabbits, but the simple truth, that civilians in uniform can suffer and die from shock disease, was horrifyingly evident in Korea. As was revealed after the war, hundreds of American captives, live-trapped while away from home and mother, had turned lethargic or comatose, or died in convulsive seizures with sudden onset. Their baffled buddies gave it the unsympathetic name of "give-up-itis."

Military interest in rodents was whipped up long before 1939, of course, but its basis, during more ingenuous ages, was not the rodents' psyches. Rats have fought successfully, if impartially, in most of mankind's wars, but the Second World War was probably the first in which large numbers of rodents were deliberately kept on active duty while others were systematically slaughtered. To explain this curious evenhandedness, and at the risk of considerable oversimplification, we may divide military rodents (including rabbits, which are not rodents, but lagomorphs, according to purists) into two platoons, or squadrons. First, there are wild, or Army-type rodents, which not only nibble at stores but carry various diseases; they are executed when captured. Then there are domestic, cabined, or Navy-type rodents; during the war these were mainly watched by Navy psychologists in an effort to understand the military mind. The story of the first kind was superbly told by the late Hans Zinsser in *Rats, Lice, and History,* a runaway best-seller in the years between World Wars. Conceivably as a result, there were no outbreaks of louse-born typhus in the Second World War, but, in the course of their vigil, wildlife men continued to run into pathologists at Army messes around the world. The yarn of the Navy's rats has never been publicized, however (except, obliquely, in such studies of mass anxiety as William H. Whyte's *The Organization Man*).

The kind of nautical problem the psychologists had in mind was not the desertion of sinking ships, but the behavior of men under tension. The crowding of anxious but idle seamen in submarines, for instance, had had some fairly unmartial effects, which needed looking into. As subjects, when mariners were unavailable, the psychologists naturally used rats, which can be frustrated into states of high anxiety that simulate combat neurosis. So now, to recapitulate, there were *three* kinds of rodent experts in the Pacific theatre—zoologists, pathologists, and psychologists—and when they met, as they often did at the island bases, something was bound to happen. What emerged was a fresh view of rats, with which some of the lonelier islands were infested. These were no ordinary rats, but a special breed, like the Pitcairn Islanders, a sort of stranded landing-party. They were descendants of seagoing ancestors, marooned when the whalers had left; but, as the only wild mammals on the islands, they had reverted to Army type. It was soon noticed that when they entered messhalls and BOQ's they solved intellectual problems with great acumen, along with some anxiety-based bravado. Outdoors, on the other hand, their populations went up and down, and when abundant they terrorized the nesting seabirds or ran in droves through the copra plantations. Often, too, they simply dropped dead of shock. In short, they were rats, but whereas in confinement they behaved like psychologists, when at liberty they acted remarkably like lemmings.

If islanded feral rats contributed to the lemming problem, biologists could take wry pleasure in the fact, for most of the rats' contributions to insular existence—to the extinction of hundreds of kinds of interesting land birds, for instance—have been a lot less positive. Then, too, a back-to-nature movement led by psychologists promised to be an exhilarating experience, especially if it included an id-hunt through Polynesia. I have to admit, though, that it didn't work out quite that way, and my account of events in the Pacific theatre may be more plausible than accurate. The published facts are scanty, and my own duty as a Navy biologist was spent amid barnacles, not rodents, on the Eastern Sea Frontier. My first-hand knowledge of Pacific islands, in fact, is confined to Catalina, where rats are visible only on very clear days. What I *am* sure of is that startling things were learned in many countries, during the war years, about the capabilities of many kinds of animals besides rats. When these were added up it was not incredible that rodents might suffer the diseases of suburbia; some students would not have been surprised, by then, if bunnies were found to say "boo" to each other in Russian.

Bees, for example, were proved to be able to tell other bees, by means of a patterned dance like a polonaise, the direction and the distance from the hive at which food could be found, as well as the kind of flower to look for and the number of worker-bees needed to do the job. For compass directions they report the azimuth of the sun, but what they perceive is not the sun itself, but the arrangement of polarized light that the sun makes around the sky.

Navigating birds, on the other hand, take bearings on the sun directly, or on the stars, but when visual cues fail they fall back on an internal chronometer, conceivably their heart-beat, to reach their destination anyway.

Prairie-dogs in their towns pass socially accepted facts, such as the invisible boundaries between their neighborhoods, from one generation to the next; they do it by imitating each other, not by instinct, and European chickadees do the same with their trick, invented about 1940, of following milkmen on their routes and beating housewives to the bottled cream.

Ravens and jackdaws can count up to six or seven, and show that they can form an abstract concept of number by responding, correctly, whether the number is cued by spots on cards, by bells or buzzers, or by different spoken commands.

A Swedish bird called the nutcracker remembers precisely where it buried its nuts in the fall, then digs them up, in late March, say, confidently and without errors through two feet of snow.

For its sexual display, an Australian species called the satin bowerbird not only constructs a bower, or bachelor apartment, decorating it with flowers and *objets d'art,* as do other members of its family, but makes paint out of charcoal or fruit-juice and paints the walls of its bower, using a pledget of chewed bark for a daub.

Bats avoid obstacles in total darkness, and probably catch flying insects too, by uttering short, loud screams and guiding themselves by the echoes; the pitch is much too high for human ears to hear, but some kinds of moths can hear the bats coming and take evasive action.

Made groggy by facts like these, most of them reported between 1946 and 1950, biologists began to feel like the White Queen, who "sometimes managed to believe as many as six impossible things before breakfast." Still, no one had yet spent a winter watching rodents under the snow, and the epicene behavior of bowerbirds was not seen, then or since, as having any direct bearing on mammalian neurosis. If anything, the intellectual feats of birds and bees made it harder to understand how rodents could get into such sorry states; one might have credited them with more sense. Until new revelations from the Navy's rats laid bare their inmost conflicts, the point was arguable, at least, that anxiety is a sort of hothouse bloom, forced in psychologists' laboratories, and could not survive a northern winter.

As a footnote in a recent article makes clear, the United States Navy takes no definite stand on rodents. "The opinions or assertions contained herein," it says (referring to a report on crowded mice), "are the private ones of the writer, and are not to be construed as official or reflecting the views of the Navy Department or naval service at large." This disavowal is a little surprising, in that its author, John J. Christian, as head of the animal laboratories of the Naval Medical Research Institute at Bethesda, Maryland, can be considered the commander of the Navy's rodents. Ten years ago, though, when he wrote what may be thought of as the Smyth Report on population cycles, his opinions were temporarily freed from protocol. An endocrinologist and Navy lieutenant (j.g.), Christian had left the Fleet and gone back to studying mice at the Wyeth Institute, in Philadelphia. His luminous essay was published where anyone at large could read it, in the August 1950 issue of the *Journal of Mammalogy,* under the title "The Adreno-Pituitary System and Population Cycles in Mammals." In it Christian said, in part:

> We now have a working hypothesis for the die-off terminating a cycle. Exhaustion of the adreno-pituitary system resulting from increased stresses inherent in a high population, especially in winter, plus the late winter demands of the reproductive system, due to increased light or other factors, precipitates population-wide death with the symptoms of adrenal insufficiency and hypoglycemic convulsions.

Dedicated readers of the *Journal* remembered the snowshoe hares' congested adrenals, and did not need to be reminded that shock is a glandular disorder. They also knew their scientific Greek, and easily translated *hypoglycemia* as "lack of sugar in the blood"; but what they found new and fascinating was Christian's clinical evidence—much of it reported by a young Viennese internist named Hans Selye—tending to show that rodents might die, of all things, from a surfeit of sexuality. Most people had thought of rabbits as adequately equipped for reproduction, but that is not the point, as Christian developed it: what does them in is not breeding, exactly, but concupiscence. Keyed up by the stresses of crowded existence—he instanced poor and insufficient food, increased exertion, and fighting—animals that have struggled through a tough winter are in no shape to stand the lust that rises like sap in the spring. Their endocrine glands, which make the clashing hormones, burn sugar like a schoolgirl making fudge, and the rodents, not being maple trees, have to borrow sugar from their livers. Cirrhosis lies that way, of course, but death from hypertension usually comes first.

In medical jargon, though the testy author of *Modern English Usage* would protest, the name for this state of endocrine strain is *stress*. As the physical embodiment of a mental state, anxiety, it is worth the respectful attention of all who believe, with mammalogists, that life can be sweet without necessarily caramelizing the liver. Despite its technicality, the subject is uncommonly rewarding. It is not only that seeing a lemming as a stressed animal goes far toward clearing up a famous mystery. And, although the how and why of psychosomatic ailments in wild rodents are undeniably important to tame men, the problems of gray flannel suits are not my main concern. The real attraction of stress, at least for a biologist, consists simply in the way it works: it turns out to contain a whole array of built-in servomechanisms. That is, the coupled oscillation of hosts and diseases, which Gause thought underlie the fluctuating balance of nature, is mimicked inside the body, and may be said to be controlled, by mutual inter-action between the glands. Biologists are impressed by abstract resemblances of this sort, which, after all, are their version of *generality*. In explaining stress by means of some fairly garish metaphors, therefore, I find it soothing to re-member that what is called "imagery" in some circles is "model-making" in others.

As it happens, the master himself is no slouch at imagery. Selye's recent book, *The Stress of Life,* is notable, among other things, for its skillful use of the didactic, or Sunday-supplement, analogy. Without plagiarizing his exposition, though, it is possible to speak of vital needs as payable in sugar, for which the liver acts as a bank. Routine withdrawals are smoothly handled by hormones from the pancreas and from the adrenal medulla, which act as paying tellers; but the top-level decisions (such as whether to grow or to reproduce) are reserved for the bank's officers, the adrenal cortex and pituitary glands. Stress, in Selye's view, amounts to an administrative flap among the hormones, and shock results when the management overdraws the bank.

If the banking model is gently dissected, it reveals its first and most important servomechanism: a remarkably bureaucratic hookup between the adrenal cortex, acting as cashier's office, and the pituitary, as board of directors. Injury and infection are common forms of stress, and in directing controlled inflammation to combat them the cortex draws cashier's checks on the liver. If the stress persists, a hormone called cortisone sends a worried message to the pituitary. Preoccupied with the big picture, the pituitary delegates a vice-presidential type, ACTH or adrenocorticotropic hormone, whose role is literally to buck up the adrenal cortex. As students of Parkinson would predict, the cortex, bucked, takes on more personnel, and expands its activities, including that of summoning more ACTH. The viciousness of the impending spiral ought to be obvious, and ordinarily it is; but while withdrawals continue, the amount of sugar in circula-tion is deceptively constant (the work of another servomechanism), and there is no device, short of autopsy, for taking inventory at the bank. If the pituitary is conned by persisting stress into throwing more support to ACTH, the big deals begin to suffer retrenchment. A cutback of ovarian hormone, for instance, may allow the cortex to treat a well-started foetus as an inflammation to be healed over. Likewise, the glandular sources of virility and of maternity, though un-equally prodigal of sugar, are equally likely to dry up. Leaving hypertension aside (because it involves another commodity, salt, which needn't be gone into just now), the fatal symptom can be hypoglycemia. A tiny extra stress, such as a loud noise (or, as Christian would have it, the sight of a lady rabbit), cor-responds to an unannounced visit by the bank examiner: the adrenal medulla is startled into sending a jolt of adrenalin to the muscles, the blood is drained of sugar, and the brain is suddenly starved. This, incidentally, is why shock looks like hyperinsulinism. An overactive pancreas, like a panicky adrenal, re-sembles an **un**trustworthy teller with his hand in the till.

Haruspicy, or divination by inspection of the entrails of domestic animals, is supposed to have been extinct for two thousand years, and no one knows what the Etruscan soothsayers made of a ravaged liver. Selye would snort, no doubt, at being called a modern haruspex, but the omens of public dread are at least as visceral as those of any other calamity, and there are some sound Latin precedents—such as the geese whose gabbling saved Rome—for the view that emotion is communicable to and by animals. More recently, thoughtful veterinarians have begun to notice that neurotic pets tend to have neurotic owners, and a report from the Philadelphia Zoo blames "social pressures," on the rise for the last two decades, for a tenfold increase of arteriosclerosis among the inmates. If Selye seems to be playing down anxiety—the word is not even listed in the index of his book—I can think of two possible reasons, both interesting if not entirely convincing. Anxiety is an ugly word, of course, and using it can easily generate more of it, just as calling a man an insomniac can keep him awake all night; Selye, as a good physician, may well have hesitated to stress it in a popular book about stress. More important, probably, is the fact that Selye, like any internist, begins and ends his work with bodily symptoms, and only grudgingly admits the existence of mind. A curious piece of shoptalk, which he quotes approvingly and in full from a San Francisco medical man (not a psychiatrist), suggests that some of his professional colleagues, like too many novelists, have read Freud without understanding him:

> The dissociation of the ego and the id has many forms. I had an American housewife with dermatomyositis [an inflammation of skin and muscles] [the brackets are Selye's] who had been taught how to play the piano when she was little, and had continued for the entertainment of the children, but didn't get very far. When she started on large doses of ACTH she was suddenly able to play the most difficult works of Beethoven and Chopin—and the children of the neighbors would gather in the garden to hear her play. Here was a dissociation of the ego and the id that was doing good. But she also became a little psychotic, and so her dosage of ACTH had to be lowered, and with every 10 units of ACTH one sonata disappeared. It had ended up with the same old music poorly performed.

The false note here, of course, is that business about "the dissociation of the ego and the id." Whatever the id may be, it is not considered innately musical, and *my* professional colleagues would count it a triumph to be able to teach it anything, even "Chopsticks." Still, we may take the anecdote as showing *some* kind of mental effect of stress; what the psychologist sees as rather more to the point is the obverse of this: moods and emotions cannot be injected hypodermically, but their cost is paid in sugar, and their action on the cortex is precisely that of ACTH. Christian finds, for instance, that crowding mice in cages enlarges their adrenals, but fortunately, in experiments of this sort, it is not always necessary to kill the animals to learn the answer. A microscope sample of blood reveals a useful clue to endocrine tension: college students at exam time show a shortage of the same type of white cell that is also scarce in the blood of crowded mice. (The skittish blood cells are called *eosinophils;* I mention this because the word is sure to turn up in detective stories before long.) The fact that tranquillizing drugs do their work by blocking various hormones opens up another line of evidence, as well as a fertile field for quackery. But the surest sign that anxiety is stress—and its most lurid property—is its ability to visit itself on the unborn. The maker of this appalling discovery, William R. Thompson of Wesleyan University, tells us nothing of the sins of his rats' fathers, but his report shows all too clearly that the offspring of frustrated mothers, part of whose pregnancy was spent in problem boxes with no exit, carried the emotional disturbance thoughout their own lives. Nestling birds can learn the parents' alarm call while still inside the egg (as the nearly-forgotten author of *Green Mansions* was among the first to notice), but the mammalian uterus is more soundproof, and the only reasonable explanation of Thompson's results is that the aroused maternal hormones perverted the silver cord, and made it a pipeline to a forbidden supply of sugar.

Circumspectly, now, so as to forestall any harumphs from the naval service at large, we may return to Christian's crowded mice. In outward demeanor the ordinary house mouse, *Mus musculus,* is the least military of rodents, but his dissembling is part of the commando tradition, and he would not have got where he is today without a lot of ruthless infighting. Nowadays house mice spend little time outdoors if they can help it, but in more rustic times they often scourged the countryside, like Marion's men, and the tenth-century Bishop of Bingen (who perished in the Mouse Tower) learned to his cost that country mice can be pushed too far. Recently, at some of our leading universities (Oslo, strange to say, has still not been heard from), mouse-watching has proved informative, if not exactly edifying, and I cull a few tidbits from the notes of some shocked colleagues:

The first thing to notice is that the old murine spirit of mass emigration is not yet dead, despite the effeteness of modern urban living. Not long ago an outbreak was observed—provoked, in fact—at the University of Wisconsin, where the scientists had set up a mouse tower, or substitute patch of tundra, in a junkroom in the basement of the zoology building, and set traps (not enough, as it turned out) in the neighboring offices and laboratories. Nothing happened for a while, except that the food—half a pound of it a day—kept disappearing. Then, in Browning's words, "the muttering grew to a grumbling; and the grumbling grew to a mighty rumbling"; and the experiment, though publishable, became unpopular; the room was simply overstuffed with mice, like a sofa in a neglected summer cottage.

Chastened, yet encouraged by this experience, the zoologists fell back on emigration-proof pens, where they could keep tab on the mice. Taking census whenever they cleaned the cages (which was pretty often, at someone's pointed insistence), they noticed that the numbers went up and down, but, as there were no seasons or predators and food was always abundant, the fluctuations made little sense at first. Gradually, though, when one of the observers, Charles Southwick, thought to count the tiffs as well as the mice, the shiny outlines of a servomechanism came into sight: as each wave of numbers crested and broke, the scuffles averaged more than one per mouse-hour, and hardly any young mice survived to the age of weaning. Putting the matter this way lays the blame, unchivalrously, on the mothers, and in fact, as the tension mounted, their nest-building became slovenly and some of them failed to nurse their litters, or even ate them (proper mouse food, remember, was always plentiful). But the males were equally responsible, though for different hormonal reasons. Like chickens with their peck-order, the buck mice were more concerned for status than for posterity, and the endocrine cost of supremacy was sexual impotence. In one of the pens two evenly-matched pretenders played mouse-in-the-manger with the females, and suppressed all reproduction until they died.

While the Wisconsin mice were either suffering from stress or practicing a peculiarly savage form of moral restraint, mice at other centers were also made unhappy, or at least infertile, by being given plenty of food, space, and sexual access. It came as no great surprise, then, when the adrenals of Christian's mice were found to swell, as he had predicted eight years before, in proportion to the numbers of their social companions. The really arresting experiment, which dilutes the inhumanity of some of the others, shows that rodents—rats, at any rate—*prefer* to be crowded and anxious. At the National Institutes of Health, in Bethesda, John C. Calhoun allowed litter-mates to grow up in one large pen, where every rat had an individual food hopper. From the start, when eating, they huddled like a farrow at a single hopper; later, though free to roam, eat, and nest in four intercommunicating pens, these rats and their descendants spent most of their time in one of the four, and as I write this they are still there, paying for their sociability in lowered fertility and shortened lives. For his part, my friend Calhoun coined a phrase that deserves to outlive his rats, and is still musing on *pathological togetherness.*

At this point in the argument, explaining the lemmings' periodic dementia should be anticlimactically easy. I seem to have overstated the case, in fact, for it seems less Gothic than *gothick,* like some of the more unnecessary behavior described by the brothers Grimm. The cycle starts where population problems always do, with the lemmings' awesome power of procreation. Nubile at the age of thirty-five days, averaging seven or eight young at a cast, a female lemming may have worries, but barrenness is not one of them, and four litters is par for a summer's dalliance. Lemming life is more austere in winter, but not much. As long as food is plentiful under the snow, the winter sport of pullulation and fighting continue as at a disreputable ski resort. The wonder is—until we remember the owls and foxes above and the weasels *in* the runways—that it takes as long as four years for the numbers to become critical, like the mass of an atomic bomb. When the Thing goes off, then, it is the younger lemmings that emigrate, in search of a patch of tundra that is slightly more private than the

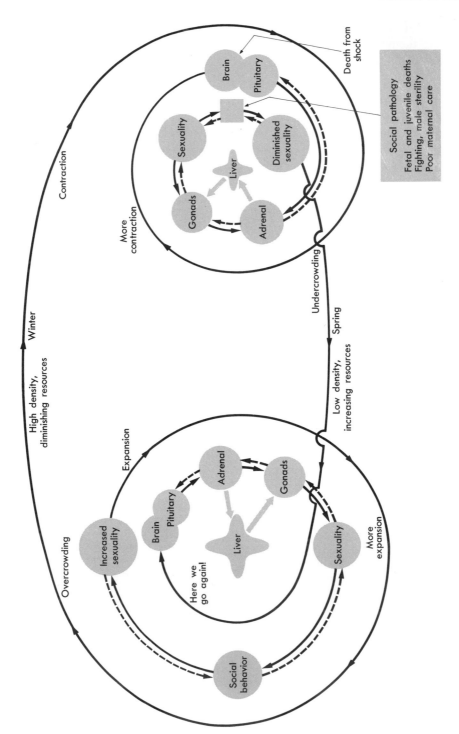

FIG. 1

beach at Coney Island; though less overtly anxious to begin with, presumably, their state of mind on reaching downtown Oslo is another matter entirely. The older, better-established residents, or those with stouter livers, stay home and die of shock—having first passed on the family disease to the next generation. Before the epidemic of stress has run its course, it spreads to the predators, too (though *this* form of lemming fever is caught, ironically, from *not* eating lemmings). The snowy owl that died at Fayal, Azores, in 1928 may or may not have known that it had really reached Atlantis, but in being shot by an anxious man it provided a textbook, or postgraduate, example of a coupled oscillation.

If all this is true, and I think it is, the Norse clergymen who exorcized the lemmings in Latin were clearly on the right track, and what the Scandinavians need is a qualified haruspex. Before they hire one, though (I am not a candidate), or resort to spraying the tundra with tranquillizers (which would be expensive), there is one tiny reservation: there is not a scrap of *direct* evidence that the lemming suffers from stress. Come to think of it, no one has yet spent a winter watching lemmings under the snow. (Some Californian zoologists lived for several winters in Alaska, trying valiantly to do just that, but the runways are pretty small for Californians, and for most of the time there was trouble finding *any* lemmings.) Except for some circumstantial lesions of the skin, which could be psychosomatic, like shingles (and which ruin the lemming's pelt), the case for contagious anxiety therefore rests on a passel of tormented rodents, but not as yet on *Lemmus lemmus*. That animal has baffled a lot of people, and I could be mistaken too. But if I am, or at least if the lemmings' adrenals are not periodically congested, I will eat a small population of them, suitably seasoned with Miltown. Fortunately, lemmings are reported to taste like squirrels, but better; in Lapland, in fact, with men who know rodents best, it's lemmings, two to one.

Sociobiology and Man

A. M. GUHL*

Man's primary need today is to cooperate with his fellow man, and all too often his failure to do so results in man's inhumanity to man. Cooperation has been a problem for primitive tribes, city-states, nations, and ethnic groups. Today, the hesitancy to cooperate on the international level threatens man's very existence. On the individual level we face criminal and social maladjustments. If the bombs don't get us, the neuroses or the stress-syndrome may. At the same time, men of intelligence, faith, and a high degree of moral and social consciousness are making remarkable contributions to man's better understanding of man. Can experimental science, especially sociobiology, contribute its share?

One may suggest as an hypothesis that man's social problems are due, in part at least, to his tendency to assume that he lives above natural laws; that his thoughts and behavior have their roots in mysticism. He does not realize that natural laws, unlike manmade laws, are never broken, but are only illustrated by the consequences. Therefore, let us explore the suggestive principles and concepts from sociobiology that are common to most vertebrates.

To a zoologist, man is an animal, a vertebrate, a mammal, and, more specifically, a primate. *Homo sapiens* has a physiology and reproductive and genetic mechanisms similar to those of animals closely related to him. He differs from them to a very marked degree in his capacity to learn and in his use of syntax; his near relatives can convey only simple signals, like those denoting the presence of food or danger, or those from parents to young. He can deal in abstractions, a trait which the chimpanzee shows to a limited extent. According to Huxley, man's future physical evolution is unpromising at best; but his social inheritance by way of libraries, machine tools, and tradition as culture is unlimited in its

* Department of Zoology, Kansas State University.

possibilities and unique in the animal kingdom. Man is highly subjective but it behooves him, as a rational being, to be very objective about his subjectivity.

There are two fundamental ways man may learn to improve his earthly status: through deductions from past experience by highly intuitive, sensitive individuals, or by scientific experimentation. We need to consider both. Even though our religious and social traditions do not permit biological experimentation with man, and we have no controls when we deal with situations as they naturally occur, we can apply our scientific knowledge to man's social welfare.

Medicine became a science when it forsook the medicine man with his shouting and drum beating and turned to animal experimentation. It learned about man's metabolic processes, hormones, the effects of drugs, and the causes and cures of diseases. Similarly, psychology became a science when it learned about mechanisms of behavior, reaction patterns, learning, frustration, and neuroses in animals. It has been demonstrated that basic principles discovered by animal experimentation can be applied to man if the animals are vertebrates and if they are closely related to man in their physical attributes. Therefore, it is relevant to discover principles in the social life of vertebrates with the hope of obtaining some inferences applicable to humans. In fact, many such studies have been made with animals ranging from fish to primates, and some generalizations are now emerging.

Territorialism and dominance

Members of many species of backboned animals are aggressive or self-assertive and threaten or attack their associates. Since they also display the trait of submissiveness, they may submit to domination or avoid their social superiors. Thus highly aggressive individuals of many species dominate most of their numbers within a given locality in competitive situations and thereby attain certain rights. Animals that live in groups may be organized on the basis of precedence through domination. The order of precedence promotes group integration as each individual learns when and where to exercise his rights. Although there is much variation between species, there are two main categories of social organization: territorialism and dominance or peck orders.

Some animals in all classes of vertebrates display territorialism. For example, many of our songbirds establish territories. A mated pair selects an area in which a nest is built and the young are reared. Others of the same species are attacked when they enter or approach the area. The male's singing on high perches serves as a warning signal and advertises the territory. Such domains insure noninterference during mating, breeding, and rearing, and maintain a feeding area. This type of organization is reminiscent of human situations in early America, in which the farmstead provided all the needs for a family and the homesteader had to be his own defender.

Marine birds, such as gulls and terns, occupy ledges on cliffs; with limited space for a large population, they reduce territories to small circumscribed areas about the nest. The parents leave alternately to forage over the water, i.e., they go to work at a distance, and when one returns to the nest it undergoes a recognition ceremony before being admitted. This is analogous to the apartment living of *homo sapiens.* Strangers use the doorbell or take the consequences. Immature young, like children, are permitted to roam over the area without attack.

Dominance orders occur among animals that live in groups: herds, flocks, schools of fish, troops of primates. These hierarchies are based on the ranking of individuals according to the number of individuals each may dominate without any retaliation. The order may be linear or it may contain pecking triangles. In groups including both males and females, the males usually show passive dominance over the females, so that each sex has its own peck order. Most males will not tolerate henpecking.

In natural situations, the young develop within an established social unit, initially in close association with the mother and gradually in relationships with other young and with adults. Thus the learning milieu develops in complexity as the young mature and establish their positions in the animal society. Simpler experimental conditions with domestic fowl have shown that chicks reared together begin to fight at about the fourth week of age, and after some sparring they soon learn which ones to avoid so that by the tenth or twelfth week an order is formed. When unacquainted adults of either sex are brought together, they immediately begin to fight or peck, and the winner of each contest establishes the right to dominate the loser. After each penmate has settled its relationship with each in the flock, the peck order is established. Any latecomers are at a disadvantage because they must engage in an encounter with each of the residents. In time, as the habits of interaction become well established by reinforcement, the threats and avoidances become symbolic, involving no more than a raising and lowering of the head as two birds meet. Thus in both natural and experimental conditions, intensities of interaction are reduced and social inertia integrates the group. In human social relations, such tolerant responses are referred to as manners.

Status and the social order

At about the time that the discovery of peck orders was stimulating experimentation with a variety of animals, R. B. Cattell made an analysis of social classes in America. His criteria for status were items that people used for estimating whether a person ranked above or beneath them in the social scale, i.e., human methods of pecking. For example: prestige of occupation judged by attempts to reach it; size of income and whether it is paid as a salary or as a wage; social status of those with whom the individual associates in private life, recreational activities, and business; neighborhood lived in, and size and type of residence; amount of conspicuous expenditures on luxuries, recreation, and leisure. That social status exists in human society is now commonly recognized.

The concept of territorialism might also be useful in the study of problems in large urban areas. It is evident in simplified form in teenage gang warfare.

Although social inertia, as tradition, is a major factor in group integration, its stabilizing influence tends to retard intellectual and social progress.

In animal societies, the fact that gregarious animals tend to organize themselves into social hierarchies drew attention to the biological significance of such societies. It soon became evident that high rank carried certain advantages in obtaining food, shelter, and mates. The question of whether an integrated social organization had any benefits for the group as a whole arose and was tested over two decades ago with hens of the common fowl.

Flocks with stable social orders were contrasted with flocks in which the peck orders were kept in a state of flux by a regular rotation of the hens. Every other day the longest resident was removed and replaced by a stranger. The reserve birds were kept in isolation. The data obtained over a period of one year showed significant differences. Aggressive acts among the controls were symbolic and less frequent than among the experimental birds, i.e., social stress was pronounced among the alternated birds. The integrated groups consumed more food, maintained or gained in body weight, and laid more eggs than those undergoing constant reorganization. One may assume that, if similar situations were found in nature, the well integrated groups would have survival value, since social organization and integration conserve energy. For humans, the indications are that in a world shrunk by modern communication and transportation, with more frequent relations among various peoples, some form of organization to maintain a satisfactory balance between competition and cooperation is worthy of the effort.

An interesting by-product of the hen experiment was the evidence of seniority right. During the first two days in the group, a hen was usually at the bottom of the peck order, and it moved up gradually as its superiors were removed and newcomers added. Some obtained top rank initially, although one individual never moved from the lowest rank even on its last day in the pen. In groups of animals living in nature, the newcomers are usually the young that tend to follow the established pattern as the older members die. Thus seniority rights in man have a biological basis; however, the criteria for status should be more characteristic of his intellectual level.

Differences: genetic and cultural

Since chickens can recognize individuals, one may wonder whether they can also differentiate between breeds. Unfortunately, little has been done in animal studies that bear on the problem of racial and other minority groups within a social structure. In small flocks of hens, the odd individual is often driven and persecuted. Some experimenters have observed that individuals of one breed treat all individuals of a different color in the same manner. Others have observed that color differences between breeds are unimportant in large flocks and that individual recognition is typical. Different breeds reared together as chicks do not draw the color line. However, mixing breeds or even strains of the same color may have undesirable effects if they differ much in rates of development or in levels of aggressiveness. It must be noted here that these observations do not include any factors related to culture.

Genetic differences between breeds and between races of animals or man have been intriguing. By means of selective breeding we have obtained high and low aggressiveness strains within two breeds of chickens. One can only wonder whether differences between various peoples also have a genetic basis or whether they stem largely from early experience within different cultures or subcultures. One avenue of approach was attempted by Dobzhansky who considered the possible genetic consequences within a society that had rigidly closed castes for about one hundred generations. He concluded that the castes did not concentrate the genes for special abilities and aptitudes in particular breeding groups. Since most of man's behavior, as contrasted with that of higher vertebrates, is developed through learning, selection may be expected to be on the basis of culture. According to Huxley, when hominids became men, the psychosocial phase of evolution was initiated on this earth. Hence man can influence his own evolution through a scientific approach to human values.

Although culture is considered a unique characteristic of human society, it has simple precursors among some animals. There is no predisposition for culture among chickens; however, learned interactions within a flock may become relatively fixed as social inertia, which has a marked effect on certain biological functions. Rudiments of culture do exist among monkeys. Reports from Japan have shown cultural transmission among free living macaques. The habit of washing food or accepting candy was traced from the practice of one or more individuals to becoming common within the troop. Washburn and DeVore have reported that troops of baboons in Africa set up group territories without intermingling. Each troop has its own characteristic daily routine. The young spend many months in close association with their mothers and are a center of interest for all adults, including the dominant male. Thus traditions become established through generations. Learned behavior integrates the group and very little social strife has been reported among free living monkeys.

Ruth Benedict compared several primitive cultures and showed that they may mold individuals into societies that may have dominant traits of nonaggressiveness, animosity, or extreme rivalry. It is what man develops and learns in his culture that determines his way of life.

Can the social inertia and the traditions of a particular culture be changed without radical upheaval or revolution? Does Spengler's *Decline of the West* suggest that civilizations pass through the equivalent successive ecological stages, or did his observations result from the general migration into new lands which enabled new cultures to develop without the restrictions imposed by ingrained traditions? The pessimist envisages the possibility of the former brought about by atomic catastrophe and a civilization reconstituted from the ashes. But man is an intelligent animal whose cultural evolution is not derived from modified DNA but from discovery and learning. Cultures can grow in the same manner as populations.

Populations, whether micro-organisms, insects, or vertebrates, tend to follow the sigmoid or Gaussian curve when changes in size are plotted against time. The acceptance of hybrid corn, farm machinery, or home appliances follows the same pattern—which has been used by industry to project its plans for manufacture. A similar projection was made by Brode for the growth of science. Each new discovery has a stimulating effect and initiates another rise at the otherwise upper asymptote. One need only recall the effects of the telephone, the automobile, electronics, the electron microscope, and atomic physics to visualize an expanding culture. Nations that have not accepted these innovations have remained on the plateau of fixed cultures. Are our sociopolitical and philosophical ideologies more resistant to such stimulation?

We may conclude that man's social behavior has some of the same basic characteristics as those of other vertebrates, although greatly elaborated in detail. Have we progressed from the peck order stage of nations? Must we learn to develop a single culture for all mankind, or can a modicum of differences be tolerated effectively through learning, much as individuals learn to respect each other's beliefs? If man's development is cultural, then there must be some variability upon which selection may operate. As Dobzhansky has pointed out, there is a feedback relationship between the biological and the cultural evolution of mankind.

Man's future rests heavily on the collective utilization of his intelligence; on his seeking verifiable truths; on his developing curiosity, satisfying motives, and the desire for understanding; and on his skill in reaching sound judgments. Each generation in its development from an animal-like infancy must pass through stages during which it acquires the uniquely human traits and ideals which give life meaning and the realization that each individual's contribution to humanity is the ultimate in life. If man is to progress, he must contribute more to the search for truths and values and to their dissemination than to the mere addition of excess protoplasm to an already swelling mass.

POLLUTION
AND HEREDITARY
CONSEQUENCES

In the past 30 years, man has poured into the atmosphere radioactive contamination, automobile exhaust fumes, and pollutants from incinerators and industrial plants. As a consequence, the pollution of the air has become a major ecological factor with which we must contend. The papers by Comar and Haagen-Smit survey the many ways in which the air we breathe is contaminated. We have become very much aware that this contamination of the air results in harm not only to ourselves in our lifetime, but also very likely to our offspring yet to be born.

One of the comments by Comar needs to be amended. We are now aware that the Red Chinese do have nuclear weapons. The paper, nevertheless, still represents an excellent introduction to radiation and man. Comar hopes, as all sane men everywhere hope, that nuclear weapons will never again be used. He is correct in pointing out that all nuclear blasts in the atmosphere involve a biological cost that must always be weighed against the benefits brought to man. Most biologists (virtually all geneticists) believe that all radioactivity, no matter what the level, brings about a biological change. These mutations from long-time study are almost always detrimental to the human system when incorporated into it.

Recent studies have shown that those individuals having long-term exposure to radiation, even those using radiation for peaceful uses, tend to have higher mortality rates. Radiologists, for example, have been shown to have more cancers of the lymphatic and blood-forming tissues and from aplastic anemia than a control population of the U.S. white male population (Appendix C).

The excellent paper by Haagen-Smit may contain some difficult passages for readers just beginning the study of biology and chemistry. Accordingly, on page 297 the paragraph beginning with "At first sight . . ." contains a discussion of ridding the air of pollutants. This is the start of an optional section and this option may be exercised until the paragraph on page 301 ending with ". . . legal and economic problems." On page 306, the section on the formation of ozone also may be regarded as optional reading.

Air pollution is not only unsightly and costly, it is also detrimental to human health. Air pollution has been indicted for problems ranging from eye irritation —in the Haagen-Smit paper—to some rather convincing evidence that detrimental mutations are established on human chromosomes—in the Muller paper. In a very brief paper, the Nobel Laureate Muller speculated on air pollutants as mutagens. Muller cites the finding that chemical mutagens produce the same general clinical effects as do ionizing radiation and ultraviolet. He suggests that air pollutants damage somatic cells as well as germ cells.

Biological Aspects
of Nuclear Weapons*

CYRIL L. COMAR

There has naturally been great public interest about the effects of radiation on the human population, past, present, and future, mainly because nuclear weapons now make it possible for practically every organism living on earth to be exposed to detectable radiation from a single event controlled by man. Lack of knowledge, misunderstandings, a new mysterious force abroad in the world, personal involvement, radioactive contamination of milk and babies—all have led to a degree of emotional controversy.

It is attempted here to present an up-to-date and balanced view of the important biological radiation problems of the day. For the purposes of clarity and not evasion it is necessary to oversimplify, restrict the discussion to the most important matters, and omit details. Hopefully, this discussion will further an understanding of the difficult problems of present-day affairs on a basis both national (should we ban nuclear tests?) and personal (should I change my dietary habits?).

Some generalities

It must be crystal clear to all sane and thoughtful people that nuclear warfare is not the means for attainment of national or ideological goals. The category of the sane and thoughtful would include all people from extreme Left to Right, the general public, military leaders, and government officials. Also included are all peoples of other countries, especially those of Russia. From news impressions, one cannot be sure that the Red Chinese have reached this degree of understanding as yet, but it is to be hoped they would by the time they are capable

* A lecture delivered January 11, 1962, as one of a series of Cornell University Lectures on *Nuclear Peril and Disarmament*.

of producing and conveying nuclear weapons. Our primary objective then must be to avoid war, but at the same time to preserve our political systems of individual rights and freedom. How best this can be accomplished is the crucial issue, and strategy is a matter to be much debated, although not here. Personally I feel that simply to display moral indignation about the seriousness and necessity of avoiding nuclear warfare provides our government leaders with little that they do not already fully appreciate.

There seems to be public consternation and confusion because reputable scientists have expressed differing views about the effects of nuclear weapons. Unfortunately, in a sense, the public seems to regard scientists as god-like in their pronouncements. Perhaps this is due to the advertising approach, where science is used to promote sales. Actually, we should be proud that anyone in this country can state his view and have his ideas represented widely, and we would not want it any other way. Also, disagreement among scientists is the rule rather than the exception, because such disagreement emphasizes the gaps in our knowledge, and very often stimulates needed research.

This places a burden on the public, the need to evaluate and judge. There is a keyword that can help, namely "credentials." From whence, and by what authority does a man obtain his information; what are his "credentials"? A reputable scientist, speaking in his own field, deserves careful attention—a scientist speaking out of his field should be given one vote, just as anyone else.

We must be especially careful about opinions and numbers presented only in part and selected to support specific points of view—for example, to prepare public opinion for nuclear war, one could in truth predict the continued existence of mankind regardless of any foreseeable dissemination of nuclear debris; in the opposite direction, one could predict, even from weapons testing carried out to date, what appears to be vast numbers of individual genetic deaths, and a vast amount of individual human suffering accumulated over thousands of years.

The credentials for viewpoints expressed here arise from a consensus gained by personal contact with various National and International Committees, reports of which are listed. Within recent years there has been developing general agreement as to the levels of radiation exposure resulting from past nuclear tests and the order of magnitude of effects expected. Disagreement arises primarily on moral issues and on the uncertainties in the necessary balancing of potential biological cost against potential benefit from a given course of action. All are keenly aware of the need for intensive research.

The nuclear weapon and fallout

When a nuclear weapon is detonated, tremendous quantities of heat are produced within a small period of time—thousandths of a second—and within a relatively small quantity of matter. As a result, all materials within the immediate vicinity of the device are completely vaporized, and raised to temperatures approaching those of the sun. The high temperature gives rise to what is known as the "fireball," which expands rapidly, heating material within the environment as it expands, and which then starts to rise. As the fireball rises, violent winds are produced which can suck large quantities of soil or water into the hot fireball and molten particles can condense onto this material. These heavy dirt particles or droplets, with their attached radioactive contamination, may return rapidly to earth and are called "local fallout." The extent and nature of fallout may vary considerably. For example, an airburst in which the explosion occurs at an appreciable distance above the earth's surface, so that dirt or water are not sucked into the cloud, produces little or no local fallout; this may be an important consideration if the strategy of an attack is to use large weapons to produce damage by fire. A land-surface explosion, on the other hand, produces a cloud heavily loaded with debris, containing relatively great numbers of the large particles raised by the surface winds. Under such conditions, it is estimated that about 80 percent of the total debris deposits as local fallout.

For purposes of discussion, then, fallout can be classified either as local or as world-wide. Local fallout, sometimes called "close-in" fallout, is defined as that which is deposited within 24 hours after detonation. Human beings have not been exposed to local fallout except for accidents such as involved the Marshall Islanders and the 23 Japanese fishermen. World-wide fallout can be classified into two categories— either as "tropospheric" or "intermediate" fallout, which is deposited within the first 30 to 60 days; or as "stratospheric" or "delayed" fallout, which may take many months or years for deposition. The radioactive iodine in our milk during October 1961, was an example of intermediate fallout from the Russian 1961 tests. Our present body burdens of radioactive strontium result mainly from stratospheric fallout from the tests prior to 1959.

Local fallout is distinguished by its settling speed and high radiation intensity, consisting of visible particles heavy enough to fall through the air. The particles are transported by winds as they settle; with light winds, they will settle close to the site of explosion and make an intense radioactive area; with heavy winds, they will be spread over larger areas, to give relatively lower radiation intensities. Local fallout is of critical importance in warfare, but of little interest from the standpoint of testing, because it is limited to the test site. The important thing about local fallout is that external radiation is the major hazard, and that the radiation intensity decreases rapidly with time, because the local fallout as produced contains considerable short-lived radioactive materials. As a rule of thumb, it is estimated that, for every seven-fold increase in time, the radiation intensity decreases by a factor of 10. For example, if the radiation intensity were 4000 units at one hour after the explosion, it would be 400 units after seven hours, and 40 units after 49 hours.

World-wide fallout is important both in warfare and in weapons testing. In contrast to warfare, about which we hope always to have to speculate, world-wide contamination is now with us. The earth and all living things on it are now contaminated to a degree with radioactive materials from past tests, and we must have an understanding of the levels of such contamination and the effects that such levels might produce in order to evaluate the biological cost of any further testing. It should also be noted that, as a result of warfare, those countries not involved will, however, be subject to world-wide fallout from the nuclear weapons used; also, areas in the warring countries that escape local fallout will be subject to world-wide fallout.

The fission products and radioactive contamination

To understand the implications of world-wide fallout which is important primarily after entrance into the body, we must consider the specific radioactive elements that are produced and their behavior. The terms radioactive elements, radio-isotopes, and radionuclides are used loosely to designate forms of elements that are unstable and give off ionizing radiation. From an atomic explosion, there can result contamination with the fissile material itself, such as uranium or plutonium, and with the so-called fission products. The primary and secondary fission products consist of about 200 radioactive species of elements. In addition, there is the possibility that some radioactive materials may be produced by activation with the neutrons from the weapons, just as in the process used for production of radioisotopes in a nuclear reactor. From the biological standpoint, perhaps the most important activation product is the radionuclide carbon 14, arising from reaction of neutrons with nitrogen atoms of the atmosphere. Of the 200 or so radioactive species produced by the weapons, only a few are of biological importance. This is because a radioactive material must possess several characteristics to varying degrees, or otherwise it cannot be potentially harmful to the human population.

First, the radionuclide must be produced by the explosion in appreciable amounts.

The second characteristic that governs the biological hazard is the so-called physical half-life of the given radioactive material, this being the time required for one-half of any given amount to disappear by radioactive decay. For world-wide fallout, which is relatively slow in coming to earth, radionuclides with half-lives of less than days or weeks are of little significance.

Another important characteristic that governs the biological hazard is the efficiency with which the particular radioactive material is transferred from the atmosphere through the food chain to the human diet. This transfer occurs primarily by two routes: contamination can stick to surfaces of plants which are eaten directly by man or eaten by animals with the passage of the radioactive elements into milk and meat; another pathway is incorporation into the soil for uptake by plants through their roots and subsequent entry into the diet of man. Knowledge of these pathways is of utmost importance for future assessments because contamination by surface adsorption is governed by the *rate of fallout,* whereas contamination through the soil is governed by the *cumulative amounts* of radioactivity deposited. The rate tends to decrease relatively rapidly after cessation of nuclear explosions, whereas the cumulative total builds up from all previous tests and decreases only by radionuclides becoming physically unavailable and by physical decay. Metabolic barriers may prevent the radioactive material from reaching locations in the body where it may cause damage, depending on the behavior of the substance in the food chain or man's system. For example, although the rare earths are common fission products, their absorption from the intestinal tract is so small in man and animals that they are of little importance as a hazard to man. Similarly, any unfission uranium or plutonium would likewise be poorly absorbed.

A final important factor that governs hazard is the length of time that a material is retained in the body. Thus, for example, strontium 90, which deposits in bone like calcium and is removed relatively slowly, would be potentially more hazardous than cesium 137, which deposits in soft tissues, like potassium, and is removed fairly rapidly.

Thus, it appears that, of all the radioactive materials produced, only a few are limiting as a potential hazard; these are strontium 90, which is a bone-seeker and could eventually lead to leukemia and bone cancer, and cesium 137 and carbon 14, which would be of interest primarily from the standpoint of genetic effects. Under certain conditions, iodine 131 could be of potential hazard from tropospheric fallout, but because of its eight-day half-life, it does not present a long-term problem.

The human population is exposed to world-wide fallout mainly by radioactive contamination of food and water, the radioactivity then being eaten and built into the body where it serves as a source of internal irradiation. Thus, from world-wide fallout the radiation for the most part will be long-term, that is, delivered over the lifetime of the individual.

During the last 10–12 years, considerable research has been done on the metabolic behavior and movement of fission products through the food chain to end up in the body of man. Suffice it to say that our knowledge of this area is reasonably adequate, coming from extensive experimental studies, collections and analyses of foodstuffs, and collections and analyses of thousands of human bones. Thus, there is reliable information on amounts of radionuclides present in the human population from the weapons tests completed in 1958.

Biological effects of radiation

The term radiation refers to the transport of energy without a material carrier, such as radiation of light rays from sun to earth, from desk lamp to desk. The type of radiation we are concerned with is of a special kind, called ionizing radiation, which has relatively large amounts of energy and has characteristic effects on biological materials. For example, if one drinks a cup of hot tea, a certain amount of thermal energy is transferred to the body as the tea cools down and reaches body temperature; that same amount of energy, delivered in the form of ionizing radiation, would end a person's tea-drinking days forever.

To discuss radiation it is necessary to deal with amounts, and therefore some sort of unit is needed. To keep matters as uncomplicated as possible, only one unit will be used, the Roentgen, named after the discoverer of the X-ray. The roentgen is based on ionization produced and can be taken to represent radiation dose absorbed in tissue. This is convenient because biological effects depend primarily on the amount of energy that is dissipated in the tissue and are governed closely by the amount of ionization. As far as we are concerned, it is important only to know what the unit means in terms of the effects of interest. For example, few of us remember what a volt is, but although we don't worry about shock from an electric train (6–10 volts), we would not change a tube in a plugged-in radio while sitting in a bathtub; and we know full well what would happen if we tangled with a high-voltage line (over 10,000 volts). To illustrate the practical meaning of the roentgen unit, consider two examples: Whole body exposure of man to a dose of about one roentgen produces no observable biochemical or clinical effect; about 400 roentgens will kill about half the individuals exposed. Later, more specific effects will be mentioned.

The whole question of biological effects is extremely complicated and space does not permit full discussion. To understand the problems posed by radiation from nuclear weapons it is essential, however, to mention three general principles.

I. Radiation effects can be classified as either genetic or somatic. The genetic effects of radiation are those which affect offspring conceived after the exposure of individuals. The effects of radiation upon the exposed individuals themselves, such as the production of leukemia or bone tumors, or the shortening of life-span—these are called somatic effects.

II. A given radiation exposure, delivered over a long period of time, produces less biological effect than when delivered over a short period of time. For example, a man exposed to a single dose of 600 roentgens of radiation over a lifetime would show effects that were scarcely, if at all, observable. This behavior comes about because of the body's capacity to recover in part from the radiation, if given time. There is recent evidence that the genetic response may also be decreased when a given radiation dosage is spread over a long period of time. Thus, if a linear extrapolation to low dose rates is made, the predicted effects will always be in error on the side of safety. This principle is of especial importance in the evaluation of effects from world-wide contamination that is built into our bodies and delivers its radiation dose over a lifetime.

III. Is there a level of radiation exposure below which no harm is caused? This is called the "threshold" question. In many studies of the effects of drugs and chemical agents, in addition to radiation, one usually gives increasing doses of the agent and measures the effect. For many substances one finds that the effect as measured is zero until a certain dose, which is called the threshold, is reached. Theoretically, any dose lower than threshold would be expected to cause no effect. It must be emphasized, however, that such behavior is entirely dependent upon the sensitivity of the methods for detecting the effect. For example, as more sensitive methods become available, the threshold dose might well be lowered, even approach zero. Where the population of the world is exposed by dissemination of radioactivity from nuclear weapons, then tremendous numbers of individuals are involved which certainly increases the sensitivity of observation. There is general agreement that genetic effects show a non-threshold behavior curve—that is, that there is no radiation dose below which genetic effects would not be observed. There is no agreement as to whether somatic effects are threshold or non-threshold in behavior. Until there is definite evidence, we must be prudent and err on the side of safety by assuming that any amount of radiation wil produce some measure of harm.

Our next task is to see what are the best estimates of how much harm results from given exposures to radiation. It is convenient to classify radiation effects either as high-level, above 50 roentgens, or low-level with especial interest below about one roentgen. Evaluation of high-level radiation effects is not particularly difficult since experiments can be done with animals, and observations are available from human beings, either accidentally exposed or treated medically.

Evaluation of the effects of radiation at low levels, especially when the exposure is over long periods of time, is much more difficult. There is no direct evidence on the effects of radiation under conditions of low-level, long-term exposure. The reason is simply that, under these conditions, experimental studies are practically impossible, requiring vast numbers of experimental animals (millions), long periods of time (decades), and sensitive criteria of damage.

The most useful approach to evaluation of low-level, long-term exposures is to consider the background radiation to which mankind has always been exposed, and simply to assume that additional exposure to radiation at about the same level as background will produce about the same harm, and always to recognize that the more we increase our exposure over background, the more uncertain are we about the effects. Essentially, this means that if any amount of radiation produces harm, then the radiation from our natural environment, background radiation, must have been producing harm to mankind through the centuries, and perhaps can serve as our best yardstick.

Since the beginning of time man has been exposed to external radiation from cosmic rays and from naturally-occurring radioactive materials such as uranium, thorium and potassium 40 in the ground, air and structures in which he lives and works. Man has also been exposed to internal radiation from radionuclides that occur universally in the body, for example, potassium 40, carbon 14, and members of the radium and thorium families. It is estimated that the typical radiation dosage from such natural sources is about one-tenth of a roentgen per year, amounting then to about seven roentgens over a standard 70-year lifetime. It must be pointed out that, in some areas of the world, in parts of India and Brazil, for example, the natural radiation exposure may be up to ten times higher than this. Population studies are being done to see if any effects can be detected. Such studies are most difficult, however, because one needs to have controlled populations for comparison: populations that have the same standard and way of living, the same nutritional plane, the same medical care, the same degree of inbreeding. As yet, in these areas there is no evidence that the backgrounds ten times higher than average are deleterious, but this does not mean that there are no affected individuals. It does mean that the number of individuals affected is too small to be detected.

Let us now consider the relationship between radiation exposure and harm to the population. For reasons of clarity, the discussion is limited to the two situations most likely to be encountered—an exposure similar to that of background resulting from world-wide fallout, and a single exposure at high levels as from local fallout. The two most important radiation effects are the production of leukemia and genetic defects; others are of much less concern.

Biological effects from world-wide fallout

Nuclear testing was stopped in the fall of 1958 and, with the exception of the French tests which did not contribute significantly to environmental contamination, there was no testing until the Russian series of 1961. There are reliable data on the present levels of radioactivity in the human population that have resulted from the tests through 1958. If one adds up all of the dosages from the radioactive materials, including carbon 14, it appears that the population exposure from world-wide fallout is about five one-thousandths of a roentgen per year—in other words, about five percent of background.

In the Western countries, exposure for medical purposes is about equal to that from background and therefore amounts to about 50% of total exposure. The medical profession is doing all it can to keep exposure to a minimum and it must be remembered that the individual who receives medical exposure expects to benefit from it. Fallout and miscellaneous peacetime uses such as from watches and luminous buttons, etc., power reactors and radioisotope usage, television, each contribute some two to three percent of total exposure.

Consequences expressed in numbers have been conservatively estimated and presented only to provide some idea of the magnitudes involved. It is emphasized that uncertainties are large.

The natural incidence of genetic defects in the world population is about four percent, which means that each year there are about three million genetic disabilities of which perhaps one million are due to background radiation. Testing through 1958 may have added as few as 2500 or as many as 100,000 cases over subsequent years. Genetic defects may be of all kinds: The innocuous defect such as the early death of an embryo that passes unnoticed; varying degrees of impaired vigor and fertility; and the worst type of defect that causes suffering but does not interfere with reproduction.

Out of a world population of three billion the natural incidence of leukemia is about 150,000 cases per year, of which some 1500 cases per year are estimated to result from background radiation. Testing through 1958 has probably added a further 75; the number will decrease with time, since leukemia incidence falls off at four to seven years after radiation exposure. Bone tumors are less frequent in occurrence than leukemia, and less liable to production by radiation.

For those not accustomed to thinking in terms of population statistics two examples are cited for comparison. In the United States alone, about 40,000 people a year are killed on the highways—a biological cost we accept for transportation. In peacetime military pursuits there are about 1400 accidental deaths per year—a biological cost for preparedness. These figures are not quoted to justify any unnecessary additions to individual suffering, but merely to emphasize that normally we do not have personal anxiety about such risks.

From a moral standpoint, we as individuals or as a nation would not want to undertake any action that would unnecessarily cause even one instance of human suffering in the world population. Realistically, we know that man has always been faced with the protection of his well-being from natural and man-made changes in his environment and circumstances. Each step forward, for example, the use of fire, electricity, transportation, medical practice, has been a great boon to humanity, while at the same time causing individual hardship that in no sense of the word is preventable. Man developed and needs fire and heat, but individuals die from fires and boiler explosions. In medical practice, uncounted lives are saved by antibiotics, but individuals have allergies and die from antibiotics. This point certainly needs no further belaboring. Even the controlled peaceful uses of atomic energy will produce some radiation exposure, and therefore by our standards will have some biological cost. But everyone, I am sure, would agree that these biological costs are far outweighed by the benefits to mankind.

As far as nuclear testing is concerned there is no question but that it has contributed in a small way to world-wide radiation exposure, and that we should therefore take the position that further production of uncontrolled radioactive contamination should not be undertaken unless this be unequivocally justifiable. In point of fact, it would seem that the decision to undertake further atmospheric testing by this country should be based primarily upon the military, political, propaganda or disarmament benefits to be obtained. At the present stage of affairs, it appears in actuality that the biological effects of further testing would be of minor consideration.

There is interest, of course, in what one might expect from the 1961 Russian series of tests. Through 1958 there had been put into the atmosphere about 100 megaton equivalents of fission products, and this produced roughly a five percent increase of radiation exposure over background. From what we know of the 1961 Russian tests, which put up about 25 megatons of fission, it is anticipated that the increase from them would be considerably less than another five percent. One may well wonder, if we are not worried about the tests up through 1958, about the Russian tests in 1961, or about another series by the United States, whether there is a point at which we should worry. The answer is, of course, yes, but settling on a given level is difficult because each country will have its own concept of benefit *vs.* cost. It is certainly to be hoped that national self-interest, if nothing else, will dictate control on an international basis.

Biological effects of high radiation exposure

What is expected to happen when populations are exposed to high levels of radiation delivered over short times? Practically all persons exposed to more than 800 to 1000 roentgens will die. About fifty percent of persons exposed to 400 roentgens will die. If pregnant women were exposed to as little as 30 roentgens there would be expected a high percentage of malformations of the newborn, depending upon the age of the unborn child at exposure.

In regard to fertility, the radiation effects are similar for both men and women. About 150 roentgens would induce brief, temporary subfertility; 250 roentgens might induce temporary sterility for one or two years; and 500–600 roentgens might well produce permanent sterility.

In regard to leukemia, it is estimated that each 100 roentgens of radiation will cause about 100 cases of leukemia per million people per year; the normal incidence is 50 cases per million people per year.

In human beings, genetic effects are difficult to evaluate since no direct observations are easily available. Social conditions interact with biological phenomena; for instance, medical care maintains genetically handicapped individuals who may reproduce themselves and transmit deleterious genes, and public health has reduced infant mortality, one of the major selective agents. Can genetic radiation damage lead to the extinction of the human species? Based on present knowledge of radiation and population genetics this is most unlikely; the levels of radiation needed to cause genetic extinction would produce obliteration of humanity by direct damage.

Some present-day problems

Since human exposure to world-wide fallout is primarily by food, a matter of primary interest is whether there is control of the food that we can buy and whether any upper limits have been set for contamination which, when exceeded, would be reason for concern and action. Levels of radioactivity are being watched very carefully by Federal agencies, especially the Public Health Service, and the categorical statement may be made that, if one can buy a food on the market, it may be eaten and enjoyed. The Government has established a body known as the Federal Radiation Council which is setting guide-lines in regard to levels of radioactive contamination in food. For example, this body has indicated that a daily intake, averaged annually, of 0 to 20 micromicrocuries of strontium 90 requires no consideration; if the intake should fall between 20 and 200 micromicrocuries, then quantitative surveillance and some routine control might be necessary; at intakes between 200 and 2000, action would be called for. (The micromicrocurie is a unit for amounts of radioactivity.)

In 1959 and 1960, when strontium 90 levels were at their highest from the tests carried out prior to and including 1958, the average dietary intake in the United States was about 15 micromicrocuries of strontium 90. It has now fallen to about nine. Next spring, we can expect to see the effects of the Russian tests and it is estimated that the new levels will be about the same as those reached following the cessation of testing in 1958.

There has been considerable publicity about radioactive iodine in milk during September and October of 1961, the main point being that the thyroids of children appear to be especially sensitive. So far the levels observed have warranted no action.

The question is often asked as to whether we should modify our diet or food technology to decrease somehow the intake of radioactive contamination, with suggestions being made to supplement diets with stable calcium which theoretically reduces strontium retention, or to give iodine drops to block thyroid uptake, or perhaps to reduce milk intake. The answer at present is categorically no. The chance of doing harm by individual and perhaps misguided modification of diets far outweighs the chance of doing any good. Paradoxically, for example, even though milk is the single largest source of strontium 90 in the diet, reducing the milk intake tends to increase the body burden of strontium to be developed. This is because milk calcium contains less Sr^{90} than does plant calcium, since the cow uses calcium more effectively than it does strontium. If the diet were to contain no milk, then the body would get all its calcium from plant sources, which are more highly contaminated. If it were not for milk, our bodies would contain three to five times more strontium 90 than at present.

Another question often raised is whether or not consideration is being given to the decontamination of land and of foodstuffs. Such decontamination measures, or as they are now called, remedial measures, are under intensive scientific investigation. Again it must be emphasized that remedial measures should be taken only when declared necessary by responsible authorities. They are mentioned here as a matter of information, since none is practical and in any event such measures would only be considered under conditions of serious accident or warfare. Remedial measures being investigated for decontamination of land are as follows:

1. Removal of recently-contaminated grass or crops;
2. Scraping off several inches of surface soil;
3. Leaching with large quantities of solvents that would move strontium down the soil profile;
4. Liming of acid soils to reduce the strontium content or the strontium-to-calcium ratio in the crop;
5. Deep ploughing to reduce the uptake of radioactive contamination by shallow-rooted grasses;
6. Using deep-rooted plants;
7. Using land for plants with low ratio of calcium-to-calories or for fiber.

Plant foods could be reduced in contamination by removing the bran from cereal products and by washing or skinning fruits and vegetables. Remedial measures for animals would consist of avoidance of surface-contaminated herbage and supplying uncontaminated calcium.

Considerable attention is being given to removal of strontium 90 and cesium 137 from milk by use of ion exchange resins. The procedure is technically feasible but as yet could not be used on a large scale without greatly increasing the cost and requiring considerable installation time and capital investment. It is emphasized that there would be greater probabilities of harm from nutritional and health problems created by attempts to decontaminate milk on a large scale, than from present levels of radioactivity. Any food problems with iodine 131 can best be handled by storage for appropriate times before use, as for example the use of canned milk.

Changes in man's diet, as already indicated, might include use of uncontaminated calcium and reservation of less contaminated food for segments of the population at greatest risk, such as children and pregnant women.

Nuclear warfare

Since there is no way of knowing the scale and pattern of attack, only non-educated guesses are possible. No attempt will be made to draw a word picture of the chaos that would ensue; none of us has a vivid enough imagination. It must be emphasized that our frames of reference would be changed completely. Previously established acceptable levels of radiation would have no meaning whatsoever. The hungry man who has to decide between starvation as against increasing his chances of developing cancer in 10 or 20 years will make that decision during the split second between the time his hand touches the food and his mouth opens to receive it.

Within close range of a surface explosion, blast and heat would be the major destructive forces and any survivors would also be at risk from external radiation. Intense fallout would cover up to hundreds of square miles nearby and persons not sheltered would be exposed to most hazardous intensities of radiation. Outside this area, there would be another zone up to thousands of square miles where a proportion of those not sheltered would be at serious risk. In areas untouched by "local fallout" the risk from radiation would be slight.

Large weapons, if used, would probably be exploded at high altitudes and this would increase the areas of fire damage (perhaps to a 50-mile radius for 100 megatons), but would decrease the areas subject to local fallout. Under these conditions, future food production would not be complicated by radioactive contamination although other ecological factors might become important. For example, there could be unchecked fires over large areas of forests and grasslands followed by spring thaws that would erode denuded slopes and flood the valleys; intensification of plant and animal disease might be expected.

If weapons were exploded so as to maximize local fallout, then future food production would depend on how much arable land was left reasonably uncontaminated. The fact that we have as much as a million or so square miles of agricultural land makes it difficult to conceive of any attack that would leave us without sufficient usable land. The major short-term problems would most likely be those of logistics and transport. Theoretical studies on the basis of attacks that were credible in past months and years indicate that life and food production would go on. For example, the latest study with which I am familiar indicated that an attack of about 1400 megatons would leave 70 percent of our cropland usable and 90 percent of our livestock alive. But the capability for destruction increases with time and predictions are meaningless.

Could then the North American man survive a nuclear attack? Certainly individuals would. Whether the survival would be 5 or 95 percent would depend on what the enemy can do and wants to do, and to a lesser degree on defensive preparedness. Whether the North American man could be well-adjusted and happy, I leave to the psychologists; whether he would again assume world leadership, I leave to the geopoliticians.

Let us now consider the situation in the areas of the world that receive world-wide fallout only. If we assume, as a point of departure, that a total of 20,000 megatons would be used in the war, and that this would involve 10,000 megatons of fission, we can estimate what the mean population exposure might be. It is recalled that previous weapon tests of 100 megatons of fission gave a radiation exposure equivalent to about five percent of natural background. This means that 10,000 megatons would increase the radiation exposure to about five times that of background, assuming the same pattern of detonations as in past tests. The exposure in the Southern hemisphere would be much less. Thus, life in the rest of the world would, to all intents and purposes, go on as usual as far as radiation damage is concerned. The greater the number of megatons, however, the greater the load of distress and suffering that individuals and all human societies would have to support.

Another generality

It has been argued that nations disappear from the world or from world leadership for one of two reasons: (*a*) the fight to achieve supremacy, or (*b*) the desire for an easy life. I have not noted any great urge to fight for supremacy. There does seem to be a desire for the easy life. . . . schooling with frills, easy programs and long vacations; spectator sports, bright youngsters who don't get to college, dull ones who do; the drive to shorten the work week, etc. These examples are not cited in criticism of any group or to belittle our great national achievements. Rather, the point is made that we have a tremendous and literally untapped reserve of creative manpower which, when coupled with productive efficiency, should permit us to accomplish whatever is needed. If we want to badly enough, we can make the sacrifices and put forth the effort to mount simultaneously a deterrent, a peace offensive, a coexistence offensive, a world leadership offensive, a space offensive, a health and education offensive, a civil defensive—whatever it's going to take to keep us out of nuclear war and to allow us to fulfill the responsibilities of world leadership.

Summary

1. Any use of nuclear energy or radiation involves a biological cost which must always be weighed against the benefits expected.

2. Controlled peacetime use of nuclear energy yields benefits far in excess of biological costs.

3. The biological cost of past weapons tests of about 100–150 megatons of fission is small enough so that individuals need have no anxiety about personal or family well-being.

4. The factor of biological cost is minor in reaching decisions about resumption of atmospheric weapons tests; other factors—military, strategic, political, propaganda—are much more important.

5. Full scale nuclear warfare means mutual destruction, certainly of highly organized social systems, although all life would most probably not be obliterated in the countries attacked, and the rest of the world might go essentially unscathed. Recognition of these facts by rational men is the hope for prevention of nuclear war.

REFERENCES

1. *The Effects of Nuclear Weapons,* by SAMUEL GLASSTONE, Editor. U.S. Atomic Energy Commission. Washington, D.C. 1957.
2. Hearings before the Special Subcommittee on Radiation of the Joint Committee on Atomic Energy. 85th Congress. First session on "The nature of radioactive fallout and its effects on man." Part 1, May 27–June 3. Part 2, June 4–7. Washington, D.C. 1957.
3. Report of the United Nations Scientific Committee on the Effects of Atomic Radiation. General Assembly: 13th session. Supplement No. 17 (A/3838). New York. 1958.
4. The Biological Effects of Atomic Radiation. Summary Reports. National Academy of Sciences—National Research Council. Washington, D.C. 1956.
5. The Biological Effects of Atomic Radiation. Summary Reports. National Academy of Sciences—National Research Council. Washington, D.C. 1960.
6. The Hazards to Man of Nuclear and Allied Radiations. Second Report to Medical Research Council. London. 1960.
7. Background Material for the Development of Radiation Protection Standards. Federal Radiation Council, Staff Report. No. 1, May 1960.
8. Background Material for the Development of Radiation Protection Standards. Federal Radiation Council, Staff Report. No. 2, September 1961.
9. *Radiation, Genes, and Man,* by BRUCE WALLACE and TH. DOBZHANSKY. Holt, Rinehart, and Winston, New York. 1959.
10. Radioactivity in Foods. C. L. COMAR. *J. Amer. Med. Assoc., 171,* 119, 1959.

Air Conservation

A. J. HAAGEN-SMIT*

Our confidence in the abundance of the four principal elements of our forefathers has been severely shaken in recent times. We have learned that the increasing population will have less and less room in which to grow its crops and keep its cattle. Coal, oil, and gas reserves have definite time limits, and we might have had to face a major war over water rights had our ancestors not been wise enough to create a United States of America. Finally, our supposedly infinite supply of air has turned out to be limited, too. With the advent of atomic energy, many of these problems can be solved, but the universal use of atomic energy will make the problem of keeping our air fit to breathe even more difficult. Now we are concerned with constituents present in concentrations of a few parts per million. The future, and part of the present, generation must worry about the removal of pollutants present in quantities smaller by a factor of many powers of ten. In this more efficient cleaning process, the theoretical knowledge and technical skill required will be far greater than the knowledge and skill available today.

Perhaps we should even be grateful that in recent years air pollution disasters and near disasters have developed on such a scale that they have attracted the attention of the whole world. Such an episode occurred in London, when, during a black fog period in 1952, some 4000 excess deaths were recorded. Other disasters drawing world-wide attention were those in Donora, Pennsylvania, Poza Rica, Mexico, and the Meuse Valley in Belgium (1). In each of these incidents dozens of people met their death by suffocation.

In recent years, the smog conditions developing in Los Angeles and in other cities on the Pacific Coast have greatly inspired a more intensified effort to clean

* Dr. Haagen-Smit is professor of biochemistry at California Institute of Technology, Pasadena.

the air all over our country (2). Keeping the air clean is expensive. In the Los Angeles area alone it is estimated that several hundred million dollars have been spent already to curtail some emissions, and many more will have to be spent before the smog will again be unnoticeable. At the present time the air-pollution-control authorities, working against a 4 percent increase in population, are doing somewhat better than holding the line. Over the whole nation the expense will be staggering and will probably run into billions of dollars.

It is understandable that there has been a great deal of resistance to the installation of costly control equipment which often does not contribute in a direct manner to profits. Some of the objections have been removed in recent years, and it is now generally conceded that damage from air pollution is large and that recovery measures often pay for themselves and in some cases may even make profits. Corrosion due to the emission of various chemicals is a source of tremendous expense to the public. Recovery methods will reduce this corrosion and will also lower the cleaning bills for the outside, as well as the inside, of our houses. But even if no direct profit is made, the many intangibles make it worth while to improve working conditions. The standard of living of the workers is raised, and possible adverse effects on their health are eliminated. This contributes to an increased efficiency on the part of the worker. It also raises the value of the industrial property and of the surounding real estate. In many cases, management has gone much further than merely curing existing air pollution problems. At the present time, climatological and topographical conditions are examined carefully in selecting the site for new industry, and in the construction of new buildings the installation of air-pollution-control equipment is considered beforehand, rather than at a time when public relations have suffered a severe setback.

The old slogan, "Prosperity is measured by the number of smoking stacks," is no longer true. Today, prosperity can be gaged by the number of strange-looking bulges protruding from the roofs of the factories. These bulges are dust- and fume-collectors and indicate that the community and its industry have progressed to a standard of living and social consciousness that does not permit objectionable emissions to spread over other peoples' property. Many modern factories and offices have installed in the air-conditioning system air-purification systems as well, since experience has shown that clean air is healthier and leads to less absenteeism and, in addition, keeps cleaning and redecorating costs at a minimum. Scientific laboratories, too, have found that the protection from plant damage, from interference in the sensitive enzyme systems, and from destruction of oxidant-sensitive organic compounds which can be obtained by air purification is worth while.

Less satisfactory, from a hygienic point of view, is the way many of us spend our day undergoing fumigations with tobacco smoke and engine exhaust—a combination which for many years has been under suspicion where its effects on health are concerned.

One of the most common forms of air pollution is that caused by smoke. A cross-country trip by airplane should convince anyone that smoke is a problem in every great city from Los Angeles to New York. Large streamers, extending for scores of miles, have their origin in open burning dumps, lumberyards, steel mills, foundries, and power plants, to name only a few of the multitude of sources. This is an old problem; some 200 years ago laws were passed in England to regulate the burning of certain types of coal. Even today, combustion is still a major source of air pollution.

At first sight this problem of controlling the emission of smoke appears quite simple—just wash it out! But we have only to think how tobacco smoke from a Turkish pipe bubbles, seemingly undisturbed, through water, to realize that perhaps this problem is not so easily solved after all. Large particles of soot and dust can readily be removed in settling chambers, or in cyclones, where gravitational or centrifugal forces are used to separate the particles by weight. Other methods consist in filtering out the dust through cloth made of cotton, woven plastics, or even glass fibers, in structures known as baghouses. For very fine

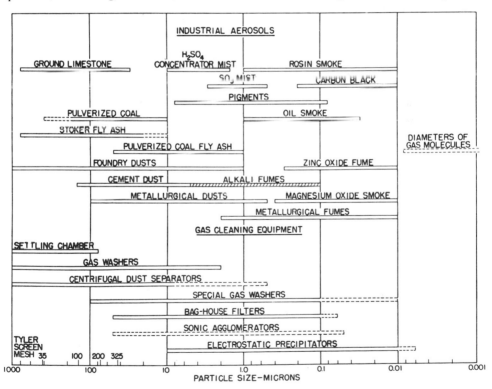

FIG. 1. Particle size chart illustrating relative size of well-known particulates and the effective range of various control methods. [H. P. Munger, "The spectrum of particle size and its relation to air pollution," in L. C. McCabe, *Air Pollution* (2, chap. 16)]

dust, of the order of from 0.5 to 1.0 micron, we have to apply processes whereby the electrically charged particle is removed by electrostatic forces by passage between electrodes kept at a potential difference of 15,000 to 40,000 volts. A comparison of particle size of effluents and the means of their recovery is shown in Fig. 1. By catching the particles of a size close to the wavelength of light, an important fraction of the dust responsible for the scattering of light is removed, and therefore the probability of visible plume formation is substantially decreased. The process is attractive to industry because of the low cost of maintenance and the negligible drop in pressure, and it is commonly used in open-hearth furnaces in steel mills and in coal-burning plants (Fig. 2). Recently its use was extended in Los Angeles to the control of stack emissions from oil-fired boilers in power plants. Each one of these dust-collection processes has found wide application in industry, but even today systematic studies to increase their efficiency would be most welcome.

The dust present in fuel is not the only agent responsible for an objectionable plume from smokestacks. Virtually all other constituents of flue gas—water, carbon monoxide, and oxides of sulfur and nitrogen—play some role. It is interesting to watch this plume formation take place in a long glass tube through which the hot stack gases are led. As soon as the gases cool below the dewpoint range, we see a deposition of metal salts, largely in the form of sulfates, along the side of the tube. Next we find a region of droplets, containing insoluble dust embedded in an acid solution of metal salts. Finally, on further cooling, the bulk of the water, containing some sulfuric acid and sulfur dioxide, condenses. When the gas stream, cooled to outside temperature, leaves the experimental stack, it escapes largely as a plume of water vapor containing trace amounts of sulfuric acid, and nearly all the sulfur dioxide and nitrogen oxide, in gaseous form. In this passage very little sulfur dioxide has been converted to sulfuric acid. The dew point of the outlet is close to that of the outside temperature, and only slight heating is required to cause the visible plume to disappear. This practice is followed in many installations where weather conditions are conducive to plume formation.

We expect that phenomena similar to those observed in the glass tubes take place when the gases are released from the stack, with the droplet size adjusting itself to the outside temperature and humidity. This is an important factor in the variability of plume density observed in otherwise identical combustion con-

---

FIG. 2. Before the installation of smoke-control equipment, the normal operation of the open-hearth furnaces at Kaiser Steel Corporation's Fontana, California, plant produced smoke which was released directly into the atmosphere. These two pictures, taken within minutes of each other, graphically demonstrate the effectiveness of the electrostatic precipitator on top of the building. (Left, above) Picture taken with all the units temporarily shut off. (Left, below) Picture taken a few minutes later with the equipment back in operation, showing clear sky. [Kaiser Steel Corporation]

ditions. The formation of droplets by condensation is not the end of plume formation, for both sulfur and nitrogen oxides, as well as metal salts, participate in a series of reactions leading to a gradual oxidation of sulfur dioxide into sulfuric acid, and of nitric oxide into higher oxides and nitric acid.

Laboratory investigations by Johnstone and Coughanowr (*3*) have shown that oxidation of sulfur dioxide takes place slowly by photochemical action. These authors estimated that about 1 percent would be oxidized per hour in intense sunlight. This would indicate that in an atmosphere containing 0.1 to 1.0 part per million of sulfur dioxide, about 100 hours of sunlight would be required to decrease visibility to about 1 mile. In continuation of these experiments it was found that oxidation occurs much faster in water solution under the influence of metal salts. Such conditions could conceivably occur in droplets present in the stack plume. The suggestion has been made that it is this reaction which is responsible for the haziness observed at considerable distance from industrial establishments. Evidence that such oxidations do take place when the gases have left the stack is found in an interesting pollution balance made at one time by the Los Angeles County Air Pollution Control District (*4*). The amount of emission of sulfur dioxide from all sources—refinery operations, oil burning, and gasoline consumption—is well known. We also know the area in which this emission is dispersed, as well as the height of the inversion layer which limits its upward movement. From these data we are able to calculate the expected sulfur dioxide concentration and compare this with the actual observed average concentration. We find, in making up this balance, that about half of the sulfur dioxide is lacking, as is shown in Table 1. This missing sulfur dioxide is found mostly as

TABLE 1. Comparison of measured and calculated concentrations of pollutants in downtown Los Angeles (*4*, p. 41).

Pollutant	Clear day* (parts per million by vol.)		Day of intense smog† (parts per million by vol.)	
	Measured	Calculated	Measured	Calculated
Carbon monoxide	3.5	3.5‡	23.0	23.0‡
Oxides of nitrogen	0.08	0.10	0.4	0.6
Sulfur dioxide	0.05	0.08	0.3	0.5
Total hydrocarbons§	0.2	0.40	1.1‖	2.6
Aldehydes	0.07	0.02	0.4	0.1
Organic acids	0.07	0.03	0.4‖	0.2

* Visibility, 7 miles.
† Visibility, less than 1 mile.
‡ The method defines the calculated value as the same as the measured value for CO.
§ Calculated as hexane.
‖ Preliminary values.

calcium and ammonium sulfates in dust settling over the country. Free sulfuric acid, except in close proximity to the stack, is virtually absent.

Research work on the effects of stack gas constituents on plants and animals is still an important field of environmental hygiene. Only recently some interesting data were revealed on the synergistic effects of aerosols and oxides of sulfur on physiological responses such as flow resistance in the respiratory system (5). This specific air pollution problem illustrates how much work has to be done before we can really understand the phenomena connected with the emission of dust and fumes. Some of this work is in the field of engineering, and other aspects deal with inorganic, physical, physicochemical, and photochemical processes. Finally, we have problems in physiology and pathology of plants and animals, as well as legal and economic problems.

Los Angeles smog

Notwithstanding its many facets, this control problem is simple compared with a more recently discovered air pollution problem which threatens to affect all metropolitan areas. It is an oxidized hydrocarbon type of pollution, better known as Los Angeles smog, from its place of discovery (Fig. 3).

FIG. 3. Dense smog over Los Angeles Civic Center. Note how the buildings project above the base of the inversion layer, while pollution remains below. [Los Angeles County Air Pollution Control District]

FIG. 4. Severe damage on the under side of spinach leaves caused by Los Angeles smog. [Los Angeles County Air Pollution Control District]

During the war years, Los Angeles was suddenly surprised to find itself engulfed in an eye-irritating cloud of chlorine-like odor. This incident lasted about a year and was generally attributed to the emissions from a synthetic-rubber plant. After the control of these emissions, complaints stopped, only to be resumed after the war. The rubber plant could not be blamed this time, for it was closed, nor could sulfur dioxide and soot be blamed for the severe eye irritation. As a matter of fact Los Angeles is a very clean city in this respect, with a dustfall of only 20 to 30 tons per month per square mile, as compared with several times this quantity in other industrial cities. There is no resemblance at all to the problems of cities in the eastern part of the United States, where coal is the major source of energy and where, consequently, soot blackens all buildings. The eye-irritating clouds in Los Angeles are accompanied by complaints from farmers about crop damage (Fig. 4) and, strangely enough from rubber manufacturers, who observed that their products cracked more heavily in this area than in other sections of the country (Fig. 5). Control of dusts and sulfur dioxide did not help, for the phenomena are due to an effect quite different from the more old-fashioned, reducing type of air pollution. Los Angeles smog, contrary to this type of pollution, is typified by its strong oxidizing action (6, 7).

For practical measurement of the typical oxidizing effect of Los Angeles smog, liberation of iodine from potassium iodide, oxidation of phenolphthalin to phenolphthalein, and many other oxidation-reduction reactions can be used. For an explanation of the effect of oxidizing smog on living tissue, its demonstrated action on amino acids such as cysteine, tryptophan, and histidine, as well as on glutathione and lysozyme, is significant and might well account for the irritating symptoms. The measured oxidant action is caused by an excess of oxidizing over reducing components in the polluted air. In Los Angeles smog

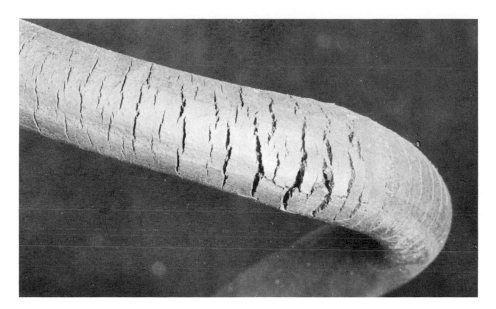

FIG. 5. Severe rubber cracking observed in Los Angeles area. [J. W. Haagen-Smit]

the concentration of sulfur dioxide, a reducing substance, is low, and its effects are usually negligible. In other areas, the presence of the oxidizing pollutants may well have escaped attention because of the masking effect of an excessive amount of reducing substances. It is quite possible that the oxidizing pollutants which characterize Los Angeles smog are of more frequent occurrence than was originally suspected.

The concentration of the oxidant varies during the day, increasing toward noon and decreasing to virtual absence during the evening and night hours. The time of increased concentration of the oxidant is invariably correlated with eye irritation and haze. The type of damage to plants from oxidizing pollutants is readily distinguishable from damage from other types of pollutants, such as sulfur dioxide or fluoride. Sensitive plants—spinach, sugar beets, alfalfa, endive, oats, and pinto beans—are used extensively to gage the spread of the pollution (Fig. 6). A major part of the oxidant consists of ozone, which is directly responsible for the excessive rubber cracking observed in the Los Angeles area. Spectrographic, as well as chemical, methods have definitely established the presence of ozone concentrations 20 to 30 times higher than those found in unpolluted air, where the normal concentration amounts to 1 to 3 parts per hundred million.

A simple and inexpensive method of measuring ozone involves the use of bent pieces of antiozodant-free rubber as indicators (Fig. 7) (8). The time necessary for the appearance of the cracks is directly related to the ozone content of the air. At night, and on smog-free days, it may take as long as an hour for the first cracks to appear; on a smoggy day, cracks are often evident in a matter

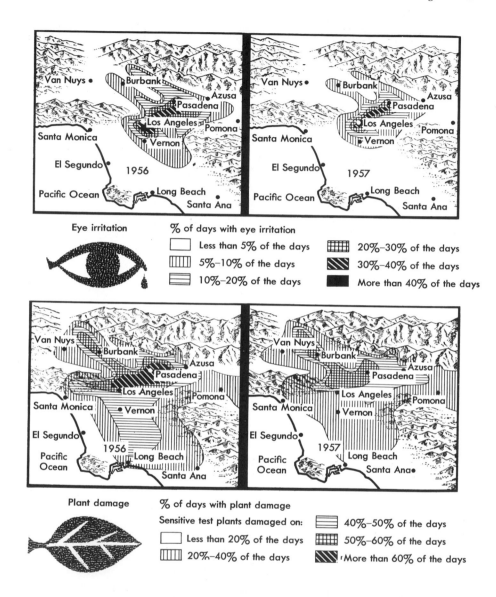

FIG. 6. The effect of air pollution control in the Los Angeles area for the period 1956–57. The intensity of eye irritation (top) has decreased, as has the area over which eye irritation is observed. Reported plant damage (bottom), too, has been less severe. [Los Angeles County Air Pollution Control District]

FIG. 7. Ozone in air is measured by its effect on rubber under strain. The degree of cracking indicates the concentration. [Los Angeles County Air Pollution Control District]

of a few minutes, under the conditions of the test. During heavy smog periods the total oxidant concentration is higher than can be accounted for on the basis of the presence of ozone alone when determined by spectrographic methods. This excess oxidant, corrected for the action of oxides of nitrogen, consists mainly of peroxidic material formed by the atmospheric oxidation of organic material. These organic peroxides are held to be responsible for eye irritation and plant damage resulting from smog. In the atmosphere over a city it is to be expected that the reactive ozone will enter into reactions with a number of other pollutants. Among the most prevalent of these groups are olefins, present in gasoline; fumigation experiments with gasoline fractions, and also with pure olefins which have been allowed to react with ozone, led to a reproduction of the typical plant-damage symptoms and to eye irritation, haze formation, and typical smog odor, as well. These experiments strongly indicated that the irritating materials were intermediate oxidation products of hydrocarbon oxidation and are of peroxidic nature, since the usual end products—aldehydes, ketones, and organic acids—are inactive in the concentration range used.

Most organic compounds are relatively stable against oxidation, when completely pure, but the presence of peroxides speeds the auto-oxidation considerably through a chain reaction initiated by hydrogen removal from the hydrocarbon chain. This effect can be accomplished also through the action of light on either the hydrocarbon or the oxygen molecule. In the latter case, the excited oxygen may remove hydrogen. Most hydrocarbons do not have absorption bands in the wavelength region of sunlight for a direct photochemical reaction. Similar reactions can be accomplished in a roundabout way by having a substance present which accepts the light energy and subsequently transfers it to the compound to be oxidized. In nature we find such substances in chlorophyll and other photochemically active pigments. In polluted atmospheres nitrogen dioxide functions as an oxidation catalyst in this way. Strong absorption of light by nitrogen dioxide occurs from the near ultraviolet through the blue part of the spectrum, and, upon irradiation, nitrogen dioxide splits into atomic oxygen and nitric oxide. Fumigation experiments with gasoline or olefin in the presence of oxides of nitrogen resulted in eye irritation and the same type of plant damage that was previously obtained with ozone acting on the olefins directly. In this case, too, we are able to calculate the concentration of hydrocarbon which should be present in a certain area and compare this with the actually observed concentration, just as we have done with the sulfur oxides. We find that the hydrocarbon concentration in the air is less than it had been calculated to be; on the other hand, the concentrations of the oxidation products—aldehydes and acids—are considerably higher than had been calculated, as is shown in Table 1. All these observed facts are in harmony with an explanation of Los Angeles smog as an oxidation phenomenon of organic material.

Formation of ozone

When all the typical symptoms of smog had been reproduced, the problem remained of accounting for the relatively high ozone content in the polluted atmosphere. It is now well established that the generation of ozone is intimately connected with the same photochemical reaction of organic material and oxides of nitrogen which causes eye irritation and plant damage. The formation of ozone is apparently a general phenomenon and is observed with many types of hydrocarbons, as well as with alcohols, ketones, aldehydes, and acids. The production of ozone has been attributed to the intermediate formation of peroxide radicals. This hypothesis is supported by the behavior of a model substance, biacetyl, upon irradiation. Years of photochemical research have shown that this diketone dissociates predominantly into acetyl radicals, which are further decomposed into methyl radicals and carbon monoxide. In most of these photochemical experiments the presence of oxygen is rigorously excluded to avoid complication. When oxygen is admitted, the free radicals will form peroxy radicals, and these apparently react with more oxygen to yield ozone:

$$H_3C-\overset{\overset{O}{\parallel}}{C}\overset{\cdot}{:}\overset{\overset{O}{\parallel}}{C}-CH_3 \xrightarrow{h\nu} H_3C-\overset{\cdot}{C} \xrightarrow{O_2} H_3C-CO\overset{\cdot}{O} \xrightarrow{O_2} H_3C-\overset{\cdot}{C}O + O_3$$

This rather surprising result can readily be verified by a simple lecture experiment in which a drop of biacetyl is introduced into a Pyrex flask. Next, a small piece of rubber with the ends tied together to form a loop is suspended in the flask. After exposure for an hour to sunlight, the rubber is heavily cracked, due to ozone attack. The rubber used should not contain antiozodants, of course. Infrared investigations have confirmed the chemical analysis and indicate that we are really dealing with ozone. Another well-known instance of radical formation is the irradiation of alkyl nitrites whereby an alkyl radical and nitric oxide are formed. When irradiation is carried out in air or oxygen, the alkyl radical forms a peroxide radical and ozone formation can readily be established. This reaction is similar to that postulated in the formation of smog of the Los Angeles type. The starting products in that case are nitrogen dioxide and hydrocarbons or their derivatives. We may visualize, first, a light-activated dissociation of nitrogen dioxide to nitric oxide and atomic oxygen, followed by a reaction of the atomic oxygen with a molecule of oxygen to form ozone. Atomic oxygen may also abstract a hydrogen from a hydrocarbon, with formation of an alkyl radical. This, in turn, can form ozone, as shown previously in the case of biacetyl. Also, reactions between nitric oxide and alkyl and alkylperoxy radicals may take place. Representatives of such combinations have been found in

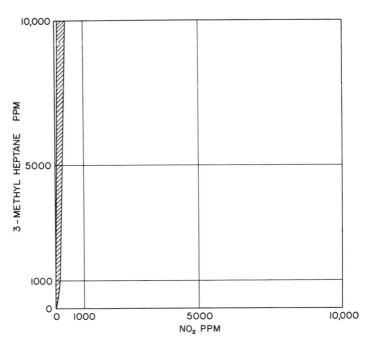

FIG. 8. Area of ozone formation with 3-methylheptane and NO_2. Ozone formation takes place only at concentrations indicated by shaded area (10,000 parts per million, volume for volume, is equivalent to 1 percent). [A. J. Haagen-Smit and M. M. Fox, *Air Repair* (7)]

long-path infrared studies conducted by workers at the Franklin Institute (*9*). Especially interesting is the formation of a peracylnitrite, a direct combination product of the photochemically produced nitric oxide and peroxy radical. This compound appears in smog atmospheres as well as in irradiation of synthetic mixtures of hydrocarbons and nitrogen oxides. It is postulated that these types of compounds play an important role as intermediates in the reoxidation of the nitric oxide to nitrogen dioxide.

A systematic study of the area of concentrations of hydrocarbon and oxides of nitrogen where ozone formation takes place showed that the reaction is limited to quite low concentrations of the reactants, as is shown in Fig. 8. Experiments of this type have focused attention on the circumstances peculiar to the problem of air pollution—that is, the extreme dilution. A chemist referring loosely to slow and fast reactions has in mind the conditions in laboratory synthesis, where concentration of about 10 percent are most commonly used. In atmospheric reactions the concentrations are in the order of 0.00001 percent— about one millionth as much. As a result, reactions which under the usual laboratory conditions are considered fast become very slow. For example, when a bimolecular reaction with participants in the concentration range of 10 percent (100,000 parts per million) requires 0.0036 second to go halfway to completion, it takes 10^6 times as long, or a whole hour, to reach the same point with a concentration of 0.1 part per million. Under the latter circumstances, not only can ozone survive attack by reducing agents but even free radicals have a far better chance of survival. It took many years to unravel relatively simple reactions such as the photodecomposition of acetone, biacetyl, and other compounds. In the air these reactions are complicated by the presence of oxygen, water, carbon dioxide, and an almost infinite variety of organic compounds from the evaporation and combustion of gasoline and from the burning of trash in its various forms.

Theoretical investigations

The field of atmospheric reactions is now being actively studied by a number of physical chemists and provides an interesting example of the way in which a practical problem has stimulated a number of theoretical investigations. Such study has familiarized a large group of physical chemists with the exciting field of extreme dilution, in which research should prove to be far less disturbed and complicated than research at higher concentrations, where molecules collide all too frequently. In addition, the practical aspects of air-pollution photochemistry have made available the instrumentation necessary to study these phenomena from a theoretical point of view. The purely theoretical physicist and chemist would have difficulty in obtaining the millions of dollars which have gone into the development of these instruments. It is gratifying to find that, as a by-product of the study of an unpleasant problem such as air pollution, a significant contribution to fundamental problems in chemistry could be made.

Automobile exhaust fumes

These remarkable reactions have now been confirmed in at least four different laboratories and provide a firm basis for control measures. We know which compounds contribute to these reactions and we know their sources, and now the Air Pollution Control District has only to control hydrocarbons, their oxidation products, and the oxides of nitrogen. Unfortunately, the necessary control equipment cannot be ordered because it still has to be invented. After hydrocarbons at refineries have been recovered, the major remaining source of hydrocarbons is the exhaust of automobiles, which amounts to 1200 tons per day. Direct and catalytic afterburners and deceleration devices are now being developed, but even after a successful device has been produced it will take many years before such devices will be installed on all the cars in the Los Angeles area. Pressing air pollution considerations can now be added to the many other arguments for streamlining our transit systems.

There are other difficulties. The major contributor to the oxides of nitrogen is, again, the automobile, and, apart from injection of water into the cylinders and the combustion of very rich fuel mixtures, no means are yet available for reducing the oxides of nitrogen. Several engineering laboratories are now searching for ways to reduce the nitrogen dioxide content of exhaust gases from gas, oil, and gasoline combustion through studies on the variable combustion conditions which can be obtained through boiler modification or changes in engine design. Often the question has come up, "Can't we do one or the other—hydrocarbon control or nitrogen dioxide control?" The answer, I believe, is "No." Most of the smog reactions are directly dependent on the product of the concentration of both hydrocarbons and oxides of nitrogen.

The private automobile is a major offender in both respects, and there is no reasonable basis for hope that control devices in the hands of the average car owner will give anywhere near the performance they give in an automobile-testing laboratory. Also, changes in gasoline composition could not be expected to have a drastic effect on smog-producing hydrocarbons in the exhaust. The steady increase in population tends to neutralize any control effort, and it is therefore evident that emissions must be controlled wherever possible. Besides being an objectionable factor in the photochemical reactions, the nitrogen oxides are objectionable in their own right and are quite toxic even in low concentrations. Fortunately we have not yet reached anywhere near the lower alert limit of 5.0 parts per million, but the concentration of this pollutant is steadily increasing, and since it appears in all combustions, the increase is practically proportional to the increase in population. Especially in areas of heavy traffic the concentration might at times surpass the safe limits, or, rather, what we now believe are safe limits. Oxides of nitrogen are rather unpleasant compounds. In concentrations of only 25 parts per million they act like war gases such as phosgene and cause lung edema. It is quite possible that, at far lower doses, objectionable damage might occur.

Cigarette and cigar smoke

Oxides of nitrogen are prominent in a quite different form of air pollution. Cigarette and cigar smoke contains from 300 to 1500 parts per million of oxides of nitrogen, which is completely removed by inhalation, through adsorption in the lungs. No attention has been given to this agent as a causative factor of respiratory ailments in smokers. Its strong toxic action should be an inducement to study more intensely the volatile components of tobacco smoke than has been done in the past, when most attention has been given to nonvolatile tars containing carcinogenic hydrocarbons.

Air pollution control administrations have a difficult task in surviving the years of waiting for engineering to catch up with the demands of the community. Programs for meeting emergency conditions have somewhat contributed to better feelings on the part of the public. It is understandable that most people not accustomed to smelling or inhaling a concoction of ozone, oxides of nitrogen, ozonides, and substances $x, y,$ and z begin to be a little worried. In recent years the medical profession in Los Angeles has set certain levels below which a catastrophe would be unlikely to occur. This is admittedly a very difficult decision to make and it has pointed to a serious deficiency in our knowledge of environmental hygiene.

Pollution levels

In studies of the health effects of air contaminants it becomes evident that there is a great difference between the industrial and general population levels. The industrial group generally represents a selected group of healthy individuals from which the extrasensitive has been removed, because the working conditions do not agree with them. For the whole population such a selection does not take place to any large degree, and we are dealing with the oversensitives—the sick, the young, and the very old. Public health officers have a most difficult task in establishing pollution levels for such a heterogeneous group, and it is a foregone conclusion that when levels are finally adopted there will be those who will maintain that they are too high, while others will charge persecution of industry because the levels are set too low. Animal experiments, and even experiments with human beings, while indicating some level of toxicity or annoyance, cannot give the answer for a general population. In urban areas we are dealing with several million people, and many would call the death of one or two persons per million, or some 20 for a town the size of Los Angeles, a disaster. The impossibility of approaching this accuracy of prediction in an experimental human, or even animal, colony is evident, for we would have to experiment with a few million individuals to get a statistically valid answer.

We come, therefore, to the conclusion that the only person able to give answers with any certainty about the result of some large-scale fumigation is the epidemiologist gathering data on death rates and general health status. It is, of course, unfortunate that this kind of study comes too late to prevent the disaster;

on the other hand, these studies furnish extremely valuable data on ways to prevent recurrence of the same series of events. It is for this reason that the study, such as that by workers at Harvard, of pretoxic effects, consisting in physiological responses warning of the danger ahead, is one of the most promising approaches to the study of pollution levels. These studies deal with the combined and synergistic effects of aerosols and sulfur dioxide. The physiological changes noted are greater flow resistance in the respiratory system, as reported by Amdur and Mead (*10*). The effects found at lower concentration do not necessarily represent toxic symptoms but may have to be regarded in the same class as sneezing, coughing, or blinking of the eye—therefore as warning signs and pretoxic symptoms.

Air pollution disaster can be prevented. Even nuisance effects can be minimized by planning at the right time. Such planning requires some basic information which can be furnished by the meteorologists. A study must be made of wind trajectories, for the progress of a package of air loaded with pollutants over the area should be known. Also needed are data on the change in concentration in a pollution cloud as it moves across a given area. This change comes about through turbulence and chemical reactions. As in the case in Los Angeles, relatively harmless gases may react to form irritants while moving across the basin. We like to know how long it takes for the pollutants to react sufficiently to give us maximum irritation.

When all these facts, plus the size and nature of the emission, are known, we can begin to think of plotting the trajectories and the isopollution lines for different substances. This kind of calculation has been described by Frenkiel (*11*) for a hypothetical case in the Los Angeles area. The calculation, which, practically, can be made only by means of electronic calculating machines, shows the fanning out of the emission from a single point of origin and its gradual dilution (Fig. 9). When we are dealing with a diffuse source such as the automobile, we can divide the area into a number of smaller areas for which traffic density, and therefore pollution, are known (Fig. 10). By calculating and integrating each one of these contributions, we arrive at the effect of a multiple source of pollution such as the automobile. This method, more than any other, shows clearly the contribution made by different sources, often miles away, to the pollution at a particular spot. Anyone enveloped by the expanding cloud will experience nuisance effects, regardless of whether or not he is in the exact center. On the basis of this concept, it is possible to express quite clearly how strongly the individual contribution from different sources may vary from one location to another, although both are in the same general area. Almost everyone is aware of this fact. Nevertheless it is quite common to refer loosely to minor and major sources, completely losing sight of the fact that in certain neighborhoods a local nuisance may have a greater effect than larger sources located far away. A great deal of friction could be avoided by recognizing this simple fact, and Frenkiel's "relative contribution charts" for different locations could be of great help in objectively settling some of the hot arguments (Fig. 11). A prerequisite for

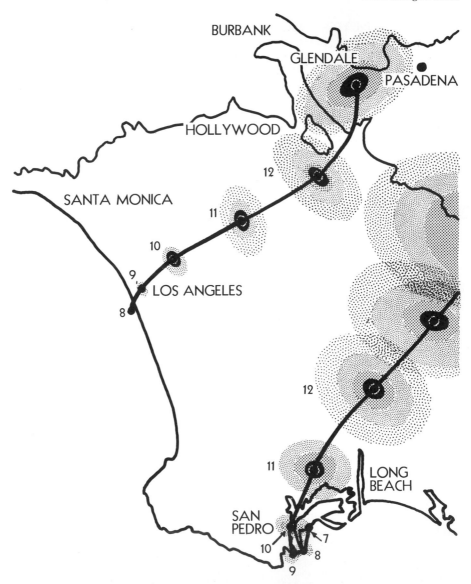

FIG. 9. Hypothetical dispersion of smoke puffs released at two points of the Los Angeles basin at 7 A.M. and 8 A.M., respectively. [F. N. Frenkiel (*11*)]

FIG. 11. Relative contributions of the three principal pollution sources to the mean concentration at California Institute of Technology. The effects of topographical features and inversion are taken into account in the mathematical model of Los Angeles County. The relative proportions of the "important" pollutants emitted by the three principal sources are based on recent studies in Los Angeles County. [F. N. Frenkiel (*11*)]

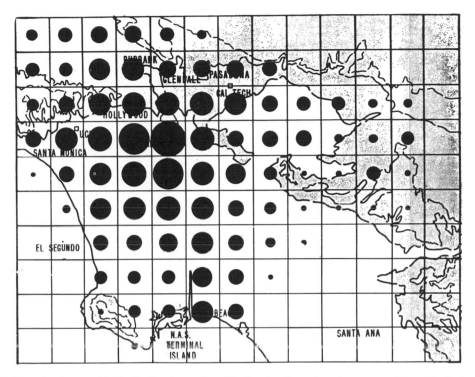

FIG. 10. Geographical distribution of traffic in the Los Angeles area. Area of circles is proportional to the number of vehicles; each square represents 16 square miles. [F. N. Frenkiel (*11*)]

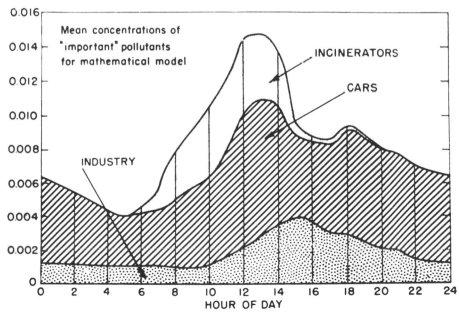

such calculations is reliable information on wind directions. Tracer studies based on the addition of easily identifiable materials such as fluorescent substances to the stack gases may be helpful. Much cheaper is the tracing of natural components specific to some of the sources. Aerial photography also offers considerable promise, especially at times when plumes 10 to 20 miles in length can be observed. Closer cooperation of other organizations, such as the Air Force and military and civilian groups, would be of great help.

Application of the methods for the calculation of pollutant distribution and movement would allow us to predict the future development of smog at a certain location and to predict what the elimination of certain sources will do as compared with the removal of others. This is especially important for a complicated case such as we find in Los Angeles. Here, most of the hydrocarbon material is emitted by the automobile, but the other components of smog, the oxides of nitrogen, are produced in nearly equal quantities by automobiles and installations burning gas or oil. The stationary installations are usually large, the trail of oxides of nitrogen is well defined, and the concentration of oxides of nitrogen may be higher than could be expected from a pollution cloud from such a diffuse source as the automobile.

Climatological conditions, and therefore air pollution moved by the wind currents, do not respect legal boundaries, nor does the pollution suddenly stop at the shore line, beyond which it is somewhat more difficult to maintain observation posts. In the Los Angeles area basin, for example, pollution from the southern industrial area can reach the Los Angeles Civic Center by either a land or a sea route. Federal and state testing programs have drawn attention to these wind movements, which cause pollutants to drift as far as islands 50 miles off the Pacific coast. These pollutants can readily be seen from the air and are quite different in appearance from low-lying clouds, due to their lack of structure and often to their characteristic yellowish-brown, off-white color, caused by refraction rather than by any color of specific chemicals.

Earlier in this article I have discussed more or less regularly occurring, or chronic, air pollution problems. There is, however, a more acute type of pollution which occurs when, through accidents such as explosions of tanks of toxic chemicals or through explosion of enemy bombs, large areas may become dangerous. In such circumstances it is of great importance to have the ability and the machinery to push a button on a computer which tells the health authorities in only a few minutes the area to which the poisonous cloud is drifting and what its concentration will be.

Conclusion

Air pollution problems are as varied as the activities of people themselves. We have looked in some detail at only two types of pollution. It has been my intent to make it clear that the problems met in air conservation are extremely complex and need the cooperative assistance of many scientific and technical disciplines. There is hardly any field of human endeavor that is not touched. The student of environmental hygiene has, as his laboratory, hundreds of square miles; as his chemicals, about everything a population emits to the air—in other words, a mixture representing a sizable portion of the inorganic and organic chemicals. His accomplishments have to be attuned to a population so varied in reactions and responses that an "average" person has no meaning in his problem. Entering into and often interfering with the normal occupations of the community, he has to be endowed with diplomatic and legal talents. The increased importance of his job in protecting the cleanliness of the air is felt in many quarters, and several universities and federal agencies have started courses in practical and theoretical aspects of air pollution control. Needed, too, are engineering studies to lead to the improvement of existing methods and to the invention of more efficient and economical processes to deal with old and new problems in air pollution.

REFERENCES

1. P. Drinker, *Harben Lectures* (1956); "Air pollution and the public health," *J. Roy. Inst. Public Health and Hyg.* (July, Aug., Sept. 1957).
2. L. C. McCabe, *Air Pollution* (McGraw Hill, New York, 1952).
3. H. F. Johnstone and D. R. Coughanowr, "Absorption of SO_2 from air and oxidation in drops containing catalysts," *Ind. Eng. Chem.* **50**, 1169 (1958).
4. *Los Angeles County Air Pollution Control District, 2nd Tech. and Admin. Rept. on Air Pollution Control in Los Angeles County* (1950–51).
5. M. O. Amdur, *Ind. Hyg. Quart.* **18**, 149 (1957).
6. A. J. Haagen-Smit, C. E. Bradley, M. M. Fox, *Ind. Eng. Chem.* **45**, 2086 (1953); A. J. Haagen-Smit and M. M. Fox, *S.A.E. Trans.* **63**, 575 (1955).
7. A. J. Haagen-Smit and M. M. Fox, *Air Repair* **4**, 105 (1954).
8. C. E. Bradley and A. J. Haagen-Smit, *Rubber Chem. and Technol.* **24**, 750 (1957).
9. E. R. Stephens, *J. Franklin Inst.* **263**, 349 (1957); E. R. Stephens, W. E. Scott, P. L. Hanst, R. C. Doerr, *J. Air Pollution Control Assoc.* **6**, 159 (1956).
10. M. O. Amdur and J. Mead, *Am. J. Physiol.* **192**, 364 (1958).
11. F. N. Frenkiel, *Sci. Monthly* **82**, 196 (1956).

Do Air Pollutants
Act as Mutagens?

HERMANN J. MULLER*

An increasing number of toxic substances that may occur as pollutants have been found to produce their chief damage by way of mutagenic action, that is, by injuring the genetic material of the cells they enter. Some substances produce this kind of effect indirectly, by giving rise to chemical reactions wherein a mutagenic substance is produced. Among the more directly mutagenic substances are those with peroxide, epoxide, chlorethyl, ethylene-imino and mesyloxy groups. In general, these are especially active when two such groups occur in the same molecule, possibly because of the greater likelihood thus afforded of both strands of the Watson-Crick DNA doublet (chromosome) being affected simultaneously at nearby points.

Thus far, all chemical mutagens intensively studied have been found to produce the same general complex of clinical effects on tissues into whose cells they penetrate as do ionizing radiation and ultra-violet; that is, they are radio-mimetic. Thus, like radiation, they produce irritation, inflammation, necrotic and precancerous changes, particularly in the more rapidly dividing cells of the parts penetrated, and they finally give rise there to malignant neoplasms. Again like radiation, however, they tend to be more injurious to malignant than to normal tissue, in correspondence with the former's faster proliferation, and they thereby act not only carcinogenically but also carcinolytically.

The carcinogenic effect is probably an expression of the production, in individual genes of individual somatic cells penetrated, of mutations that reduce the cell's susceptibility to inhibition of its proliferation. In cases where the agent reaches the germ cells, the mutations induced by it are manifested mainly as inheritable impairments, usually slight but of the most diverse kinds, that afflict

* The late Dr. Muller of Indiana University was a Nobel Prize Laureate.

256

the descendants through an indefinitely long succession of generations. On the other hand, the irritating and destructive effects of mutagens, including their carcinolytic action, on organisms exposed to them, are expressions of the genetic impairment and death of scattered somatic cells that have experienced chromosome loss or nuclear entanglement, in the course of mitoses undergone after one or more of their chromosomes had been broken by the mutagen. Recent studies indicate that the generalized long-term rise in morbidity and mortality, amounting to a decrease in longevity, of individuals exposed to penetrating mutagenic agents, are also expressions of scattered cell losses caused by chromosome breaks.

Many mutagenic substances are destroyed or rendered innocuous before attaining circulation in the body, as for example when a peroxide molecule is attacked by catalase, but sometimes such defenses are incomplete or may be used up by near-saturation doses. Especially in the portals of entry, such as, in the case of air pollutants, the lungs, would the concentrations be more likely to be high enough to succeed in reaching the cell nuclei and there exerting their mutagenic influence. In such cases the chief visible signs of their action would be a shorter term irritation and edema of the organ of entry, a longer term scarification and reduction in its functional capacity, vigor and resistance to challenges, and ultimately, in some cases, carcinogenesis.

THE MARTIAN
ENVIRONMENT

Interestingly, the newest of scientific and technological developments—space exploration—has made many individuals conscious of ecology. One reads of possible life on other planets in our galaxy and on planets in other galaxies.

Before we consider the problems of possible life on Mars, it seems appropriate to consider the spaceship in space. This vehicle is a remarkable container having very sophisticated machinery, a well-trained pilot, and an intricate system of ecological relationships involving man and machine. Within a few years, one will probably read of the construction of a spaceship as a self-contained ecological unit, dependent only upon the energy from the sun and independent of earth.

Two interesting papers concerning possibilities of life on Mars are included in this section. Horowitz holds out the possibility that Mars may have had life at one time and that there is no convincing evidence, at present, that life does not still exist on Mars. The existence of life on Mars, according to Horowitz, is neither proven nor unproven.

Siegal and his colleagues showed that many complex terrestrial organisms can survive and grow under experimental atmospheric conditions which simulate the Martian atmosphere. If this were the only environmental factor with which to be concerned, human beings from Earth would have an acceptable vegetarian diet on Mars.

The paragraph on p. 333 beginning with "Comparative chemical and biochemical tests . . ." may be regarded as an optional reading on techniques.

The Search for
Extraterrestrial Life*

N. H. HOROWITZ

The discovery of life on another planet would be a monument to our age. Not only would it be an unparalleled technological achievement, but it would be a momentous scientific event that would enlarge our view of nature and ourselves and provide unique evidence bearing on the origin of life. In this article, I am going to discuss the coming search for life on Mars. Venus, our other close neighbor among the planets, has been excluded from consideration, for the time being at least, because its high surface temperature—in the neighborhood of 400°C—seems incompatible with life or, for that matter, with much organic chemistry of any kind. The planets of the solar system beyond Mars are out of reach for the present.

The Martian environment

I have given the reason for thinking that if life ever existed on Venus, it does so no longer. What can be said about Mars? We can say that although the situation is not brimming with hope, neither is it hopeless. The Martian environment is a harsh one by terrestrial standards. The mean temperature is −55°C, compared to +15°C for the Earth. The atmosphere is thin and very dry; it contains carbon dioxide and a small amount of water vapor, but no detected oxygen. Owing to the low density of the atmosphere and the absence of a magnetic field, the surface of Mars is bombarded by cosmic rays and solar radiation in an almost unattenuated form, as O'Gallagher and Simpson have recently pointed out (1). Finally, the Mariner IV photographs give the definite impres-

* The author is professor of biology at the California Institute of Technology and chief of the Bioscience Section, Jet Propulsion Laboratory, Pasadena, California. This article is based on a talk given at the dedication of the Laboratory for Astrophysics and Space Research, University of Chicago, 13 October 1965.

sion that Mars is geologically a dead planet whose surface has been undisturbed by anything except meteorite impacts for a very long time and which lacks the great variety of ecological habitats that characterize the Earth (2).

This is all very depressing news for biologists, but if I have learned anything during 6 years of association with the space program, it is that people with manic-depressive tendencies should stay out of it. Our knowledge of planetary environments is still fragmentary, and one's subjective estimate of the likelihood of finding life on Mars is liable to undergo violent fluctuations from time to time as new data accumulate. The fact is that nothing that we have learned about Mars—in contrast to Venus—excludes it as a possible abode of life. Martian temperatures are not very different from those of Antarctica, where a varied microbial life, and even a few flowering plants and invertebrate animals, have been found (3). Although the mean temperature on Mars is low, the seasonal and diurnal fluctuations are great, and temperatures as high as 25°C have been measured near the equator.

Radiation flux on Mars

The ionization produced at the surface of Mars by cosmic rays is several hundred times greater than that found on Earth, which is shielded by 1033 grams of atmosphere per square centimeter, but it is still far below a level that could be considered hazardous for life—even a slowly reproducing form of life. The dose rate calculated from O'Gallagher and Simpson's estimate of the ion density at or near the Martian surface is about 20 millirads per day, whereas the mean lethal dose for a typical bacterium (*Escherichia coli*) is in the neighborhood of 5000 rads. A greater potential hazard is posed by the solar far-ultraviolet light which, according to a recent report (4), penetrates to the Martian surface. Wavelengths in the neighborhood of 2600 angstroms are highly lethal for unprotected cells. On the Earth, these wavelengths are removed by ozone in our upper atmosphere. At the distance of Mars, the flux of solar ultraviolet in the 2400- to 2800-angstrom range exceeds 20 ergs per square millimeter per second (5). This quantity of radiation is sufficient to kill the most resistant terrestrial bacteria in a matter of minutes. Ultraviolet is strongly absorbed by many substances, however, so that it would not be difficult for Martian organisms to be protected against it. If a substantial fraction of this radiation reaches the surface of Mars, it would be a significant factor in protecting the planet against accidental contamination by terrestrial microorganisms, and it obviously should be taken into account in determining spacecraft sterilization standards. This is a large and complex subject which I will not attempt to discuss here.

Scarcity of water

The scarcity of water is probably the most serious limiting factor for any Martian biology. The atmosphere of Mars contains approximately 14 microns of precipitable water, or roughly 1/1000 the amount found in our atmosphere (6).

Polar ice caps that wax and wane with the seasons are seen on the planet, and it has been suggested that permafrost may be found beneath the surface. No permanent bodies of liquid water can exist there, however, because Mars is below the triple point for water. It has been argued that the lack of water excludes the possibility of life as we know it on Mars. It is certainly true that no terrestrial species could survive under average Martian conditions as we know them, except in a dormant state. But if we admit the possibility that Mars once had a more favorable climate which was gradually transformed to the severe one we find there today, and if we accept the possibility that life arose on the planet during this earlier epoch, then we cannot exclude the possibility that Martian life succeeded in adapting itself to the changing conditions and survives there still.

Many terrestrial species are adapted to life in dry environments—in deserts, for example, or in saturated brine, as in the Dead Sea or the Great Salt Lake. One of the most interesting drought-loving forms is the kangaroo rat of the Mojave Desert in Arizona and Southern California. This little animal has been studied by Schmidt-Nielsen (7), who finds that it can live indefinitely on air-dried barley without ever drinking water. All its water is produced metabolically by the oxidation of carbohydrates. It can survive in this way at relative humidities as low as 20 percent—that is, in an atmosphere in equilibrium with 60 percent sulfuric acid. If the kangaroo rat is fed on soy beans, it requires water in order to excrete the extra urea produced by this high-protein food; but it can then thrive on sea water. The urine of the animal contains twice as much salt as sea water does.

Even Southern California is not as dry as Mars, and I am not suggesting that Mars is inhabited by kangaroo rats and that the first life-detection device on Mars should be a mousetrap. I am citing this example merely in order to show what evolution can accomplish. The point was made very clearly in a recent cartoon by Mauldin in which a flying saucer carrying two obvious Martians is shown. One Martian is inspecting the Earth through field glasses and is saying to the other: "A planet three-quarters covered with water couldn't possibly support life."

The biological implications of the Mariner IV photographs of Mars have been widely discussed. These photographs show a densely cratered surface resembling that of the Moon. If the rates of meteorite impact on Mars and the Moon are the same, then the Mariner pictures mean that the craters seen on Mars are the same age as those on the Moon—that is, up to 5 billion years old. The fact that such ancient craters are still visible would imply the virtual absence of weathering on the face of Mars; this, together with the failure to detect any signs of river valleys or ocean beds, would lead to the conclusion that the condition of Mars as we see it today is not very different from that of primordial Mars. If this were so, there would be little reason to suppose that life had ever evolved on the planet. The question of the relative rates of meteorite impact on the Moon and Mars is critical for this argument, however. Recent discussions of this problem (8, 9) indicate that in all probability Mars has been subject to a much higher rate of crater-forming impacts than the Moon. It follows that the craters seen on

Mars are younger than those of the Moon, and no conclusions can be drawn from the photographs about the nature of earlier Martian environments. The greatest possible age for the Martian craters, according to Anders and Arnold (8), is 800 million years. But fossil remains of highly evolved types of microorganisms have been found in Precambrian rocks approaching 2 billion years old (10). Clearly, then, it would be dangerous to conclude from the evidence now available that life never evolved on Mars.

I cannot leave this subject without emphasizing that not all the evidence bearing on this question is negative. The phenomenon that first led astronomers to suggest that Mars is an inhabited planet—the seasonal change of color in the maria, or dark regions—is still unexplained. This effect is described as a wave of darkening that starts at the edge of the melting polar ice cap in the spring and progresses toward the equator as the season advances. The color of the maria changes from grayish to violet, although some observers have reported vivid greens and blues. By midsummer, the wave reaches the equator; then, with the approach of winter, the color fades. It is generally agreed that the phenomenon is associated with the seasonal translocation of water vapor from one pole to the other. It could thus reflect the growth of vegetation, stimulated by the availability of water, or it could result from an inorganic process such as the uptake of water by hygroscopic salts. The biological explanation readily accounts for one striking fact; namely, that the maria continue to reappear despite the great dust storms that sometimes obscure the entire disc of the planet. This regenerative capacity suggests that something in the maria is capable of growing up through the dust layer. It is of interest to note that there is an indication in the Mariner IV photographs, supported by recent radar experiments, that the maria correspond to heavily cratered regions.

Objectives and tactics of Martian biological exploration

Coming now to the tactics of Martian biological exploration, let me first state the initial objectives. They are twofold: first, of course, to determine whether there is life on the planet; second, and equally important, to learn whether Martian life, if it exists, is independent in origin from life on the Earth. I will consider here only the first of these twin objectives, since this is the only one we can hope to accomplish in the next decade. Current theories about the history of the solar system and the origin of life suggest that conditions on primitive Mars may have been sufficiently like those of the primitive Earth to have made possible an independent origin of life (11). But if life is found on Mars, it cannot be *assumed* to have had an independent origin. To get the answer would require a careful study of the chemical organization of Martian life. We would want to know, for example, whether Martian protoplasm contains nucleic acids and proteins, and if so what their composition is. We would have questions about the optical activity of Martian amino acids, about the Martian genetic code, and so forth. These are difficult questions. To get answers to them in a reasonable length of time may require the return of Martian samples to the Earth for study in terrestrial laboratories. This may not be so far-fetched as it sounds; informed people are already talking about manned missions to Mars by 1985. In this discussion, however, I will consider only life-detection experiments that could be carried out by unmanned spacecraft that land on the surface of Mars. The possibility of performing an unambiguous life-detection test from a flyby or an orbiter is remote. To solve this problem, we will probably have to land a capsule on Mars and have it survive long enough to make some measurements and transmit them back to Earth. This is not an easy task, but no Mars mission is easy.

In designing life-detection experiments, certain fundamental principles have to be observed. In the first place, the best experiments are those that make the fewest unsupported assumptions about the nature of Martian life and the Martian environment. Second, it is essential that the program of life-detection tests be of such a nature that positive results will be strongly indicative of the presence of life, and cumulative negative results will provide credible evidence of its absence. On both scores, a series of high-resolution visual scans of the Martian terrain, including a TV-microscope system, would be nearly ideal. Such scans of a number of selected areas would be of great interest not only for biologists, but for other scientists as well—and, I imagine, for nonscientists, too. Unfortunately, the same quality that makes photographs so valuable—their high information content —also makes them very expensive to transmit, in terms of the power required. The capacity of the communication link to transmit information—its bit rate capability—may not be high enough on early missions to send many pictures. Besides, we need more information than pictures alone can produce. For these reasons, it is desirable to develop low-bit-rate experiments which are capable of yielding useful data. As an example of such an experiment, I will mention one whose development I have been associated with. This device, which has been called "Gulliver" by its inventor, Gilbert V. Levin (12), is representative of a number of experiments being developed under the sponsorship of the National Aeronautics and Space Administration to detect microbial life in Martian soil. By searching for microorganisms, it is hoped to maximize the chance of success. Microorganisms are ubiquitous on the Earth, and they survive in extreme environments. Microbial life could conceivably be the only form of life on Mars, but it is hard to imagine there being life on Mars without microbes. For the purposes of fundamental biology, it would be just as valuable to find microbial life on Mars as higher forms. Any form of Martian life would be intensely interesting to science. From a fundamental viewpoint, there is only one form of life on the Earth. All species are constructed out of the same few building blocks; despite appearances, the differences between species are relatively superficial. The question we ask is whether another form of life exists on Mars.

The "Gulliver" experiment

"Gulliver" is a culture chamber that inoculates itself with a sample of soil. The sample is obtained by two 7½-meter lengths of kite line wound on small projectiles. When the projectiles are fired, the lines unwind and fall to the ground. A small motor inside the chamber then reels them in, together with adhering soil particles. The chamber contains a growth medium whose organic nutrients are labeled with radioactive carbon. When the medium is inoculated with soil, the accompanying microorganisms metabolize the organic compounds and release radioactive carbon dioxide. This diffuses to the window of a Geiger counter, where the radioactivity is measured. Growth of the microbes causes the rate of carbon dioxide production to increase exponentially with time—an indication that the gas is being formed biologically. Provision is also made for the injection, during the run, of a solution containing a metabolic poison which can be used to confirm the biological origin of the carbon dioxide and to analyze the nature of the metabolic reactions.

The choice of nutrients for the Gulliver medium—especially the organic nutrients—is obviously a matter of central importance. I will not take time here to explain why we assume that Martian life would be based on carbon and not, for instance, on silicon. This question has received considerable attention in the past (13). There is general agreement that carbon is uniquely qualified among the elements for forming the large and complex kinds of molecules that we associate with life. We know also that the Martian atmosphere contains large quantities of carbon dioxide—in fact, this is its principal constituent. If there is life on Mars, then it is a reasonable assumption—indeed, I believe it is a necessary consequence—that its carbon cycles through this atmosphere. We would expect to find on Mars, as we find on Earth, a continual exchange of carbon between the atmosphere and the biosphere.

The problem of selecting organic substrates is common to Gulliver and other experiments designed to culture Martian microbes. What we need are organic substances that are widespread in the solar system and that are known to have a biological function on the Earth. This problem can be approached experimentally. In fact, the experiment has already been done: It is the well known Urey-Miller spark-discharge reaction (14). This experiment demonstrated the production of a variety of biologically important organic compounds when a spark discharge was passed through a mixture of gases believed to resemble those of the Earth's primordial atmosphere. Since the primitive atmospheres of Mars and Earth were probably similar, it is reasonable to suppose that the same compounds were formed in large amounts on primitive Mars. Many of these substances—for example, formate, lactate, and glutamate—are readily metabolized to carbon dioxide, and they are therefore a natural choice for a cosmic culture medium.

Photosynthesis

Radioactive carbon can be used in another kind of experiment that makes even fewer assumptions about the nature of Martian life than does Gulliver. It can be used to detect photosynthesis—that is, the light-dependent fixation of carbon dioxide. A number of instruments specially designed to detect photosynthesis are currently being developed under NASA sponsorship. One of the strongest statements that can be made about Martian biology is that if there is life on the planet there must be at least one photosynthetic species. This is so because the sun is the only inexhaustible source of energy in the solar system. All life on the Earth depends ultimately on those species which are capable of utilizing solar energy. This includes the chemoautotropic bacteria which obtain energy by the oxidation of inorganic matter; these organisms would soon exhaust their sources of supply if they were not continually replenished by the activity of photo-synthesizers. Since photosynthetic organisms must receive light from the sun, this argument leads to the corollary that, if there is life on Mars, some of it must live on the surface. There is no use imagining that if there is no life at the surface it may be found under rocks or in caves. The presence of little or no oxygen in the atmosphere of Mars does not, of course, rule out the possibility that photosyn-thesis is occurring there. On the Earth, green-plant photosynthesis produces oxygen, but bacterial photosynthesis does not. This difference results from the fact that bacteria do not use water for the reduction of carbon dioxide, but other reducing agents. The same could be true on Mars, but since the planet is ap-parently hydrogen-poor, the nature of the reducing agent poses a major problem.

Other experiments being developed for the biological exploration of Mars include automatic instruments for the analysis of the atmosphere and soil, with special reference to substances of biological importance, and for detecting net optical activity in soil extracts (15).

Summary and conclusions

In summary, current theories about the history of the solar system and the origin of life suggest that conditions on primitive Mars may have been sufficiently like those of the primitive Earth to have made possible an independent origin of life. The present environment of Mars is extremely harsh, but our knowledge of it does not permit the conclusion that, if life ever existed there, it is now extinct. Indeed, certain phenomena associated with the change of seasons suggest the growth of vegetation on Mars, although other explanations are not excluded. A number of automatic devices designed to detect microbial life, or the products of microbial activity, in Martian soil are currently being developed. It is hoped that these instruments, combined with high-resolution photography, will give an answer to the question of life on Mars in the next decade. A positive answer would immediately pose questions concerning the chemical nature of Martian life. How we will go about getting answers to these questions, should they arise, we cannot now predict.

In closing, let me say that, in my personal opinion, the chance of finding life on Mars is clearly not zero, but neither is it very high. Certainly, there is little in the Mariner IV and other recent data to make one confident on this score. It is not optimism about the outcome that gives impetus to the search for extrater-restrial life; rather, it is the immense importance that a positive result would have.

One has to multiply the first of these somewhat subjective quantities by the second to find the scientific worth of the Mars undertaking. The argument of this article is that the value so obtained is high.

Of course, even a lifeless Mars could be of great biological value if it yielded fossils or yielded organic chemicals of a prebiological era. In respect to the latter point, the Moon, too, may be of considerable interest. These are questions for the future. For the present, we can say that while Mariner IV neither proved nor disproved the existence of life on Mars, it did demonstrate that we now have the technology necessary to get the answer; indeed, this demonstration was the most important result of the mission. Whatever the final answer to the question of life on Mars may turn out to be, the search will be one of the great scientific and engineering enterprises of the 20th century.

REFERENCES

1. J. J. O'GALLAGHER and J. A. SIMPSON, *Science* **149,** 969 (1965).
2. R. B. LEIGHTON, B. C. MURRAY, R. P. SHARP, J. D. ALLEN, R. K. SLOAN, *ibid.,* p. 627.
3. G. A. LLANO, *Sci. Am.* **207,** 212 (Sept. 1962).
4. D. C. EVANS, *Science* **149,** 969 (1965).
5. C. W. ALLEN, *Astrophysical Quantities* (University of London Press, London, 1955), p. 139.
6. L. D. KAPLAN, G. MUNCH, H. SPINRAD, *Astrophys. J.* **139,** 1 (1964).
7. K. SCHMIDT-NIELSEN, *Desert Animals* (Oxford Univ. Press, Oxford, 1964).
8. E. ANDERS and J. R. ARNOLD, *Science* **149,** 1494 (1965).
9. J. WITTING, F. NARIN, C. A. STONE, *ibid.,* p. 1496; R. B. BALDWIN, *ibid.,* p. 1498.
10. M. F. GLAESSNER, *Biol. Rev.* **37,** 467 (1962).
11. N. H. HOROWITZ and S. MILLER, *Fortschr. Chem. Org. Naturstoffe* **20,** 423 (1962).
12. G. V. LEVIN, A. H. HEIM, J. R. CLENDENNING, M. F. THOMPSON, *Science* **138,** 114 (1962).
13. J. T. EDSALL and J. WYMAN, *Biophysical Chemistry* (Academic Press, New York, 1962), vol. 1. chap. 1.
14. S. L. MILLER, *Ann. N.Y. Acad. Sci.* **69,** 260 (1957).
15. F. H. QUIMBY, ED., "Concepts for Detection of Extraterrestrial Life," (National Aeronautics and Space Administration, Washington, D.C., 1964).
16. I am indebted to Dr. Paul Howard-Flanders and Richard W. Davies for helpful discussions in regard to radiation fluxes at Mars.

Martian Biology:
The Experimentalist's Approach

S. M. SIEGEL, L. A. HALPERN,
C. GIUMARRO, G. RENWICK
AND G. DAVIS

Recently, Salisbury, in a provocative article,[1] has constructed a speculative picture of possible Martian life-forms, and of possible biogeochemical cycles in which such forms might participate.

We are in general agreement with the concepts which Salisbury has presented; as experimentalists, however, we question his reservations about the use of simulated environments. Speculation or even sound theorization notwithstanding, the sole model for life now available to us is life on Earth. Because statistical factors influence evolution, one would expect even identical planets to exhibit appreciable divergences in life-forms. Nevertheless, Earth and Mars might contain local environments in which convergent forms could arise. Thus, Salisbury suggests that the higher terrestrial plant, rather than the lower forms traditionally postulated in astronomical circles, is a good model for explaining some of the phenomena which have been held to indicate the presence of life on Mars. On the other hand, he distinguishes higher plants as plants which "universally require oxygen." This distinction suggests a divergence between the terrestrial model and its Martian counterpart which we believe may not exist.

Higher plants at low oxygen pressures

Mature air-grown plants, including *Coleus,* marigold and *Alyssum,* can survive many days under near-anaerobic conditions in spite of their aerobic history.[2] Lettuce, tomato, cucumber, bean, marigold, *Zinnia,* rye, corn, *Ageratum, Dian-*

* Union Carbide Research Institute, Tarrytown, N.Y. Reprinted from *Nature*, Vol. 197, No. 4865, pp. 329–331, January 26, 1963.

TABLE 1. Germination percentage after 3–6 days.

Kind of seed	Argon (or nitrogen)	Atmosphere 2% oxygen + 98% argon	5% oxygen + 95% argon	Air
Lettuce	0	78	78	98
Marigold	0	33	—	57
Zinnia	0	22	—	57
Celosia	22	81	—	89
Alyssum	0	21	—	80
Portulaca	0	50	—	55
Carrot	0	50	—	32
Onion	0	65	—	69
Cucumber	17	88	96	100
Bean	0	—	60	53
Coleus	0	—	54	91
Tomato	0	—	33	91
Dianthus	7	—	50	82
Ageratum	—	—	33	84
Cabbage	0	9	71	95
Turnip	0	16	21	90
Beet	0	—	40	50
Rye	40	50	95	95
Barley	—	—	28	80
Corn	29	—	—	80
Rice	17	24	24	23

thus, Celosia, rice, turnip, broccoli and other common plants germinate well and produce sizable seedlings in an atmosphere containing 5 percent oxygen or less (ref. 3, Table 1). Several of these plants—notably cucumber, rye, corn, rice and *Celosia*—produce some seeds which are facultative anaerobes.

If our results with more than 30 higher plant species are at all representative, they indicate that, among terrestrial plants, many (perhaps most) require little oxygen; some (perhaps many) might qualify as microphilic aerobes; and a sizable minority, perhaps 10 percent, can function anaerobically.

Low oxygen-low temperature interaction

Many terrestrial plants are hardy enough to survive freezing and to grow during the more moderate phases of the extreme diurnal temperature cycles reported for Mars. The south tropical latitudes of Mars are notably mild.[4,5] Furthermore, we have found that cultivation of seeds in atmospheres containing little oxygen enhances the resistance of the seedlings to freezing and lowers the minimum temperature required for germination. Three-week-old cucumber seedlings grown from seed in air or in an atmosphere of 2 percent oxygen and 98 percent argon were cooled to −10°C., kept at that temperature for 1 h, and then allowed to

FIG. 1. Left: freeze-resistant cucumber seedlings grown for 3 weeks in an atmosphere of 2 percent oxygen plus 98 percent argon. Right: air-grown 3-week-old cucumber seedlings damaged by freezing (−10°C.). Both groups had been kept at −10°C. for 1 h and allowed to thaw for 1 h before being photographed.

thaw. As the air-grown seedlings thawed, they collapsed, presumably because of mechanical damage by ice crystals (Fig. 1, left). In contrast, the sturdy seedlings grown in an atmosphere of 2 percent oxygen were not damaged (Fig. 1, right). At temperatures below 10°C., cucumber seeds will germinate in air to an extent no greater than 10 percent in 10 days. If, however, the seeds are incubated in an argon atmosphere (containing only 0.005 percent oxygen) 50–90 percent germinate in 20 days at 6°–7°C., and subsequent shoot extension at a rate of 10 mm a day has been noted. Even under aerobic conditions, germination of cucumber seeds exposed daily to temperatures of −7°C. for 8 h and 23°C. for 16 h was about 30 percent in 2–3 days and 50 percent in 4 days. Cucumber is not noted for its resistance to cold.

Hardier species can germinate when exposed daily to temperatures of −7°C. for 16 h and 23°C. for 8 h. For the common 'rock garden' species, *Dianthus* and *Ageratum,* germination is 10 percent in 3–4 days in these temperature conditions. Germination for these species was doubled or tripled when the daily freezing period was shortened to 8 h.

We have already reported[6] the germination of winter rye and the development of green winter rye seedlings under a synthetic atmosphere which simulates in most respects the atmosphere believed to exist on Mars,[5] using a temperature-cycle of $+20°C$. (day) and $-10°$. (night). In one respect our synthetic atmosphere differs considerably from the real Martian atmosphere in that we added 1–2 percent by weight of water in the soil, which results in a substantial partial pressure of water in the enclosed atmosphere. The best available information indicates a much lower (perhaps 2 orders of magnitude) average water content in the Martian atmosphere than is present under our conditions. However, it must be borne in mind that astronomical observations of the Martian atmosphere as a whole would not, in all probability, reveal the presence of localized bodies of water, or of microclimates at the surface of Mars which are much higher in water content than for the total Martian atmosphere.

Xerophytes

Xerophytes are also markedly conditioned by their gaseous environment. Only a few specimens, of *Euphorbia clandestina* and *Gymnocalycium friederickii,* were tested, but the results were none the less striking.

In this experiment, specimens were grown in 16–1. jars either in air or in a synthetic atmosphere of volume composition as follows: oxygen 0.09 percent; carbon dioxide, 0.24 percent; argon, 1.39 percent; and nitrogen, 98.28 percent.

This gas mixture was used at a total pressure of 0.1 atmosphere (after De Vaucouleurs,[5] who provides a good general treatise on aereography). The plants were placed in a 1 : 1 mixture of potting soil and 'Perl-lome' ('Perl-lome,' a product of Certified Industrial Products, Inc., Hillside, New Jersey, is a derivative of perlite. De Vaucouleurs suggests that a felsitic rhyolite covers the Martian surface, and perlite is such a volcanic mineral). The water content of the soil and 'Perl-lome' mixture was about 1–2 percent by weight.

After about a month at $25°C$., the jars were transferred to an unheated greenhouse. Temperatures were recorded and observations on plant conditions were made during January, February and March 1962. The mean daily maxima for these months were $+5°C$., $-2°C$. and $+8°C$., respectively. The mean nightly minima were $-9°C$., $-12°C$. and $0°C$.

By the end of February the four *Euphorbia* specimens grown in air were dead, but the four grown in the synthetic atmosphere were normal in appearance —green and erect by contrast with the yellow, shrivelled group grown in air. At the end of March, only one of the plants in the synthetic atmosphere appeared normal. The remaining three were no longer erect, although they retained green coloration and were not desiccated. Six *Gymnocalycium* plants were grown in each atmosphere. Three of those grown in air survived through February, and all those grown in the synthetic atmosphere still appeared normal at the end of

TABLE 2. Changes in weight and size of xerophytes under experimental atmospheric conditions.

Height (cm)			Diameter (cm)			Fresh weight (g)			Dry wt. (g)
Initial	Final	Change	Initial	Final	Change	Initial	Final	Change	
Euphorbia*, grown in air									
11.4	10.1	−1.3	1.0	0.5	−0.5	12.0	5.4	−6.6	4.7
Euphorbia*, grown in synthetic atmosphere									
11.6	11.9	+0.3	1.0	1.1	+0.1	12.0	12.5	+0.5	5.5
Gymnocalycium†, grown in air									
						13.9	5.2	−8.7	2.2
Gymnocalycium†, grown in synthetic atmosphere									
						14.5	6.3	−8.2	1.7

* Four specimens in each atmosphere.
† Six specimens in each atmosphere.

February. During March, the remaining plants grown in air died, while only one of those grown in the synthetic atmosphere died.

After 3 months of cold, the plants were examined and analysed. The *Euphorbia* plants grown in air had lost height, diameter and fresh weight (Table 2). Plants grown in the synthetic atmosphere showed a gain in these measurements, and all had retained some green coloration, even though only one out of four was scored as 'normal.' All the *Gymnocalycium* plants lost weight, regardless of the atmosphere in which they were grown.

Comparative chemical and biochemical tests made on *Euphorbia* plants grown in the two atmospheres revealed an interesting pattern of similarities and differences. Spectrophotometric determination of chlorophylls[7] in acetone extracts of the leaves (which form an apical whorl) showed that none were present in the group of dead plants that had been grown in air. Chlorophylls *a* and *b* were present in the usual 3 : 1 ratio in extracts from plants grown in the synthetic atmosphere. Longitudinal sections (3–5 mm) from the aerial portions of the plants were tested by immersion in several common reagents. Tissues from the two groups were similarly treated. Marked differences were observed in peroxidase activity and in the results of non-carbohydrate aldehyde determinations. (A mixture of 10^{-3} M pyrogallol and 10^{-3} M hydrogen peroxide in phosphate buffer (*p*H 4.5) was used as the peroxidase developer.) Even sharper were the distinctions in the results of tests for reducing sugar, starch, phosphorylase activity (tissues were immersed in 1 percent glucose-1-phosphate at *p*H 6.6 for 1 h at 25°C., then stained with KI_3 [after S. Siegel, *Bot. Gaz.*, **114**, 139 {1952}], and indole; all results were negative for the air-grown group and positive for the test group. Determinations of element composition for the two groups reflected no striking differences. [The determinations were made by Micro-Tech Laboratories, Skokie, Ill.])

TABLE 3. Germination of seeds in water vapour in air at 25°C.

Kind of seed	Germination after 13 days (percent)	Root-length after 13 days (mm)
Phlox	52	7.3
Cucumber	37	7.7
Marigold	18	1.0
Portulaca	63	4.9
Alyssum	26	8.3
Turnip	88	16.5
Carrot	40	18.3
Celosia	100	18.2
Rye	100	30.5

TABLE 4. Germination of rye in experimental atmosphere in water vapour at 25°C.

Incubation time (days)	No. Germinated	Germinated (percent)	Longest roots (mm)
1	6	4.5	1
4	45	33.8	5
5	100	75.3	15

Germination without liquid water

Xerophytism is a relative condition, and it seems reasonable to suppose that plants other than typical desert forms may be able to adapt to dry conditions. The seed, generally a rich source of hydrophilic colloids, is well known for its imbibitional powers. Accordingly, some experiments were carried out in which dry seeds were supported in closed jars, in air at a pressure of 75–125 mm of mercury, above a source of liquid water. Germination was slow as compared with usual rates, but the results (Table 3) show that a number of species can germinate and produce seedlings without difficulty under such conditions. When winter rye was placed in the synthetic atmosphere at a total pressure of 75 mm of mercury, 150 mm above a source of liquid water, germination was reasonably prompt and considerable root growth was noted after several days (Table 4).

Other factors

In our laboratory we are also investigating the effects of substratum and of ultra-violet radiation on plant growth under conditions of low temperature and low oxygen supply. We have observed that remarkably high levels of ultra-violet radiation are sometimes needed to suppress the growth of higher plants (energy of 10^8 ergs/cm^2 is only marginally effective as an inhibitor of growth in bean embryos).

Animal forms

Most of our investigative efforts have been concerned with the flowering plant. Other plants also show promising behaviour at low oxygen-levels. The fungus *Alternaria* and gametophytes of the fern *Pteridium* have been grown in an atmosphere of 5 percent oxygen and 95 percent argon.

Among animal forms, the ciliate *Colpoda* grows in hay-infusion cultures prepared and maintained under the synthetic atmosphere. HeLa cells, which can grow for 4 days under strictly anaerobic conditions more rapidly than in air, are being examined for adaptability (including clonal selection) to anaerobic culture of indefinite duration at low temperature in media of high osmotic concentration. *Planaria* have thus far shown rigidly aerobic behaviour, but they have been maintained for as long as 23 days in 5 percent oxygen and 95 percent argon and 16 days in 2 percent oxygen and 98 percent argon, as compared with 93 days in air.

The most striking results have been obtained with the common brine shrimp, *Artemia salina.* In sea-water (salinity 3 percent) or diluted sea-water (salinity 1 percent) in both liquid and agar media, active, viable *Nauplius* larvæ have been hatched in approximately equal percentages in air, in air reduced to 0.03 atmosphere, and in the synthetic gas mixture of 0.1 atmospheres. Typical values for hatching, based on findings with several hundred eggs per trial range from 35 to 45 percent in 2 days.

It seems likely that marine organisms could adapt to the requirements of existence in a variety of synthetic environments   existence in a medium which is 'dry' in the physiological sense and has a depressed freezing point.[8] If, as in the case of *Artemia,* such organisms were also facultative anaerobes or near anaerobes, their prospects for survival would be good indeed.

Members of other invertebrate phyla also possess unusual ranges of tolerance to low pressure, low oxygen, and low temperature. The small black ant, *Monomorium minutum,* retains general activity and positive phototaxy after more than 15 h in 1 percent oxygen and 99 percent argon. The nematode *Cephalobus* remains active indefinitely under anaerobic conditions or at total pressure of 0.03 atmosphere and shows remarkable tolerances to freezing and to salinity well in excess of that of sea-water.

Conclusions

Our results show that complex terrestrial organisms can survive and grow under conditions which constitute an extreme departure in one or more respects from the normal terrestrial environment. Of particular importance was the finding that tolerance of plants to low temperatures could be conditioned in a favourable manner by synthetic atmospheres low in oxygen. It would be reasonable to expect other combinations of stress factors to give rise to unusual and exciting biological responses.

While it is impossible to project these findings on to present-day attempts to anticipate the nature of life elsewhere in the solar system, it is reasonable to conclude that the 'plasticity' of organisms as we recognize them is far greater than the teachings of modern biology indicate. Thus, whatever environments may be encountered during future explorations of the solar system there is every prospect that those which are not too extreme relative to Earth, for example, those expected on Mars may well support forms of life that we could recognize readily.

REFERENCES

1. SALISBURY, F. B., *Science,* **136,** 17 (1962); this article contains an excellent bibliography.
2. SIEGEL, S. M., *Physiol. Plantarum,* **14,** 554 (1961).
3. SIEGEL, S. M., and HALPERN, L. A., *Physiol. Plantarum* (in the press). SIEGEL, S. M., ROSEN, L. A., and RENWICK, G., *ibid.,* **15,** 304 (1962).
4. KIESS, C. C., and LASSOVZSKY, K., *The Known Physical Characteristics of the Moon and Planets,* Publ. No. *ARDC-TR*-58–41 (*ASTIA* Doc. No. *AD* 115–617) (Air Research and Development Command, Andrews Air Force Base, Washington, 1958).
5. DE VAUCOULEURS, G., *Physics of the Planet Mars* (Faber and Faber, London, 1953).
6. SIEGEL, S. M., ROSEN, L. A., and GIUMARRO, C., *Proc. U.S. Nat. Acad. Sci.,* **48,** 725 (1962).
7. LONG, C. (edit.), *Biochemists Handbook,* 1029 (Van Nostrand, Princeton, 1961).
8. SCHMIDT, K., and ALLEE, W. C., *Ecological Animal Geography* (Wiley, New York, 1949).

Appendixes

Appendix A
Glossary of Terms

Acetone	Technically called dimethyl ketone. Small quantities are found in normal urine, but larger quantities may be found in the urine of persons with diabetes.
Allometric	Different parts of organic beings may change with proportionate or disproportionate rates in time.
Amenorrhea	Absence of menses.
Anti-Rh	Human serum that contains Rh antibodies.
Autochthonous	Usually a disease found in that place in which an individual normally lives; aboriginal.
Beryllium	One of the elements; has the symbol Be.
Buccolingual	The region of the cheek and the tongue.
Carcinogenesis	The origin of cancer.
Carcinolytic	Represents destruction to the cells of carcinoma.
Caries	Usually a localized destructive disease of the teeth which starts at the enamel surface. It is believed that masses of microorganisms are responsible for this destruction.
Cavernous angioma	An enlarged area due to the dilation of blood vessels. Usually, it contains many cavities.
Cesium	Belongs to the alkali metal group.
Corticosterone	Obtained from the adrenal cortex and induces hyperglycemia and is also involved in the deposition of glycogen in the liver.
Cryptorchid	Occasionally one or both of the testes do not descend into the scrotum.

279

Diastrophyism	The process whereby the earth's crust is deformed. This may produce mountains, continents, etc.
Duodenal stenosis	A stricture or a narrowing of the duodenum.
Endogenous	Usually produced within the organism.
Epidemiology	Originally limited to the medical science dealing with epidemics, but in recent times, its definition has been broadened to include population studies, ecological studies, etc.
Ergosterol	An unsaturated hydrocarbon, similar in composition to cholesterol.
Etiology	The causes or the beginnings, usually of a disease.
Fumarole	Usually a hole in a volcanic region from which come forth hot gases and vapors.
Hydrocarbon	A compound containing only hydrogen and carbon.
Hydrocephaly	Collection of fluid in the cerebral ventricles. This causes a dilation of these cavities and a thinning of the brain.
Isohyet	A line on a chart connecting those places having the same rainfall.
Isotherm	A line on a chart connecting those places having the same temperature.
Ketonuria	The excretion of acetone bodies in the urine.
Ketosis	Acetone substances or ketone bodies are found in the body.
kg/dm^2	Kilogram per square decimeter.
Klinefelter's disease	Chromosomal males, usually with XXY condition, and defective hormonal condition, frequently sterile.
Kwashiorkor	A disease usually limited to African natives, particularly children. It may be regarded as malignant malnutrition. Characterized by anemia, edema, pot belly, loss or change in hair color, etc.
Lithosphere	Sometimes referred to as the earth's crust. This consists of an outer layer of surface soil lying upon a mass of hard rock several miles thick.
Lymphoma	A general term that includes neoplastic diseases of the lymphoid tissues.
Lysis	A gradual alleviation of the symptoms of an acute disease.
Micromicrocurie	A measure of radium emanation, specifically one-millionth of a curie.
Mutagenic	An agent which can cause mutations.
Necrosis	Death of a tissue or of a body.

Neolithic revolution	A culture which is characterized by the use of polished stones, implements, and many cultural advances.
Neoplasms	In a specific sense, it means a new growth of cells or tissues, but now generally used to designate a comparatively unlimited or uncontrolled new growth that seemingly has autonomy in its growth patterns.
Olefins	Any one of the group of hydrocarbons, possessing one or more double bonds in the carbon chain.
Osteomalacia	A disease characterized by a gradual softening and bending of the bones; generally more common in women than in men.
Oxidant	Agent which receives the electrons in an oxidation-reduction reaction.
Oxides	Compounds of oxygen with another radical or element.
Oxidizing	Chemical change in which electrons are transferred from the reducing agent to the oxidizing agent.
Perinatal	A period of time before, during, and after birth.
Phocomelia	An individual having hands and feet attached directly to shoulders and hips. The arrangement bears a resemblance to the flippers on a seal.
Phototaxis	Reaction of living protoplasm to light. If attracted, a positive phototaxis; if repelled, a negative phototaxis.
Pyrexia	An acute inflammation.
Radioisotopes	Isotopes showing radioactivity.
Reducing agent	Agent which gives up the electrons in an oxidation-reduction reaction.
Radiomimetic	Showing similarities to radio waves.
Scarification	Making a number of superficial incisions in the skin.
Slash and burn	A primitive method of cultivation.
Specific heat	A characteristic amount of heat which changes the temperature of a unit mass of a specific substance by one degree.
Specific heat of fusion	The characteristic amount of heat required to change a unit mass of a specific substance from solid to liquid at its melting point.
Specific heat of vaporization	The characteristic amount of heat required to change a unit mass of a specific substance from liquid to vapor.
Spectrograph	An instrument for dispersing light radiation into a spectrum and recording it photographically.

Stillbirth	The birth of a dead fetus.
Synergistic	Usually denotes cooperative action of certain muscles.
Toxoplasmosis	Induced by protozoan parasites which provoke an accumulation of lymphocytes around affected cells. The parasitized cells become necrotic.
Triple point for water	Mathematical representation of the conditions at which the three phases of water—solid, liquid, and vapor—can exist together in equilibrium.
Turner's disease	Chromosomal females with unusual XO condition. Usually sterile.
Volcanism	Volcanic power or action.
Varicocele	A tumor or an enlargement of the veins.

Appendix B
Statistical Principles

Many of the articles in this book employ simple statistical procedures. It is the purpose of this short appendix to provide the beginning reader with a generalized understanding of some statistical procedures. It can hardly take the place of one of the many excellent textbooks available. One of the more useful texts for elementary students is by N. J. Moroney entitled, *Facts From Figures,* 1956, Penguin Books.

The question of probability is very important in statistics. A probability figure indicates that a certain occurrence may have taken place by virtue of chance alone. The probability figure is found between 1.0, or the probability that an observation or set of observations will occur every time, and 0.0, or the probability that an observation or set of observations will never take place. For example, $P = 0.15$ means that an observation or set of observations by chance alone could have taken place 15 out of 100 tries. The statistician believes that such an observation can easily take place by chance alone and that there are apparently no hidden directive factors working. A probability figure of 0.15 is regarded as not significant.

It is important to understand how a statistician uses the term "significant" because it has a special meaning. We can say that an observation is significant because it did not occur by chance alone. For example, if we read a probability figure of 0.03, we understand that an observation has taken place only 3 times in 100. All this indicates that chance alone is very likely not operating in this observation. Some factor other than chance or a directive factor is causing the development of such a low probability. Usually, in biological materials, probability of 0.05 or less is regarded as significant. We may also designate a probability of 0.01 or less as very significant.

Throughout this volume, references will be made to two statistical tests which can provide significance or nonsignificance. These are the Chi-square or χ^2 test and the *t*-test. This is not the place to elaborate on the methods involved in the obtaining of certain probabilities. However, the reader may see statements which read "The Chi-square test or the *t*-test provides a *P* of . . . ." The paper may, on the other hand, indicate that the test provides an index figure which, with the use of proper tables, may be converted into a *P* of . . . . If the decimal is in two places, it will indicate the number of times out of one hundred that the *P* could be exceeded by chance alone. If the decimal is in three places, it will represent the number of chances in 1,000 that it could be exceeded.

Usually, an author will provide the reader with sufficient data to indicate that his statistical analysis results in significance. Virtually all authors will also provide supporting evidence which is also biologically important. This coupling of statistical calculations and biological data is crucial because a significance figure alone does not, in itself, rule out the possibility that the observation being reported could have taken place by chance alone.

In statistics, the term correlation has a specific meaning. When the recordings of two variables are shown to have dependency, that is, shown to have some degree of relationship, we may say that the results are correlated. The correlation may be a positive or it may be a negative one. For example, one investigator may show that the malformation rate in children increases with maternal exposure to radiation. This is a positive correlation because it shows that increase of one variable is related to increase of another variable. Let us suppose, on the other hand, that a researcher shows that the greater the rainfall in an area, the less an area is needed for tribal occupancy for food requirements. In this instance, one variable is increasing, whereas another variable is decreasing. The correlation representing dependency is still there and is regarded as a negative correlation.

A sample or population of figures representing characteristics such as rainfall in inches or human weight in pounds, tends to cluster around the average of the given population. The average value, or statistically speaking, the mean, is used frequently. Usually the figures cluster around the mean in a configuration called a normal distribution since it will frequently take the shape of a bell-shaped curve. One important measure of variability around this mean may be represented as a standard deviation or S.D. In a technical sense, it is equal to the positive square root of the variance. This definition is too complex to elaborate more fully in this appendix. About two-thirds of the individual figures have values within one standard deviation above and one standard deviation below the mean of the distribution. Approximately 95% of the figures fall within two standard deviations above and below the mean, and over 99% within three standard deviations above the mean and below the mean. These are rough rules but they work well in practice.

If one were able to take many samples of the characteristic being tested, he could assemble many mean calculations. It is a fact that the means of samples also tend to cluster around a bellshaped distribution. One may ask how the mean of one given specific sample is related to the mean of a "population of means" from which the sample mean has been taken. For this problem, sophisticated mathematical procedures are employed, and the standard error of the mean may be obtained. A good indication of the relationship of the given sample mean to the "true mean" is supplied by the standard error, usually designated by the ± symbol. Accordingly, it is customary to describe any sample in terms of its mean value ± the standard error. This will give an indication of the sample's reliability. It may be shown that the larger the sample, the more likely its mean will be closer to the true mean, and the smaller will be the standard error.

A number of symbols are used in these papers: > indicates greater than, and < is less than.

Appendix C
Supplementary Readings

Introduction

BARTHOLOMEW, GEORGE A., JR., and JOSEPH B. BIRDSELL, "Ecology and the Proto-hominids," *American Anthropologist,* **55:** 481–498, 1953. (Application of ecological concepts developed by vertebrate zoologists to protoliominids. Strongly recommended.)

BIEL, E. R., "Microclimate, Bioclimatology, and Notes on Comparative Dynamic Climatology," *American Scientist,* **49:** 325–357, 1961. (Compares macro- and micro-climatic conditions. Strongly recommended.)

*DORF, ERLING, "Climatic Changes of the Past and Present," *American Scientist,* **48:** 341–364, 1960. (Excellent review of climatic changes. Has climatic zone maps of North America. Strongly recommended.)

KENDEIGH, S. CHARLES, *Animal Ecology,* 1961, Prentice-Hall. (Human ecology draws heavily upon animal ecological principles. Kendeigh's text is an excellent source book of these principles.)

*LANDSBERG, H. E., "Trends in Climatology," *Science,* **128:** 749–758, 1958. (Reviews current mechanisms for studying climatic conditions. Discusses climatic changes produced by cities.)

Adaptation to soils

ALBRECHT, WILLIAM A., "Soil Fertility and Biotic Geography," *Geographical Review,* **57:** 86–105, 1957. (A still useful paper on soil conditions in the United States and its effects on protein potential, plants, wildlife, and man.)

BRONSON, BENNETT, "Roots and the Substance of the Ancient Maya," *Southwestern Journal of Anthropology,* **22:** 251–279, 1966. (Reviews the importance of root crops in agricultural potential.)

---

* Indicates that reading may be found in an anthology, *Human Ecology,* Jack B. Bresler (Editor), 1966, Addison-Wesley Publishing Co., Inc., Reading, Mass.

CADELL, P. B., "Geographic Distribution of Dental Caries in Relation to New England Soils," *Australian Dental Journal,* **9:** 32–38, 1964. (Supports thesis of Ludwig that prevalence of caries is related to the soils.)

FERDON, EDWIN N., JR., "Agricultural Potential and the Development of Cultures," *Southwestern Journal of Anthropology,* **15:** 1–19, 1959. (Believes man's ingenuity may overcome the environment's theoretical limitation over agricultural yield.)

*GENTRY, JOHN T., "An Epidemiological Study of Congenital Malformations in New York State," *AJPH,* **49:** 4, 1–22, 1959. (Study suggests that geological areas of probable radioactive materials were associated with high rates of congenital malformations.)

Adaptation to physical factors

BAKER, PAUL T., "The Biological Adaptation of Man to Hot Deserts," *American Naturalist,* **92:** 337–357, 1958. (An acclimatized man with brunette skin and low body fat appears to be best suited for work under hot desert conditions. Excellent study in human ecology.)

GOLDSMITH, R., "Use of Clothing Records to Demonstrate Acclimatization to Cold in Man," *Journal of Applied Physiology,* **15:** 776–780, 1960. (Reports that the number of layers of clothes is reduced as acclimatization takes place.)

*NEWMAN, MARSHALL T., "The Application of Ecological Rules to the Racial Anthropology of the Aboriginal New World," *American Anthropologist,* **55:** 311–327, 1953. (Believes that body form distribution of New World aborigines supports Bergmann's and Allen's rules.)

NEWMAN, RUSSELL W., and ELLA H. MUNRO, "The Relation of Climate and Body Size in U.S. Males," *American Journal of Physical Anthropology,* **13:** 1–17, 1955. (Further support for Bergmann's rule of body size relationship with environmental conditions.)

SCHOLANDER, P. F., "Evolution of Climatic Adaptation in Homeotherms," *Evolution,* **9:** 15–26, 1955. (Believes that mammalian physiological features, not body forms, is key to human temperature adaptation.)

The environment, other organisms, human diseases

BURKITT, DENIS, "A Children's Cancer Dependent on Environment," *Viruses, Nucleic Acids and Cancer,* 1963. (A fuller treatment of the study reported by the Burkitt paper in the reader.)

VOLPE, E. PETER, *Understanding Evolution,* Wm. C. Brown Co., 1967. (Cites a number of references to humans and ecological factors.)

Food, water, and energetics

BURKHOLDER, PAUL R., "Drugs from the Sea," *Armed Forces Chemical Journal,* **17:** 1–8, 1963. (Well-written, easy-to-read review of 80 articles on the riches from the sea.)

MAXWELL, JOHN C., "Will There be Enough Water?" *American Scientist,* **53:** 97–103, 1965. (Raises questions dealing with where and how we are going to find large quantities of water.)

MERTEN, D., and O. SUSCHNY. "Some Factors Influencing the Food-Chain Transport of Radioactive Materials into Cow's Milk," *Nature,* **189:** 806–808, 1961. (Traces radioactive materials from origin to human consumption.)

PHILLIPSON, JOHN, *Ecological Energetics,* St. Martin's Press, 1966. (A fuller and slightly more difficult treatment of energy transformations which occur within ecosystems.)

Reproduction

CHANG, K. S. F., S. T. CHAN, W. D. LOW, and C. K. NG, "Climate and Conception Rates in Hong Kong," *Human Biology,* **35:** 366–376, 1963. (Study shows conception rates highest in winter and lowest in summer. External temperature is thought to be major factor in conceptions.)

COWLES, RAYMOND B., "Hyperthermia, Aspermia, Mutation Rates, and Evolution," *Quarterly Review of Biology,* **40:** 341–367, 1965. (An excellent in-depth paper on temperature and its relations to mutations and evolution in plants, animals, and humans. Should follow the reading of paper by Glover and Young.)

LUCEY, JEROLD F., and RICHARD E. BEHRMAN, "Thalidomide: Effect upon Pregnancy in the Rhesus Monkey," *Science,* **139:** 1295–1296, 1963. (Thalidomide apparently kills embryo prior to implantation.)

Cycles

ASCHOFF, JÜRGEN, "Circadian Rhythms in Man," *Science,* **148:** 1427–1432, 1965. (Believes that a self-sustained oscillator underlies human 24-hour periodicity. A difficult but rewarding paper.)

BAILER, C., BAILER III, and JOAN GURIAN, "Congenital Malformations and Season of Birth: A Brief Review," *Eugenics Quarterly,* **12:** 146–153, 1965. (The paper not only reviews the latest studies in the field, but also raises some questions that need answers.)

LANDER, ELVIR, HANS FORSSMAN, and HANS OLOF AKESSON, "Season of Birth and Mental Deficiency," *Acta Genetica et Statistica Medica,* **14:** 265–280, 1964. (A negative reaction to the paper by Knobloch and Pasamanick.)

MACMAHON, BRIAN, and JAMES M. SOWA, "Physical Damage to the Fetus," *The Filbank Memorial Fund,* **39:** 1–60, 1961. (A positive reaction to the paper by Knobloch and Pasamanick.)

Ecology and genetics

MATSUNAGA, EI, "Intra-Uterine Selection by the ABO Incompatibility of Mother and Foetus," *American Journal of Human Genetics,* **7:** 66–71, 1955. (Fetal intrauterine death may take place because fetal gene develops in an incompatible environment.)

VOLPE, E. PETER, "Understanding Evolution," Wm. C. Brown Co., 1967. (Cites a number of references to humans and ecological factors.)

Population and society

*BIRDSELL, JOSEPH B., "Some Environmental and Cultural Factors Influencing the Structure of Australian Aboriginal Populations," *The American Naturalist,* **87:** 171–207, 1953. (Indicates how rainfall, tribal area, and culture are related. Excellent study.)

BIRDSELL, J. B., "Some Population Problems Involving Pleistocene Man," *Cold Spring Harbor Symposia on Quantitative Biology,* **22:** 47–69, 1957. (Discusses population growth, migration patterns, and elapsed time in Australia.)

CALHOUN, JOHN B., "Population Density and Social Pathology," *Scientific American,* **206:** 139–148, 1962. (Discusses the consequences of pathological "togetherness.")

*HOAGLAND, HUDSON, "Cybernetics of Population Control," *Bull. Atom. Sci.,* 1–6, 1964. (Another view of overpopulation and stress with emphasis on human population.)

Pollution and hereditary causes

*BOCHE, ROBERT D., and J. J. QUILLIGAN, JR., "Effect of Synthetic Smog on Spontaneous Activity of Mice," *Science,* **131:** 1733–1734, 1960. (Smog appears as an agent which reduces activity in mice.)

CANNON, HELEN L., and JESSIE M. BOWLES, "Contamination of Vegetation by Tetraethyl Lead," *Science,* **137:** 765–766, 1962. (Study indicates that plants near highways are showing lead contamination.)

GOULD, A. R., "A Cumulative Deposition of Fallout Within Buildings," *Nature,* **193:** 1152–1153, 1962. (Cites preferential deposition of radioactive fallout around doors and windows.)

*HAMMOND, E. CUYLER, "Smoking and Death Rates—A Riddle in Cause and Effect," *American Scientist,* **46:** 331–353, 1958. (An excellent review of pollution by smoking and its consequences.)

*LEWIS, E. B., "Leukemia, Multiple Myeloma, and Aplastic Anemia in American Radiologists," *Science,* **142:** 1492–1494, 1963. (Study suggests that radiation exposure is related to cancerous conditions.)

The Martian environment

BIERI, ROBERT, "Humanoids on Other Planets?" *American Scientist,* **52:** 452–458, 1964. (Presents a thesis that beings on other planets may look like us.)

*GLENN, JOHN H. and JOHN A. O'KEEFE, "The Mercury-Atlas 6 Space Flight," *Science,* **136:** 1093–1099, 1962. (A still fascinating account of the first American space flight and the first published report of a space flight.)

LOVELL, BERNARD, "The Challenge of Space Research," *Nature,* **195:** 935–939, 1962. (Discusses the scientific dividends and tasks for future in space research.)

REA, D. G., "Evidence for Life on Mars," *Nature,* **200:** 114–116, 1963. (Reviews some of the arguments for life on Mars.)

A B C D E 6 9 8

This anthology-text is composed of current papers which have been drawn from many science and social science journals. The readings, which are presented in a loose historical approach, are based upon established—almost classical—principles from animal ecology. The volume presents human ecology as a way of looking at the various aspects of biological, physical, and social sciences. As an auxiliary text at the freshman or sophomore level, the book is meant to show how the subject under discussion is related to other sciences. Content areas address such questions as: how does environment affect man, how does he affect his environment, and how does man affect man in the context of the environment? The material presents an in-depth background to daily problems such as air pollution, population studies, fertility problems, human diseases, and space.

ADDISON-WESLEY PUBLISHING COMPANY
READING, MASSACHUSETTS
MENLO PARK, CALIFORNIA · LONDON · DON MILLS, ONTARIO